COLUMBIA COLLEGE CHICAGO

W9-DJO-050

H . D .   A N D   P O E T S   A F T E R

ENTERED JUN 2 4 2005

Edited by **DONNA KROLIK HOLLENBERG**

COLUMBIA COLLEGE LIBRARY
600 S. MICHIGAN AVENUE
CHICAGO, IL 60605

H.D.

AND POETS AFTER

UNIVERSITY OF IOWA PRESS

IOWA CITY

University of Iowa Press, Iowa City 52242

Copyright © 2000 by the University of Iowa Press
All rights reserved
Printed in the United States of America

Design by Martha Farlow

http://www.uiowa.edu/~uipress

No part of this book may be reproduced or used in any form or
by any means, electronic or mechanical, including photocopying
and recording, without permission in writing from the publisher.
All reasonable steps have been taken to contact copyright holders
of material used in this book. The publisher would be pleased to
make suitable arrangements with any whom it has not been
possible to reach.

Printed on acid-free paper

LIBRARY OF CONGRESS CATALOGING-IN-PUBLICATION DATA
H.D. and poets after / edited by Donna Krolik Hollenberg.
   p.   cm.
Includes bibliographical references and index.
ISBN 0-87745-709-3 (cloth), ISBN 0-87745-721-2 (pbk.)
   1. American poetry—20th century—History and criticism.
2. H.D. (Hilda Doolittle), 1886–1961—Influence.
I. Hollenberg, Donna Krolik.
PS325.H43   2000
811'.509—dc21   99-058110

00 01 02 03 04 C 5 4 3 2 1
00 01 02 03 04 P 5 4 3 2 1

TO LEN

Contents

Acknowledgments

A panel at the American Literature Association meeting in 1996 led to the making of this book, and collecting the essays in it was like being at the center of a friendly force field. I especially want to thank all of the contributors for their energy and effort, as well as Holly Carver, the director of the University of Iowa Press, for her support. I am also grateful to the University of Connecticut Research Foundation for awarding me a grant and to Allison Hild, my research assistant. Most of all, I'd like to thank my husband, Leonard M. Rubin, for many hours of technical assistance.

I want to mark the passing of Frances Jaffer (b. 1921), whose death on January 20, 1999, was a loss to the whole poetry community. Her essay here was her last piece of writing.

Grateful acknowledgment is given to New Directions Publishing Corporation for permission to quote from the following copyrighted works of H.D.: *Collected Poems 1912–1944* (copyright © 1925 by HD, copyright © 1957, 1969 by Norman Holmes Pearson, copyright © 1982 by Perdita Schaffner); *End to Torment: A Memoir of Ezra Pound* (copyright © 1979 by New Directions Publishing Corporation); *The Gift* (copyright © 1969, 1982 by the Estate of Hilda Doolittle, copyright © 1988 by Perdita Schaffner); *Helen in Egypt* (copyright © 1961 by Norman Holmes Pearson); *Hermetic Definition* (copyright © 1958, 1959, 1961, 1972 by Norman Holmes Pearson); *HERmione* (copyright © 1981 by the Estate of Hilda Doolittle, copyright © 1981 by Perdita Schaffner); *Notes on Thought and Vision* (copyright © 1982 by the Estate of Hilda Doolittle); *Tribute to Freud* (copyright © 1956, 1974 by Norman Holmes Pearson); *Trilogy* (copyright © 1973 by Norman Holmes Pearson); *Vale Ave* (copyright © 1992 by Perdita Schaffner).

Introduction

DONNA KROLIK HOLLENBERG

H.D. has long been considered a "poet's poet" in the best sense. From her work's first appearance under the Imagist label to its later development in innovative long poems and prose, its excellence was recognized by her peers and successors.[1] The most obvious reflection of that recognition was, of course, her award in poetry from the American Academy of Arts and Letters in 1960, its first to a woman (Hollenberg 1997: 261). In the next generation, her work was also acclaimed. The most extensive and influential discussion of its importance is Robert Duncan's *The H.D. Book*, published in parts in several "little magazines" between 1966 and 1988.[2] In this important series of meditations, Duncan reconceptualizes modernism so that H.D.'s contribution is central, providing a new intellectual context for contemporary poetry. In fact, in the decade following H.D.'s death, when several of her major texts were out of print or not yet published, Duncan's work inspired other members of the younger generation to pressure Norman Holmes Pearson, her literary executor, to get them published. When Pearson wrote to publisher James Laughlin in 1971, proposing the publication of H.D.'s manuscripts by New Directions, he stressed the requests of Robert Duncan, Denise Levertov, and Robert Kelly (Hollenberg 1997: 293). In addition to these three and to those besides Kelly included in this volume, other contemporary poets who have acknowledged H.D.'s work elsewhere in books, essays, reviews, epigraphs, and poems include Robin Blaser, George Bowerings, Hayden Carruth, Robert Creeley, Jane Cooper, Beverly Dahlen, Diane Di Prima, Sandra Gilbert, Judy Grahn, Barbara Guest, Thom Gunn, Donald Hall, Lindy Hough, Susan Howe, Dale Kushner, Dorothy Livesay, Charlotte Mandel, Hilda Morley, May Swenson, Joan Rettallack, Adrienne Rich, John Peck, Robert Pinsky, Lola Lemire Tostevin, Edith Walden, and Anne Waldman.

The voices of these poets are part of a growing body of commentary accompanying the ongoing publication of H.D.'s work. This latter project reflects the fact that, while H.D. is among the last of the major American modernists to have entered the literary canon, her place there is now secure enough to be contested.[3] In fact, since her centennial in 1986, the occasion of several memorial volumes, the field of H.D. scholarship has burgeoned, a fact documented by Michael Boughn in *H.D.: A Bibliography, 1905–1990*.[4] A survey of the literature since 1990 indicates the publication of both important new primary sources and new critical studies. Primary sources include several editions of previously unpublished prose fiction, as well as reissued editions of poetry and autobiography, most with substantial new annotations and introductions.[5] In addition to the reissued stories, *Kora and Ka with Mira Mare*, introduced by Robert Spoo, we now have H.D.'s previously unpublished early novels, *Paint It Today* and *Asphodel*, edited and introduced by Cassandra Laity and Robert Spoo, respectively, as well as the previously unpublished stories of *Within the Walls*. Reissues of H.D.'s poetry include *Vale Ave*, introduced by John Walsh, and an annotated *Trilogy*, edited by Aliki Barnstone. Also, Jane Augustine has edited and annotated the full text of H.D.'s autobiography, *The Gift*, with its accompanying "Notes." Further, several book-length, annotated editions of correspondence supplement the two earlier biographies (Robinson 1982; Guest 1984). Caroline Zilboorg has edited two volumes of the letters between Richard Aldington and H.D., I have edited the letters between H.D. and Norman Holmes Pearson, and Robert J. Bertholf has edited those between Robert Duncan and H.D. An edition of letters between H.D. and Bryher during H.D.'s analysis with Freud, edited by Susan Stanford Friedman, is forthcoming.[6]

The critical reception of H.D.'s work in the last decade reflects an increasing understanding of both her historical situation (including her biography) and her intellectual context.[7] Indeed, since H.D. was well read in classical and modern languages and was connected with several important twentieth-century movements (such as psychoanalysis, occultism, the Harlem Renaissance, and avant-garde cinema), her engagement with intellectual history is a particularly rich line of inquiry.[8] H.D.'s position as a woman writer recording the spiritual impact of violence and war in their cultural, personal, and spiritual meanings is a central preoccupation of her texts. It is thus appropriate that much of the critical response to her work—including biographical, contextual, textual, new historicist, psychoanalytic, and poststructuralist—has been integrated with a feminist foregrounding of gender.[9] Critical response since 1990 also reflects a new awareness of H.D.'s achievements in experimental prose (fiction, autobiography, memoir, essay) as well as in poetry. For example, building on her earlier study of H.D.'s poetry, Susan Stanford Friedman showed the ways in which H.D.'s experimental prose fiction was pivotal in her artistic development as well as comparable in philosophical preoccupation and narrative technique to that of such other innovators as Stein, Woolf, Joyce, and Faulkner (1981, 1990).

Recent trends in feminist theory are also evident in the reading of H.D., particularly the French poststructuralist emphasis on the self as a linguistic construct rather than the source of language and agency. For example, incorporating poststructuralism into the methodology of her book on H.D.'s prose, Friedman argues that, in its very reflexivity and excess, H.D.'s prose deconstructs her textualization as "woman" in existing culture even as it reconstructs the story of her own subjectivity. Here Friedman is in dialogue with her own earlier work and with ongoing Anglo-American feminist critique based in women's psychosocial experience, such as my book on H.D.'s "poetics of childbirth and creativity" (1991). Several books, influenced particularly by Lacan and Kristeva, take a more uniformly poststructuralist stance, valuing H.D.'s work for the symptomatic quality of its crises and slippages, particularly with regard to her responses to Freudian psychoanalysis. For example, as part of her argument that H.D. successfully confronts woman's exclusion from the universal symbolic order, Dianne Chisholm discusses her use of the figure of the hysteric, linking hysteria with witchcraft and mystical ecstasy (1992). And Claire Buck values H.D. for her representation of a split subjectivity and her depiction of "an oscillation" that makes bisexuality the mark of "the difficulty or uncertainty of sexual identity, rather than the foundation of an alternative identity" (1991: 89). Rafaella Baccolini also situates her book within the tradition of gender critique, arguing that H.D.'s confrontation with male modernism produced formal as well as thematic revisions (1995). Building on the work of these critics but complicating their desire to recuperate H.D. as a model for later generations, Susan Edmunds claims that "the visionary politics of H.D.'s long poems cannot be reconciled with [these] liberal-feminist and post-structuralist-feminist agendas." Instead, she argues that "H.D.'s visionary solutions reveal fully historical patterns of political bias, ambivalence, and incoherence" (1994: 5). In support of her argument, Edmunds places H.D.'s work in two new contexts besides her engagement with psychoanalysis: the film theory and practice of Sergei Eisenstein and the African independence movements of the 1950s and 1960s.

Three new books offer sustained attention to previously unexplored aspects of H.D.'s avowed literary and intellectual heritage. Cassandra Laity offers an account of H.D.'s relationship to the writers of the Victorian fin de siècle, especially Rossetti, Pater, Swinburne, and Wilde. She argues that H.D.'s loyalty to these "decadent writers," particularly to their representations of the androgynous boy and the femme fatale, differentiates her work from that of her male modernist contemporaries (1996). Eileen Gregory analyzes the important subject of H.D.'s classicism, that is, her lifelong engagement with classical texts, art, religion, and mythology. Moving beyond earlier accounts that explain H.D.'s classicism as a product of late-nineteenth-century decadence or modernist poetics and beyond those that see it simply "as a set of masks or personae, unreal disguises for a real, biographically or historically contextualized subject," Gregory interprets H.D.'s "fictions of the classical" within the history of "precedent classicisms." She argues that, in this context, H.D.'s relation to ancient writers is deliberately nonlinear. In her words, "H.D. consistently veers from the linearity, seminality, and totality of certain classical models, preferring in her affiliations and in her imagination of literary history something like an antimodel involving dissemination, dispersion, and diaspora" (1997: 2). Diana Collecott builds on this rereading of H.D.'s classicism in her book, *H.D. and Sapphic Modernism* (1999). Arguing that Sappho's presence in H.D.'s work is as important as that of Homer in Pound's or that of Dante in Eliot's, she develops a lesbian poetics not only for H.D. but also for such contemporaries such as Bryher, Amy Lowell, and Virginia Woolf. The essays in two recent special issues of *Sagetrieb*, devoted solely to H.D., show a parallel development in reading practice, in that the majority foreground historical considerations or continue to illuminate H.D.'s place in intellectual history.[10]

H.D. and Poets After collects twenty new essays about H.D.'s influence on contemporary American poetry. Half are by American poets

writing about their literary engagement with H.D., and half are by critics writing about H.D. in relation to these same poets. A dialogue is
thus built into the structure of the book between two perspectives: the
first, autobiographical testimony, and the second, critical analysis by
scholars attuned to both modern and contemporary poetries. When I
read them as a group, it became clear that these essays were also inherently dialogic, not only with each other but with H.D. That is, as the
contributors considered H.D.'s relationship to themselves or to each
other, they became aware not only of specific aspects of her work's continuing vitality but of their role in maintaining it and shaping its reception. Thus, we have sustained discussions of the work of the ten poets
included here as well as new insights into H.D.'s oeuvre: she becomes
not only a major progenitor but our contemporary. Already canonized
by the literary community, her work is now an occasion for a fruitful
exchange of perceptions among this and future gatherings of readers.

By bringing together poets and scholars in alternating exchanges, the
volume calls into question both traditional notions of literary criticism
and earlier theories of literary influence. First of all, almost half of the
contributors are poet/scholars, and their essays tend to collapse the distinction between creative and scholarly essays, host and parasite, preva-
lent since the heyday of the New Critics.[11] In fact, all these essays show
that, when deeply imagined, these two kinds of engagement with a predecessor are complementary. In most cases, the critics wrote their essays after having read the autobiographical testimony of the poets, and
thus I have placed the poets' essays first, but I could have reversed the
order. For the critics here *chose* the contemporary poets they wished to
compare with H.D., writing in a kind of triangulated, imaginative sym-
biosis. That is, both poets and critics endeavored to grasp the entelechy
of H.D.'s work, what it aims to be, across their own generation from
a shared perspective. Further, read as a group, these pairs of essays do
not confirm earlier theories of poetic influence, such as Harold Bloom's
Freudian model of Oedipal struggle with a masterly predecessor, a
study in literary psychohistory that does not consider the possibility of
women as literary precursors (1972). In fact, the concept of "influence,"
in the sense of an influx or pouring in of external power (male or female), does not best describe the dynamic here. Rather, the idea of "affiliation" is more serviceable. It implies possibilities of choice and continuity that, as Sandra Gilbert and Susan Gubar have noted, enable the

construction of new genealogies that are open to historical flux (1988). Here we see that H.D.'s poetry finds readers of both sexes and various ethnic backgrounds (who may be poets and/or critics) because those readers need these poems in order to articulate their own deepest thoughts and feelings, otherwise inaccessible, about the moment in which they live. Thus, these paired essays dramatize the fact that the literary tradition is not reducible to any essential psychological scheme. It is open to anyone capable of an imaginative response to language.

What do these essays tell us about the nature of H.D.'s enduring appeal and about her special relevance to us now? I find several recurrent, overlapping motifs. First of all, her poetry is powerfully erotic in the radical sense; that is, the contributors feel Eros present, not only as sexuality but as a multifaceted life force, a primary affirmation that enables spiritual growth and change. As Alicia Ostriker puts it, remembering her first, deeply intuitive response to the "ravishing, cerebral, sexual" beauty of H.D.'s *Helen in Egypt*, which seemed to represent a hitherto repressed female subjectivity: "It was uncannily like a half-remembered dream from my own history." For Ostriker, H.D.'s heterodox vision rivals Blake's, and today, twenty years later, H.D. continues to inspire her to risk being "a fool for poetry," to "give all for love." Similarly, Robert Kelly recounts the "special intensity" he felt when he first read H.D.'s long poems, then largely unpublished, in the office of Norman Holmes Pearson. She seemed then to be there in the room in person, and he remains attracted to the "sheer protean nature of the beloved" in her work. Jane Augustine, commenting on Kelly's poem inspired by H.D., places this poem in the context of one of H.D.'s profoundest themes, the "desire for a pure and redeemed, physical sexuality, sexual union inseparable from divine love." Also, through H.D., Sharon Doubiago comes to recognize "the Helen situation in all women," which she describes as psychic wounding in romance and marriage and reconceives in her poetry as an opening for transformative vision. And Frances Jaffer connects the life force in H.D.'s poetry with the ability of all great art to mediate sorrow. As a child, she visited the Parthenon with her father, a structural engineer, and his death soon thereafter became forever connected with the perfection of this temple. "A spreading sense of spirit," she calls this experience, and it enabled her later to comprehend H.D.'s similar response to classical subjects.

Indeed, as Kim Vaeth points out, H.D.'s poetry came to provide Jaffer with a model of courage, enabling her to express in her own poetry "adverse, out-of-control events" related to her life as a cancer patient.

Not surprisingly, given H.D.'s revisions of central myths about the position of women in Western culture, she is a strong precursor and role model for a generation of feminist poets represented here. This protofeminism constitutes a second important motif. Several contributors came into their own during the height of the feminist movement in the 1970s. They associate their discovery of H.D.'s major work with the excitement of consciousness-raising in that period, with new questions about the origins, dynamics, and consequences of gender roles. As Rachel Blau DuPlessis puts it, "[H.D.'s] whole work was answering questions we had just begun to formulate, we were hot with it, and in that heat H.D. emerged. . . . We had opened [Queen Tut's] tomb." Of course, during that excavation process, they also recognized the ways in which H.D.'s aesthetic values and goals differed from their own, a difference inevitable given their later positions in history. As Burton Hatlen points out, noting that the shift in philosophical and political awareness from H.D. to DuPlessis was mediated by the Objectivists, DuPlessis's work "enacts an open engagement with H.D." that "encompasses resistance as well as influence." In her later writings, he continues, DuPlessis has become "increasingly suspicious of [H.D.'s] transhistorical and archetypal rhetorics, even when mobilized for feminist purposes." What she retains from H.D. is a sense of writing as an "act of discovery, a venture forward into the unknown."

H.D.'s appeal as a precursor and foil to feminist poets in the seventies is further elaborated in this collection in the essays by Alicia Ostriker, Sharon Doubiago, and Kathleen Fraser, as well as in the companion pieces to those essays. For example, H.D.'s revisionist mythmaking, grounded "in a woman's body and mind" rather than in conventional dogma, makes possible Ostriker's comparable imaginative rebellion against the subordination of women in Judeo-Christian tradition and in the patriarchal family. In my essay on Ostriker and H.D., I discuss the ways in which the experience of motherhood, central to both as a moral force, becomes the source of Ostriker's parallel but divergent stance as a social poet. Similarly, Sharon Doubiago's two long poems are woven together with H.D.'s *Helen in Egypt* in a "web of corresponding myths" that are matrifocal, writes Kathleen Crown. In the course of this literary engagement, Crown continues, Doubiago shifts the structure of address in her poems, shaking off "male-oriented paradigms of conscious influence." The result is a "new set of textual relations in the reading process," one that seeks to "in-form the reader by incorporating the reader's voice and desire." Exploring another feminist idea, sisterhood without sameness, Kathleen Fraser views H.D.'s gift as the "ability to see the empty page waiting to be inscribed" by a plurality of women writers and readers different from herself, and Cynthia Hogue comments that H.D. gave Fraser the means to "generate her own poetic structures." In fact, as Hogue points out, in the hands of Fraser, DuPlessis, Jaffer, Ostriker, and other feminist poets and critics who contributed to Fraser's journal *HOW(ever)* in the eighties, H.D.'s dramatization of a transformed and transformative spirituality in *Trilogy* became an invitation to pursue a new feminist poetics. All of these poets extend the feminist critique of culture to their handling of form, deliberately challenging established reading patterns and habits of consciousness.

Brenda Hillman and Leslie Scalapino, who represent a younger generation of women poets, continue to read H.D. as a precursor and foil for their own experimentation. However, their essays foreground a philosophical skepticism, rooted in postmodern awareness, that eschews archetypes and other fixed categories, including gender identity itself. This epistemological restlessness constitutes a third motif. Brenda Hillman offers three "appreciative thoughts" about H.D. and "three complaints." For example, she appreciates "the largeness of [H.D.'s] use of various orthodoxies" and writes, "I learned that the human imagination, when it confronts what it might think of as godness . . . doesn't have to be the agent of an impossible narrowness that we usually associate with belief." However, Hillman also complains about this very largeness: she finds H.D. "singularly disconnected from the minute noticings that make for the most engaging forms of spiritual insight." In her companion piece on Hillman and H.D., Aliki Barnstone responds to Hillman's ambivalent affiliation, pointing out that for Hillman, the concept of influence itself is "not monolithic, nor is it easily traceable or linear." She also analyzes the points of likeness between the two poets: both are Gnostics, "driven inward by crisis," she writes; in both, "writing is a way of knowing and coming into light." For Leslie Scalapino also poetry is a means of epistemological speculation. She focuses on the ways in which language constructs human reality, and she traces back to H.D. her idea that "'reading' is interior scrutiny" that is at once observation of the outside. Unlike H.D., who regarded ancient myth as a repository of sacred revelation, Scalapino regards meaning as inherently relative. She finds H.D.'s writing "revolutionary in investigating one's own mind being present action." In her companion essay on H.D. and Scalapino, Elisabeth Frost shows that although Scalapino writes "highly fractured serial compositions" and H.D. writes mythic epic poems, they have a "shared view of the contingent, shifting nature of gender and the self." Further, Frost points out that, when read through Scalapino, H.D. becomes "a deconstructive poet" whose daring uses of "the structures of 'illusion' challenge the nature of identity."

Perhaps the most compelling aspect of H.D.'s continuing appeal, as it is represented here, lies in her efforts to express the unprecedented threat to selfhood and memory inherent in twentieth-century moral disaster—war, genocide, the atomic bomb. A response to this third motif in her work appears in several essays, including those by and/or about DuPlessis, Fraser, and Ostriker. These essays express concern about the inadequacy of the romantic lyric "I" in the face of unprecedented human catastrophe, a concern related to the authors' feminist analysis of the linked realities of war and sexual violence. This assault upon the lyric subject is foregrounded and more broadly contextualized in the final two pairs of essays by Nathaniel Mackey, Adalaide Morris, Carolyn Forché, and Eileen Gregory. As Mackey writes, he has been drawn to H.D. most recently through her articulation of "a coastal poetics, a coastal way of knowing." He explains coastal knowledge as "dissolute knowledge, repetitive, compulsive . . . repeatedly undone and reconstituted." It is knowledge in which the poet is aware of the limits of art as sublimation of social violence and in which the poetry expresses that awareness in the "need for a cross-cut or cross-accentual tug between rapture and erosion." H.D.'s late poetry seems driven by "apprehensions of desertion or destitution" that are as important as its affirmations, he continues. In her companion piece, Adalaide Morris compares central books in serial compositions by H.D. and Mackey in which such knowledge is explored. Morris argues that "the extravagant, self-reflexive, mythopoetic word-work" characteristic of such writing "exceeds not only the gendered and racialized vocabularies so often deployed to analyze it but also the modernist and postmodernist paradigms most frequently used to position it." Instead of regarding words as neutral, transparent instruments through which to transmit messages or engaging in random postmodern epistemic play, H.D. and Mackey practice "a discrepant engagement" between world and word that insists on a fit, albeit an imperfect one. Morris calls this epistemological drive "radical modernism," and she explains its roots in the "operations—operatic extremity, operatic tilt—of language." In the improvisational practice of both poets, she argues, "sound leads thought," and verbal play (such as puns or chordal words) enables "polyphonic thinking" that is innovative and regenerative.

Similarly, Carolyn Forché provides a new political and ethical context within which to read H.D. She writes that her second engagement with H.D.'s work was in the context of preparation for her anthology of international twentieth-century poetry "marked by the impress of extremity." Like herself but more obliquely, she finds H.D. "struggling with the insurmountable difficulty of writing her way toward restoration, while conceiving a poetic form that would somehow display the ruin." Finally, in her essay on H.D. and Forché, Eileen Gregory focuses upon the intertextual relationship between *Trilogy* and Forché's *The Angel of History*, arguing that although both poems are "metaphysical or spiritual in their response to conditions of extremity," H.D. speaks in a language of "visionary transformation" that is no longer available to Forché. However, read through Forché, the very idiosyncrasy of *Trilogy* can be seen as an aspect of its resistance to extremity; "its aim is finally one of advocacy" and not escape. In fact, as Gregory points out, Forché's placement of H.D. within a "global record of cultural and linguistic displacement," rather than in the more limited context of Anglo-American modernism in which she is usually read, is particularly generative and telling.

The ways in which H.D.'s work resonates with (postmodern) discontent and doubt, while still affirming life and the resourcefulness of language, inform all of these essays. In maintaining this lineage, we honor a vision of humanity that enables us to withstand the troubling realities of the contemporary world.

NOTES

1. Among her contemporaries, those who have commented on H.D.'s work include Ezra Pound, T. S. Eliot, William Carlos Williams, Marianne Moore, Bryher, Amy Lowell, John Gould Fletcher, Horace Gregory, Marya Zaturenska, May Sinclair, Maxwell Anderson, Mark Van Doren, Archibald MacLeish, Lola Ridge, William Rose Benét, Conrad Aiken, F. S. Flint, Richard Aldington, Louis Bogan, Osbert Sitwell, Babette Deutsch, Randall Jarrell, John Berryman, D. H. Lawrence, Ford Madox Ford, Robert McAlmon.

2. For a description of *The H.D. Book*, with dates and places of publication, see Duncan (1983: 65).

3. For a discussion of the literary politics that caused H.D.'s neglect by the literary establishment, see Susan Friedman's essay, "Who Buried H.D.?" Friedman argues that H.D.'s work was imperfectly considered and irregularly available in the first era of the academic canon formation of modernism (the 1940s, 1950s, and 1960s), in part because women writers were scarcely read from informed gender perspectives. More recently, Lawrence Rainey has attempted to rebury H.D. by dismissing her as a minor coterie poet.

4. The memorial volumes include the books *H.D.: Woman and Poet*, ed. Michael King, and *Signets: Reading H.D.*, ed. Susan Stanford Friedman and Rachel Blau DuPlessis. They also include the following special issues of journals in England and America: *Agenda* 25 (autumn–winter 1987–88); *Contemporary Literature* 27 (winter 1986); *(HOW)ever* 3 (October 1983); *Iowa Review* 16 (1986); *Poesis* 6 (fall 1985); *Sagetrieb* 6 (fall 1987); *San Jose Studies* 13 (fall 1987). Also, the *H.D. Newsletter* (1987–91) was undertaken in this spirit. These volumes are particularly valuable because they include the publication of letters and other primary sources as well as criticism and poetry.

5. For a discussion of the impact of these new editions of H.D.'s prose fiction on reading practice, see Spoo (1997).

6. Although it is not devoted to H.D. alone, the anthology *The Gender of Modernism*, ed. Bonnie Kime Scott, contains several important primary sources, that is, previously unpublished letters and reprinted essays and reviews by H.D.

7. A full survey of the literature on H.D. since 1990 is beyond the scope of this introduction: the *MLA Bibliography* lists 188 records. Thus I will give priority here to books that focus on H.D. alone and to special issues of journals devoted to her work. An indication of expanding contexts is the fact that chapters on H.D. have been included in books on the following subjects: new approaches to modernism; writing on World War I; literature and science; modern poetry and prophecy; modern poetry and the occult; the construction of a tradition of women poets; rereadings of Sappho; innovative poetics; major modernist contemporaries and successors (such as Ezra Pound, Wallace Stevens, Kay Boyle, Virginia Woolf, May Sarton, Gwendolyn Brooks).

8. Gary Burnett's book, *H.D.: Between Image and Epic*, is an example of this criti-

cal inclination in its focus on H.D.'s poetry between the wars in the context of her interest in the mystery cults at Eleusis.

9. Friedman and DuPlessis (1990) sets the tone in this respect.

10. See Hart (1995) and Twitchell-Waas (1996).

11. Two of the poets represented here (Ostriker and DuPlessis) have written influential scholarly works on H.D. in addition to their several books of poetry, and several of the scholars (Augustine, Barnstone, Crown, Frost, Hatlen, Hogue, and Vaeth) are themselves published poets. For examples of innovative "essays in poetics" by other poet/scholars, see Bernstein (1992) and Howe (1993).

H . D .   A N D   P O E T S   A F T E R

"A Wish to Make Real to Myself What Is Most Real": My H.D.

ALICIA OSTRIKER

I
I see what is beneath me, what is above me,

what men say is-not—I remember,
I remember, I remember—   H.D., *Trilogy*

It was the middle or late seventies before I first read her. What I knew about her was what anyone knew: H.D. was that Imagist poet who wrote small, contained, elliptical poems. I had often glanced past them in anthologies. Flounced past, seeking bigger game. Always you would see the same little H.D. poems. "Whirl up, sea." They were vivid but appeared to lead nowhere. No professorial wand pointed at them as "In a Station of the Metro" and "The Red Wheelbarrow" were pointed at. Sharp little oddities, they snagged the mind like burrs, clinging a moment, producing a faint perplexity, falling away.

A graduate student, Joe Boles, came saying that he wanted to write a dissertation on modernist poetic historiography comparing Auden and H.D. Auden and who? What? Joe had taken my Blake seminar while I was still a Blake fanatic. He had pointed out to me, in the gentlest possible manner, that my protofeminist Blake had a darker twin, a Blake who dreaded female power. Because it was not an insight I wanted, I resisted for a time what glares from Blake's titanic work: a milewide streak of misogyny, existing alongside his equally forceful protofeminism. A teacherly joy is to have a student drag you kicking and screaming into a higher enlightenment, and Joe had been in a feminist reading group with his girlfriend for five years. So I asked if he could tell me something about H.D., and he tossed *Trilogy, Tribute to Freud, Helen in Egypt*, and *Hermetic Definition* into my lap.

During the following fall and winter, Joe wrote his opening chapters on Auden, then abandoned them and wrote the dissertation on H.D. We read, brooded, and learned together. I remember the summer following that first conversation, however. Each day I would take my children and a large satchel containing fruit, suntan lotion, towels, bathing suits, and books to the pool. It was a good erotic place to be, among all those attractive healthy young bodies, and the light like the blue in David Hockney's sybaritic California paintings, even though we were in New Jersey rather than California. I began, absurdly enough, with *Helen in Egypt*.

Day after brilliant hot day I sat on the grass beside the Community Park swimming pool, puzzling over *Helen in Egypt* while my children swam. The poem was utterly mysterious to me, although I thought I knew the Greek material if not the Egyptian. I had no clue what was happening from one line to the next, much less what the prose headings were for, as they were no more rational than the poetry. The work was also exquisitely beautiful. Ravishing, cerebral, sexual as the July bath of sun, it held me as a dream seductively holds us when we are half-awakened. It was uncannily like a half-remembered dream from my own history. I lay on the grass in a trance the background to which was the splashing and shouts of children, the heated dance of adolescents and read of Helen and Achilles. Hieroglyphs. A temple, a beach marked by sandals, a swirling concatenation of gods. The sensation repeated my initial encounter with Blake's prophecies a decade and a half earlier. It was, in fact, a double sensation. Here was this entire bafflement, and twined or twinned with it was the foreknowledge that I would understand what I was reading. I would press forward, I knew, and when I had penetrated these poems I would possess a treasure for the rest of my lifetime.

So it was. "The heart accepts, // encompasses the whole / of the undecipherable script," and the mind trails after (H.D. 1961: 86). Something must be said for coming to works of vast and mysterious power naively, lacking the crutch of commentary. In the embrace of language, before a word is comprehended perhaps, something crucial may already be known. Perhaps everything. A quality of aura or energy is transmitted. The preverbal, or the nonverbal, that intelligent feeling-entity that has translated itself through the vessel of the poet into poetry: that mysterious quality enters you, you enter it. You perceive again that "all myth, the one reality / dwells here." Whatever comes afterward is gloss. H.D.'s theories in *Notes on Thought and Vision*, on the over-mind and the womb-mind, are entirely relevant here. Having allowed yourself to be entranced, after you somehow feel the new sensation, when the thrill has composed itself into a recursive pattern, that is the time to analyze and to see what the critics say.

Fortunately for me, and for other H.D. addicts, Susan Stanford Friedman materialized at just that moment, first with "Who Buried H.D.?" which deftly disposed of the then-dominant psychoanalytic readings of H.D. (readings that explained that the girl wrote poetry to compensate for her missing penis), and then with that noble, generous, and path-breaking volume on the poet's struggle with Freud and with Western religion, *Psyche Reborn*. Aided by Friedman on H.D. much as I had been aided at an earlier moment by Northrop Frye on Blake, I crept through her labyrinth. Dimly lit though it was, I felt unafraid. At the core, there would be no Minotaur but another heterodox visionary. Like Whitman, like Blake, but a woman.

At last, in the line of visionaries given to us in English, a woman.

The relief and release of that! Here at last, a scrupulously refined poetics, taut as a bowstring whose arrow aims at the mists of the future, produced by a woman. An acutely subtle sense of form and diction, rich grounding in classic poetry and art, along with a refusal to submit to Western culture's classic dualisms. "Chasm, schism in consciousness," she declared, "must be bridged over." Hers was a traditionalism wrestling with tradition, unsubmissive, laced with a subversiveness grounded in a woman's experience of the body and sexuality, frustrated eroticism, childbirth, and the aching self-doubt born of habitual rejection and misunderstanding. "All men say 'what' to me," Emily Dickinson wrote to Higginson, pained that her lucidities appeared incomprehensible to normal people. In H.D.'s case, what seems simple and obvious is the insistence on transcribing ecstatic, or terrifying, spiritual experience without a frame of conventional religion or dogma and defiantly grounding that experience in a woman's body and mind. The poems were, first to last, liminal. Whether her images and discourse drew from the natural world, or ancient myth and literature, or esoteric Christianity, or the nets of love, their subject was the psyche in extremis, in passionate pursuit of itself, of wholeness, in pursuit of the divine.

I was at the time reading women's poetry voraciously. I was rubbing the salts of anger in my own wounds. But I also wanted my poems to swing between mythology and the kitchen and bedroom. I meant to bend heaven and earth until they touched and melted into each other like wax. If God is anywhere, I thought, God is in my body. I needed a life in the kitchen and the bedroom, and I needed a life in God; I wanted them to be inseparable. The same place and time, or spacelessness, timelessness. Elsewhere, in what is called "the other world," and here. Like the tree whose invisible root system mirrors its branching crown (an image I would later use to conclude the poem "A Young Woman, a Tree"), reality is below as above. Reaching toward the beard, reaching to the feet, like Whitman's soul at the moment of its fusion with the body on that transparent summer day.

Where were the female models for such a fusion? Where were the women who remembered it? Except Plath, and despite Plath's extraordinary seductiveness (join me, join me in drinking this poison, admit your rage, your pain, your demonic fury), no contemporary woman's poetry embodied what a woman perceives as sacred. There was Plath, electric and deadly. There was Sexton, raw, thrashing, insisting that "the body does not lie," trying and failing to imagine a God the Father she could both believe in and be loved by. There was Levertov, somehow too—shall I say it—nice. There were other poets able to analyze the oppressiveness of patriarchy, to remind us that our professors were not always right, to explore female experience with a vengeance. But where was a vision that could respond to what Virginia Woolf called Milton's bogey, on its own terms and at its own level? Where was the woman poet able not only to "break the lie of men's thoughts" but to imagine a power that might "cherish and shelter us" without erecting new dualities and exclusions?

When I first read H.D. the second wave of feminism was cresting. We believed that change was possible, in art and in life. As artists, we wanted to turn our suffering into soup, our sap into language. To be useful and beautiful. To read H.D. after Plath, Sexton, Rich, Piercy, Kumin, Kizer, Rukeyser, that set of explosions, was to have one's eyes opened. It was to feel that certain things have already been explained in the only way that poetry can explain them. Not slant in Emily's sense, but at a certain metaphysical angle to the world. It was like turning a corner on a bombed-out street and finding ourselves in a temple on a promontory. A glittering blue-green sea lies below; the temple contains in its archives the architectural plans of the city in which we have been living and a long-forgotten promise of redemption.

The poems did not surrender themselves to me immediately but gradually over a period of years continued yielding as I continued inquiring. The experience was like that of intimacy rather than scholarship, and in some sense H.D. offers an intimate exchange despite the seeming remoteness of tone and absence of personal detail in the poems. She speaks for herself but also to us. So many of her poems address a "you" with whom we can identify and invite us to dialogue and trust. The poems seem not merely read but spoken, almost wordlessly spoken, communicating something that is beyond words. Beyond, within, beneath, behind words. Communicating with the intensity of a cat's body vibrating as it purrs. Communicating the tension of the bowstring. Yet one would understand these poems only on condition that one worked at them.

For what use is poetry to women if it fails to imply the terrible need to work? Adrienne Rich speaks of her childhood desire "to change the laws of history." That is the dream of feminism. But to make the future swerve a millimeter from its current course requires and will require the most formidable and thankless labor on the part of dedicated women and their allies. "We know each other by secret symbols," perhaps, but are we prepared to engage in the many kinds of difficult work—psychic, political, rational, emotional—we will be obliged to perform, for the indefinite future, if we wish to transform the world? That H.D. would be difficult would make her a more strengthening ally. To track her invisible footsteps would stretch our sinews.

II   *But symptom or inspiration, the writing continues to write itself, or*
            to be written.   H.D., *Tribute to Freud*

It feels strange to speak of H.D.'s influence on my poetry, in part because I have written several essays about her that may make the present effort superfluous and in part because I hold her in such awe. She is so like a goddess to me, shameless and radiant. I am embarrassed by the question of affinity. Yet how can I avoid offering the homage of attempting to see just where she has aided me? And then, how can I avoid seeing where and how I deviate, and how far I fall short?

The first book of my poems that contains her blood flowing in my veins or her wine in my bottles is *A Woman under the Surface*, published in 1982. Less crude and colloquial than my earlier work, smoother, yet avoiding the air of the elevated or sublime, its general air is one of intimacy, of the personal, combined with a certain distance, implying that the personal is valued because it may speak to the condition of others beyond the self. When I look at it now I see there is a certain silver sheen to it, a bit tarnished. There is a certain economy. This tone and compression I learned from H.D.

Close to half the poems in this book are in two- or three-line stanzas, of fluid line length, and in these I feel the music of H.D. has helped me shape my music and find my meaning. For any music bears a meaning, and we may violently or gently bear it away to other regions. During my school years I wrote poems that appropriated the cadences of T. S. Eliot but twisted angrily away from his meaning. Writing what he would hate, in forms approximating bits of his rhythms, was a form of battle. With H.D. came no friction, no sense of agon. Rather, she offered the sense that to compose in a music similar to hers would bring me closer to my own meanings, which would not be identical to hers but would resonate with them, tone alongside tone.

A group of these two- or three-line-stanza pieces in *A Woman under the Surface*, including "After the Shipwreck," "Fisherman," "The Raven of Death," "The End of the Line," "In Spring Rain," are imaginary scenes in two senses. They develop images I have imagined rather than physically observed, and they are also scenes that attempt to describe the imagination in certain of its myriad aspects. "The Runner" is dedicated to Muriel Rukeyser, but its tempo and shaping, as well as its extended figure of the runner and the association with the battle of Marathon, derive from H.D. "Moon and Earth" uses its astronomical metaphor as a figure for mother-daughter relations, another H.D. motif. In addition to liminal poems like these, in which (I hope) the material world becomes transparent to the world of the spirit, *A Woman under the Surface* includes several poems with themes taken from classical mythology. Of these, the six-part sequence "Message from the Sleeper at Hell's Mouth," a retelling of the Eros/Psyche story, is most clearly inflected by H.D. The erotically charged lyrics in *Heliodora*, where romantic enthrallment (Rachel DuPlessis's fine term) is interpreted as worship of Aphrodite and the drama of love is limned with exquisite and chaste elegance, excited me. The enchanting idea cited by Norman Holmes Pearson in the preface to *Hermetic Definition*, that "women are individually seeking, as one woman, fragments of the Eternal Lover," spoke to me of an impulse in my own life that I was prepared to believe universal. If in my private experience the rapture of art and the rapture of love were almost identical, if the lover and the work of art or poetry were two parallel windows into eternity, if erotic encounter yielded illumination and the life of the creative mind felt always saturated by the erotic, was there not a single divine reality underlying these twinned manifestations? And were not Eros, Jesus, Krishna all names for the Eternal Lover, sought by the soul?

The poem begins with a lyric in the voice of the author, imagining the god Eros, the lover, as baby and father, sower of seed and giver of gifts who "shoots in every living thing." Aware that the overwhelming majority of love songs are songs of suffering, that tales of love are usually about delusion, the poet takes her stand for a Psyche who is not destroyed but succeeds. She addresses her book on behalf of Psyche: "Go, book, and say this time she conquers." The premise of the sequence, that Psyche is soul-butterfly-woman, is inspired by Apuleius and his commentators up through Freud and Neumann perhaps, but also by the epiphany scene in "Tribute to the Angels."

I have elsewhere described the process of self-analysis involved in completing "Message from the Sleeper at Hell's Mouth." Poems in the voices of Psyche's mother, her two sisters, and her mother-in-law, Aphrodite, delineate relationships and aspects of female roles and personalities that seemed to me common to the world of myth and to our own time. Writing these was relatively easy. The final poem, in the voice of Psyche, was almost insuperably difficult for me, because to write it I needed to acknowledge and accept the actuality of evil as well as good, motives of cruelty as well as kindness, in what I called "my Psyche." Surely I could not have broken through my own resistance to self-knowledge without the example of *Trilogy* and, still more, of *Helen in Egypt*, in which Helen's innocence and her guilt coexist. What is reality and what is illusion? The poetry of spiritual struggle, in which the soul attempts in obscurity and through flashes of illumination to comprehend itself, read its own hieroglyphs, accept itself, reconstruct and redefine itself, to make wholeness of fragments in a world and culture that adamantly resist wholeness, without—at the outset—any clear sense of its path: H.D.'s work from the period of World War II onward undertakes this task over and over, defying exterior and interior doubt. Walking my own path, I had knelt to sip from her wellspring of courage.

In *A Woman under the Surface*, then, what I retrieved from H.D. was a music, a mode of liminality, and the uses of myth to uncover or recover a woman's psyche. In my later books, *The Imaginary Lover*, *Green Age*, and *The Crack in Everything*, these limpid strains continue. The stream rises to its fullest in "A Meditation in Seven Days," a sequence that broods over the meanings of femaleness in Jewish tradition, from the "tangle of sandy footprints" of Abraham, Sarah, and Hagar—obviously an H.D.-derived image—until the present moment. It is a mixed tradition in which woman's powerlessness is streaked with certain kinds of power. The final poem, like the final poem of "Message from the Sleeper at Hell's Mouth," is a dream poem. A titanic male God lies lost in his own drunkenness in a house with three abused children whom I take to be the three monotheistic religions. He dreams of a woman in a yellow dress he has locked out of the house who rises with the springtime and threatens to return; I too dream of her, I dream that I myself am that rejected woman, my hand at his door, about to enter. For the theme of the exiled Shekhinah, the kabbalistic feminine side of God, there are many sources. I had been reading Patai and Merlin Stone, among others. But in what poetry, save H.D.'s, could I have found the Lady whose potential power is our own, whose book is our book?

The limpid style of these poems represents one of my cherished modes. Beginning with *Imaginary Lover*, there is also a kind of thickening, stylistic and thematic, in some of the work that means the most to me. Here it seems that I differ from H.D. Instead of gliding along with the slenderness and lightness of two- and three-line stanzas, poems like "Surviving," "The War of Men and Women," and "The Book of Life" are, so to speak, lumpy. Less like bouillon, strained and distilled, more like stew. Solid sections of varying shapes and sizes jostle against stanzas; lyric and discursive sections interrupt each other; bits of dialogue, bits of comedy, invade the poem; I have become a poet of impurity—even, deliberately, of ugliness. "Is the dung greater or less than the rose?" H.D. asks in *Notes on Thought and Vision* and adds, "If you cannot be seduced by beauty, you cannot learn the wisdom of ugliness" (1982: 32). In "The Book of Life," a poem addressed to a sculptress friend, I find myself describing my friend's art as "a register / Of pain and anger poured into ugly beauty. / The body's loop from clay to clay." Perhaps the thickness of my writing in these poems, the bulkiness of them, the avoidance of limpidity, is a means of confronting and embodying the world's intractable horror. Perhaps it is a means of drawing attention to the awkward multiplicity of fish I try to drag into my net. Paula Modersohn-Becker and her mother, the birthing of her art as a modernist painter interrupted by her death following complications in childbirth, myself and my own difficult relations with my mother, my grief over the curtailment of a sister artist's career, my guilt over my mother's inability to fulfill her own gifts, our collective guilt as survivors of "the broken mothers," and the ongoing craving to be taught and healed by them in a poem called "Surviving." The history of gender war and its more overt political analogues and consequences, the imperative and impossibility of joining "our life with the dangerous life of the other," geology and archaeology, the exasperation of our inability to recover the illumination of paradise lost, viewed through the lens of a younger male poet's crumbling marriage in "The War of Men and Women." Friendship, art, motherhood, Jewishness, aging, and death in "The Book of Life." Perhaps the form of these poems is an objective correlative for the exhausted and unsatisfied perception that, as "The War of Men and Women" puts it, "diagnosis is easy, cure impossible." Perhaps, too, the untransparency of the form is a way of bringing body into the poems. Here I deviate from H.D. Her verse stems from and sublimates body. It may indeed be that the dung yields the rose, but we find an abundance of roses in the poetry and little dung; "the reddest rose unfolds" with a vulval vibration that is a shade more mystical than biological. For me, biology is precious; I want not to neglect it. Yet I think these poems and others like "An Army of Lovers" or "Everywoman Her Own Theology," notwithstanding their differences in form and tone, yearn in the same direction as H.D. yearns. They behave as if they remembered a prior existence more joyous and more organized by love than our own. They behave as if they thought that lost world could be rebuilt.

The closest I have come to combining the thick and the limpid is in *The Nakedness of the Fathers*, a book of many combinations: prose and poetry, commentary and autobiography, history and myth. I follow the trajectory of the Hebrew Bible, from Creation into the compelling stories of Abraham, Isaac, Jacob, and so on, along with their wives, sisters, daughters, on through David and Solomon, and on into fantasies of the return of the mothers who have been so terribly—but not entirely—erased from our founding scriptures. I experience the men and women of the Bible as my own fathers and mothers, as portions of myself. I plunge into the stories to find these links. I love the men—they are such mixed characters, every success pierced with some sort of pain, that is what it means to be Jewish—and I try to retrieve the women, the female power. I try to remember it. I reread and rewrite these stories until I remember. All the while that I worked on this book, off and on for almost ten years, it was my spiritual path. It was my obsession. I used to laugh to myself, thinking the book would be too Jewish for Christians, too heterodox for Jews, too feminist for almost everyone, and too heterosexual for most feminists. For whom was I writing it, then? I thought I was writing it for God. For the God who at the end of days is to be united with his exiled Shekhinah. In Lurianic Kabbala it is believed that when we perform deeds of goodness, we help bring that reunion about. I thought I was working toward that imaginary conclusion. Like H.D., I had no map. Unlike H.D., I do not actually "believe" in God. Neither do I "believe" in a goddess. What was I doing, then? What does it mean, when we pursue these imaginings?

III   *And what there is to conquer*
           By strength and submission, has already been discovered,
           Once or twice, or several times, by men whom one cannot hope
           To emulate—   T. S. Eliot, *Four Quartets*

These lines make clear enough why H.D. is of such value to a woman poet. When Eliot says "men" he means "men." We need a woman poet whom we cannot hope to emulate.

I write this essay as I prepare, in a state of considerable confusion, a volume of selected poems representing thirty-odd years of work. I have just turned sixty. Who am I? Which of my selves belongs in this book? What is the value of such a book? Do any of these poems live? How many marriage poems should I include? How many about my mother, my children? Will the political poems offend the aesthetes? And of those unclassifiable liminal pieces that tend to slip from the grasp and can never please a crowd, yet are perhaps my purest compositions as poems, how many dare I include? Who would read them? I have belonged to no school. I have written, for the most part, in a state of loneliness that has also at times been ecstasy. As a child I was silent, as a young woman inaudible. Entering the moment of cronehood in which I am supposed to be a wise woman, I shake my raddled locks. I wish to make myself heard. Let me contribute my drop to the general bucket, praying that the ripples spread.

What a peculiar thing it is to say. To say that I am finalizing the text for my *Selected and New Poems*, which Pitt did in the fall of 1998. Finalizing thirty years' worth of poems. It is exciting and frightening as I come down to the wire of determining who I am or have been. Please let it be a book that yields meaning, I find myself praying. Please let the poems be good, stay good and do good. Let them be formally excellent compositions, and let them also be life-giving. Is it too much to ask? I realize as I write that I have hardly confided the depth and quality of my caring about this book to anyone, except in the most superficial terms. I have hardly confided it to myself. Perhaps the desire for "immortality," that chestnut, must be confessed to.

Unlike H.D. I have no belief whatsoever in a personal afterlife, and perhaps as a consequence I have placed great stock in my parenting, my teaching, and my writing. I wish these investments to be growth stocks, as it were. How embarrassing to admit it. But one sees so little of the results of one's labors in one's lifetime. What my children have become I partly see. Intelligence, talent, sweetness beam from them. Much too is hidden. What has become of my students I scarcely know, except for a very few with whom I have become friends. What will become of my writing I cannot know at all. I peer into the dark.

The best of it, I think, comes from the dark. From the unknown, from what I am not conscious of, not quite, into the light of the knowable experience that can be shared and felt by others. I cannot do much more than whisper or speak in a voice as to a friend in conversation, there is not much barbaric yawp in me, perhaps there is a little of the oracular. A little. Like H.D. I have no map. I try to reach beyond this world, to what exists within or behind or beneath it—never above it, however. Whatever divinities I divine in the universe, they are not above but within us. It is why I cannot be orthodox or even conservative in my writing or my life. The only thing I actually trust, and then only some small part of the time, is my inner self, with which I hope the Great Self communicates. Wordlessly or in language. Perhaps this is what the Bible means by the still, small voice. H.D. in "The Walls Do Not Fall" identifies Dream with the third person of the Trinity, the holy ghost, and insists on its authority. This makes complete democratic sense to me if I can substitute the term "inspiration" for "Dream." Still, I need the poems to feel as if they were written by someone who spends time in a kitchen. Who has cleaned baby shit. Who lives in a material world, in a material body, in history. The beyond and the here, I want them both in my poems. The coarse and the fine. Both. Both.

And I want a mind to be in them, thinking. And I want a heart in them, caring. I feel quite the fool saying these things. Let me caper in my motley, then.

Recently a very old and distant poet friend, Jack Micheline, died. I met him first in New York, where he was on leave from being a San Francisco Beat poet, a man maybe ten years older than I who didn't shave much, wore old, stained clothes, drank like the Irishman he was, tended to rant. He was sentimental, a talker, a street poet. I would drink beer with him and a student who'd introduced us. When my family was on sabbatical for a semester in Berkeley in 1973, Jack showed up there, as luck would have it. I used to bump into him on Telegraph Avenue. He would be striding up and down shouting out his poems and hustling broadsides of them at a buck apiece. I was still very close to being the excruciatingly shy girl of my childhood. At that point in my life, when I read poems in public, I read them into my collarbone. Watching Jack, I was embarrassed for him, sad for his poverty, ashamed of the crude Beatnik sentiments in his shouts. But somewhere during that time I realized something of great importance to me: Jack was not just a bum, he was a fool. He was letting himself be a fool for poetry. Same as Ginsberg, who was one of my post-Blakean heroes. Ginsberg was a better poet, but the motivation was the same. Give all for love. Transform your anger, your pain, shame, suffering. Give it away. Turn it into love like a fool. I realized that I wanted to do that too and have done as well as, within my middle-class professorial life, and struggling against the barrier of a still imprisoning shyness, I have been able.

But H.D. too has said it: "in me (the worm) clearly / is no righteousness, but this / persistence" (H.D. 1973: 11). She has invoked "my mind (yours), / your way of thought (mine)" and argued in the face of racking contempt and self-doubt that each "personal approach / to the eternal realities" has its place, if only as a leaf in the forest (H.D. 1973: 51–52).

Blake has said, "If the fool would persist in his folly he would become wise" (1964: 96). Foolishness may be a form of self-protection that enables a woman to place in the mouth of another woman a declaration like "I will encompass the infinite / in time, in the crystal, / in my thought here." Could anything be more absurd? Well, perhaps the stubborn eroticism of the aged poet addressing the young Lionel Durand as yet another Eros to her Psyche, or Osiris to her Isis, is even more magnificently ridiculous. A woman over seventy to a man not yet forty? Persistence, persistence. The reddest rose keeps unfolding.

A final reason I so enjoy H.D. is that hardly anyone read her during the time she was writing her best work. She was far too difficult to be read. Ezra and the others labeled her and then crowded her out. She wrote what? What she needed, for herself: "One writes the kind of poetry that one likes. Other people put labels on it." And in *End to Torment*, she speaks of a place in the mind like "the orange groves of Capri, of arcades and arches of Padua and Vienna. Let go, it says, the grandiose, let go ambition; scribble and write, that is your inheritance, no grim compulsion. . . . Others may use our invention, extension, communication. We don't care anymore" (H.D. 1979: 56). Will I, I wonder, ever arrive at that serenity? Meanwhile, the folly remains and is encouraged by this woman I cannot hope to emulate. Our idols have achieved, in the art, far more than we hope to achieve; all the more do we need them in order to produce whatever is latently in us. Here is how it works, for each of us who has been inspired/inspirited by a former artist:

> She draws the veil aside,
>
> unbinds my eyes,
> commands,
> write, write or die.   (H.D. 1972: 7)

And then, and then, the foolish hope that the poems will live for others, will filter and fiber their blood, that others will wish to drink from my stream, and that I'll be an accompanying shadow somewhere.

NOTE

H.D.'s words in the title were quoted by Horace Gregory in his preface to *Helen in Egypt* (1961: ix).

Motherhood/Morality/Momentum: Alicia Ostriker and H.D.

DONNA KROLIK HOLLENBERG

Keep Lilith in a cage, curse Lilith in a Tree?
no; no barbaric hordes nor gods can yet prevail
against the law that drags the snail across the grass,

that turns the falcon from the course,
that drives the lion until he finds
the lioness within the cave;

. . . .

but those prayers are worn threadbare;
there must be others, bright with vivid fire,

revolatilizing, luminous, life-bearing   H.D., "Vale Ave"

We keep pushing
Child, we keep dropping
The seeds

And being part of mystery that is
Bigger than language
And changes the language
And bursts it apart
And grows up and
Wildly away out of it   Alicia Ostriker, "Lilith Says
                              Where Trees Come From"

Alicia Ostriker began to write out of the experience of motherhood well before she read H.D. She was committed early to being a poet who would write about the body and completed "Once More out of Darkness," a poem about pregnancy and birth, in 1965, a year after graduate school. In 1970 she began *The Mother/Child Papers*, galvanized by the experience of bearing a son during the Vietnam War. As she later wrote, considering the historical fact of recurring wars from the dual perspective of poet and mother:

> The advantage of motherhood for a woman artist is that it puts her in immediate and inescapable contact with the sources of life, death, beauty, growth, corruption. . . . if she is a moralist it engages her in serious and useful work. . . . we can imagine what it would signify to all women and men, to live in a culture where childbirth and mothering occupied the kind of position that sex and romantic love have occupied in literature and art for the last hundred years, or the kind of position that warfare has occupied since literature began. (Ostriker 1983: 130–31)

Similarly, concern with motherhood in the context of war was central to H.D. During World War I, when she was establishing herself as a poet, H.D. had two traumatic pregnancies, the first ending in stillbirth, the second in the birth of her daughter, Perdita, in the setting of her own grave illness and the deaths of her brother and father. Everything she wrote later reacted to that trauma. She wanted to restore, through the power of imaginative vision, what had been lost in her own life and, indeed, in the life of Europe. In increasingly female-centered texts, she came to connect the "family romance" and female oppression with the warrior ethos in Western culture and, ultimately, to reappropriate the childbirth metaphor for women writers in the name of love and the hope of social reform (Hollenberg 1991). As Ostriker comments, claiming her as a precursor, "It is appropriate that H.D. is our first poet to imagine a female being in whom a biological life, a life of feeling, and a life of dedicated spirituality and artistic creation are not divided but one" (1983: 40).

In this essay I will explore the implications of motherhood as a moral force in the work of Alicia Ostriker within the context of her literary engagement with H.D. The experience of motherhood, which Ostriker describes as an "extraordinary sensation of transformation from being a private individual self to being a portion of something else," informs her view of the woman poet's role in culture and tradition in ways that parallel but diverge from H.D. (1983: 127). Ostriker's reading of H.D., part of an immersion in women's poetry begun during the height of the feminist movement, prepares her to write out of the (often transgressive) intellectual and emotional depth of her experience and gives her conceptual and formal means of doing so. H.D.'s religious heterodoxy and revisionist mythmaking are particularly instructive: her recovery of a repressed maternal principle in Western culture enables Ostriker's comparable revision of androcentric Jewish myth. However, Ostriker's poetry engages history more directly than H.D.'s. Most recently, she has written in a mode of post-Holocaust apostasy that contradicts H.D.'s commitment to a predetermined cosmic order and spiritual transcendence. Indeed, unlike H.D., for whom poetry is the expression of a sacred "inner world of defence" (Hollenberg 1997: 10) and childbearing a metaphor for salvation, the experience of motherhood is a source of Ostriker's use of poetry as social protest, and she rejects the conversion of human life into the discourse of the sublime.

The first book that Ostriker wrote after reading H.D. was *A Woman under the Surface* (1982), in which both the experience of motherhood and her engagement with H.D. are expressed subliminally. The moral imperative of the mother-child bond, that sense of the self's transformation, is experienced at a primitive level. The book's title is taken from the poem "The Exchange," which records the fear of and desire for chthonic female power, which is transgressive in a world limited by stifling gender roles and male domination. The poet imagines changing places with a strong woman who swims "below the surface" of the water. If she "dives down," this double might climb into the boat she inhabits with her children, strangle and dispose of them, take her car, drive to her home, and confront her husband. When he answers the doorbell and sees "this magnificent naked woman, bits of sunlight / Glittering on her pubic fur," past insults will be avenged while she swims coolly "out of reach" (Ostriker 1982: 7). In other poems, the feeling of being part of a larger whole informs the poet's concern for the well-being of other women, particularly those on the social margins. For example, there is a poem in the voice of a "crazy lady" who insists on being embraced, another about "three women" who have been neglected or misled by men, and one that recounts a daughter's nightmare invasion by the bedraggled specter of her mother. Particularly reminiscent of H.D., still other poems engage in revisionist mythmaking; that is, mythmaking that alters existing myths for the purposes of cultural reform. For example, there is a poem sequence, based on the myth of Eros and Psyche, that questions the inevitability of female masochism embedded in Apuleius's version of that myth.[1]

Further, in this book Ostriker internalized the shape of H.D.'s mature poetic stanza, the formal correlative of her radical stance as a visionary modernist in a world shattered by war: two or three nonmetrical lines that nevertheless are gracefully cadenced, suggesting traces of primal order. As H.D. put it in her early novel, *Paint It Today*, anticipating the limpid stanza form she would create in *Trilogy*: "Large, epic pictures bored her, though she struggled through them. She wanted the songs that cut like a swallow wing the high, untainted ether, not the tragic legions of set lines that fell like black armies with terrific force and mechanical set action, paralyzing, or broke like a black sea to baffle and to crush" (1992b: 12). Like H.D., Ostriker became adept at this stanza form and at the subtle use of off-rhyme as well as of other kinds of interior sound linkages.[2] In this book, poems about the liberation of her dream life are reminiscent of H.D. in sound as well as theme. Consider these lines from the opening and closing of Ostriker's "The Diver":

> Giving the self to water, a diver
> Lifts from stone, sails through the air,
> Hits, goes under.

> Now, she remembers everything, this cold
> Sweet privacy, the instantaneous
> Loss of her name. She remembers that drowning
> Is a possibility, like not drowning.   (1982: 63)

Though grounded in experience and thus in loss, they are buoyant and fluid. Like the following lines by H.D., they invite us to trust our own inner lives, suggesting that resilience and spiritual regeneration lie there, not in outside authority:

> let us go down to the sea,

> gather dry sea-weed,
> heap drift-wood,

> let us light a new fire
> and in the fragrance

> of burnt salt and sea-incense
> chant new paeans to the new Sun
>
> of regeneration.   (1973: 26)

Ostriker's reading of H.D. is directly acknowledged in her next book of poems, *The Imaginary Lover* (1986), in which the epigraph, from *Trilogy*, expresses a desire for spiritual wholeness and autonomy that Ostriker shares:

> Chasm, schism in consciousness
> must be bridged over;
> we are each householder,
> each with a treasure.   (H.D. 1973: 49)

Both poets locate the impediments to that wholeness in the dualities authorized by culture and tradition. Among these is a socially constructed contradiction between creativity and procreativity, motherhood and authorship. In fact, a "quest for autonomous self-definition" is central to the women's poetry movement that Ostriker describes in her groundbreaking book of literary criticism, *Stealing the Language: The Emergence of Women's Poetry in America*, published the same year. Not surprisingly, many of Ostriker's observations about the work of her predecessors and contemporaries apply to her own poetry as well. In fact, the main categories she ascribes to this poetry movement—the ways in which women write about the body and nature, the meanings of anger and violence in one's work, the "imperative of intimacy" that marks the expression of female desire, revisionist mythmaking as attempts at self and cultural reform—are exemplified in *The Imaginary Lover*.

This book is divided into four sections, all of which contain poems that could be placed in the categories above. What distinguishes Ostriker's work, however, are qualities of sensuality, humor, courage, exuberance, and a range that extends from the natural into the political and metaphysical. Ostriker enters into the political realm (defined broadly to include management of the family and the self) in many poems throughout the book. There are poems about the politics of creative expression, the politics of marriage, the politics of parenthood, particularly as children grow up and away, as well as the politics of historical events. Some cover several of these subjects simultaneously. Among my favorites is "Surviving," a ten-part sequence about a subject also central to H.D., who prays, after having survived the Blitz in London, *"we pause to give / thanks that we rise again from death and live"* (1973: 110). H.D.'s prayer follows her vision of a Lady whose precise and unconventional definition—culminating in a revised Nativity—signals spiritual renewal and growth. Like *Trilogy*, "Surviving" responds to the violence and displacement that mark our century and spotlights a revised conception of motherhood. However, unlike H.D., who wrote under the direct stress of wartime bombardment, Ostriker writes from the postwar perspective of those who feel that "to survive is to be ashamed" (1986a: 44). This survival guilt is worse for women, she claims, for it becomes fused with histories of biological vulnerability and social subordination. Continuing H.D.'s urgent opening questions, "what saved us? what for?" (1973: 4), Ostriker asks, "Who can urge us to pull ourselves onward? / How can the broken mothers teach us?" (1986a: 44).

In the body of the poem, Ostriker answers these questions and tests the assumption behind the second one. Unlike H.D., who employs techniques of trance and verbal alchemy (repetition, etymology, phonic overlap), attempting to transcend the historical moment to effect spiritual transformation, Ostriker writes a series of meditations that draw on cultural and personal history. Set in an art gallery, half of the poems are about the artist Paula Modersohn-Becker, who died after complications in childbirth, and half are about Ostriker's own mother, whose domestic duties defeated her artistic aspirations. In the fourth section, a surrealist dreamscape, the tragedy of Modersohn-Becker's short life and the wry comedy of her mother's long one become fused in the mind of the poet-onlooker, enabling her to proceed beyond guilt or self-pity. Having realized that despite her premature death, Modersohn-Becker's last paintings were "survivors / Without malice," the poet imagines herself going up in an elevator, into which her mother steps, "carrying her shopping bags" and "talking, talking" (Ostriker 1986a: 47). What follows is a tragicomic immigrant litany: details of her mother's heroism and self-sacrifice on behalf of her family:

> Did I ever tell you
> I fought the doctors and nurses
> The very day you were born. They said

> "You'll stick a bottle in her mouth"
> But I nursed you, I showed
> Them. And did I tell you
> When I was hungry because your father
> Didn't have a job, I used to feed you
> That expensive beef puree, spoonful by spoonful
>   (Ostriker 1986a: 48)

The poet's response to this litany and to her mother's stories about the blighted youth of her grandmother, with their further suggestion of collective guilt, is renewed resolution. After all, risk and the "promise of cruelty" and "impoverishment" are conditions of life common also to artists. But they did not prevent Keats from writing "The Eve of St. Agnes" or Hart Crane *The Bridge*. With this realization, the poet remembers her mother's inspiring qualities: her playfulness in the public swimming pool, the way the other kids flocked around her, her courage, and her songs:

> You get even the smallest ones to duck
> Heads under water, bubbling and giggling
> *Don't be afraid! Breathe out like this!* Then we all sing.
>   (Ostriker 1986a: 50)

This memory enables her to break the hold of histories and theories of women's weakness and tears that are *"maps to nowhere"* (Ostriker 1986a: 50). At the end, calling upon "Mother my poet" to help her to understand more fully "the duty / Proper to the survivor," she concludes, "Tell me it is not merely the duty of grief" (Ostriker 1986a: 51).

Several poems in this book are inspired by the words of past writers to whom Ostriker feels connected. "An Army of Lovers" opens with an epigraph from H.D. on the secret kinship of pacifist artists during wartime censorship. They pass each other on the pavement, "remote, speechless," but they are "nameless initiates, / born of one mother" (H.D. 1973: 21). She compares their shared concern with that of contemporary women poets who write prayers for peace, hoping to counter the ongoing linked realities of war and sexual violence. Other poems begin with epigraphs or lines by Ezra Pound, June Jordan, Fitzgerald/ Hemingway, Franz Kafka, and Emily Dickinson. The poem inspired by Dickinson, which begins with Dickinson's "After great pain a formal feeling comes," takes off from that proposition to explore its opposite. The result is a poetics of exuberance and hope that depends upon the achievement of community and is founded in the responsibility of motherhood:

> If that is the case, then after great happiness
> Should a feeling come that is somehow informal?

> Yes, yes, a thousand times yes.   (Ostriker 1986a: 57)

The poet's associations fly from the intense happiness of Catullus and Lesbia, engrossed in each other, to her own pleasure after teaching a successful seminar on Blake's *Four Zoas*, in which her students make new discoveries and come "closer together." "Scrubbing perception's doors," she calls this, and then she imagines, as a final triumph, having patiently charmed her young son out of a temper tantrum.

Ostriker's sense of art as personal liberation, as well as a powerful socially constitutive force, also informs "Everywoman Her Own Theology," a poem that foreshadows her most recent work on feminist revisions of the Bible. Here she critiques the inhumanity of abstract, dualistic belief systems in which believers construct themselves in violent opposition to "infidels." Instead she imagines "something sacred" that wants to "materialize, / Folding its silver wings, / In a kitchen, and bump its chest against mine" (Ostriker 1986a: 65). This domestication of the sacred is continued in her next volume, *Green Age* (1989), in which the personal-as-political-as-sacred marks key sequences in each of the book's three parts. In "A Birthday Suite," dedicated to her daughter Eve, Ostriker dramatizes the intense yearnings for relationships defined by mutuality and interpenetration that, she says, characterize the poetry of many women writing today (Cook 1992). Stemming from the intensity of the mother-child bond, this blurring of boundaries between self and other is not without conflict and pain during the phase of separation, but it is also mutually empowering. As Ostriker's "Happy Birthday" wish to her daughter concludes: "On your mark, get set, // We give birth to each other. Welcome. Welcome" (Ostriker 1989: 21). In her sequence "A Meditation in Seven Days" (in *Green Age*) Ostriker extends this desire for mutuality and equality to the traditional Jewish concept of a male God, imagining instead "the meanings of femaleness in Jewish tradition" (see the previous chapter in this volume). This poem's assumption, "that we may find in the text of the Bible and throughout Jewish tradition faint traces of a Canaanite goddess or goddesses whose worship was forbidden with the advent of monotheism," is based in the scholarship of feminist theologians who have likewise challenged the androcentrism of mainstream religious ideas (Ostriker 1989: 73). It is also based in her reading of H.D. As she points out in her essay in this volume, "in what poetry, save H.D.'s, could I have found the Lady whose potential power is our own?" In the last step of this poem, the poet's recognition of this (suppressed) female presence in Jewish lore and life foreshadows the feminist revision of biblical myth in her later work.

As this sequence in *Green Age* promises, Ostriker engages her Jewish heritage more fully in the two books that follow: *Feminist Revision and the Bible* (1993) and *The Nakedness of the Fathers: Biblical Visions and Revisions* (1994). In both of these books, her allusions to H.D. strengthen a revisionary impulse rooted in the experience of the mother-child bond. In the first, a series of three "lectures" (the last in the form of a poem sequence), Ostriker directly cites H.D. as a major influence on religious poets in our time because she is "the most seriously engaged in spiritual quest" and "the most radically transgressive." As Ostriker explains, H.D.'s "explicit goal is to recover, in a moment of apocalyptic revelation, as the blasting open of cities in war becomes the blasting open of intellectual and spiritual paradigms, at the heart of the worship of the Father and Son, an older worship of the Mother" (1993: 79). Following this example, Ostriker points out several types of biblical revisionism in contemporary poetry by women since the sixties. These include many poems that angrily indict God the Father, that regard the "religion of patriarchy" as "a projection of masculine ego, masculine will to power, masculine death-worship," as well as "a tremendous outpouring of comedy, shameless sexuality, an insistence on sensual immediacy and the details belonging to the flesh as holy" (Ostriker 1993: 81). There is also much poetry connected with the women's spirituality movement that "avoids and evades biblical texts," drawing instead on pagan, Native American, African, and Hindu traditions. Common to all these types are the following "motifs and motivations": "the return of immanence and nature, the reconnection of body and spirit, the rejection of dogma and the embrace of syncretism, and an insistence on the unmediated personal experience of the divine" (Ostriker 1993: 83). Ostriker concludes this discussion by citing the poetry of Lucille Clifton, an African-American poet whose religious syncretism is like H.D.'s but whose vernacular style is bolder. In one of her earliest poems, Ostriker points out, Clifton "defines an outrageous female holiness" in a tone that "fuses celebration, defiance, and humorous sympathy" (1993: 83).

In "The Lilith Poems," the poem sequence that follows this discussion, Ostriker employs this mode and tone herself. These six poems imagine the legendary Jewish outcast, Adam's first wife who refused to lie beneath him, as a black woman who composes a vigorous, syncretic "New Song" (Ostriker 1993: 98). Stronger, bolder, sexier than Eve, Lilith is the latter's cleaning lady by day, but at night she steps out in "high heels," "jumps the fence" of Paradise, and dares to defy Adam. As she says, "Nobody gives me orders / Now or ever" (Ostriker 1993: 94). Moreover, she "deconstructs scripture," finds a *"mother / Tongue"* within this "curse, discourse," and inspires her conventional sister with courage (Ostriker 1993: 95). In fact, the last is her most important function. Sympathetic to the concern for her children that keeps Eve obedient, Lilith brings forward her own "ancient angers"—the hundred babies she bears every day that are condemned to "die by nightfall" (Ostriker 1993: 96). In their memory she teaches Eve a lesson about "changing the language" (Ostriker 1993: 97). In "Lilith Says Where Trees Come From," from which I quote more fully in the second epigraph above, she cites the weeds "pushing / Busting with lust" as an example of the resiliency and potential of the life force outside the dubious protection of the garden enclosure. Ostriker's use of black vernacular as well as open form in these poems is doubly appropriate. Not only does it fit the sense of otherness she feels as a woman within Judaism ("I am and am not a Jew," she writes in *The Nakedness of the Fathers*), it also deliberately breaks down barriers between self and other, a central tenet of her poetics and moral stance.

For H.D. as well, as exemplified in the above epigraph from her poem "Vale Ave," the powerful, subversive law of Eros is associated with Lilith (and Lucifer) and not Eve (and Adam). That is, a felt connection with a marginalized woman opens a path to the redemptive power of communal memory.[3] Significantly, in her case, the paradigmatic "other" woman is a Semite. Think, first, of the psychological connection between Raymonde Ransome, the neurasthenic heroine of the central story in *Palimpsest* who has repressed her husband's betrayal dur-

ing the war, and Ermentrude Solomon, "the Hampstead Jewess . . . in a
world of conscious pain" (H.D. 1968: 111). In the course of this story,
Raymonde acclaims her Jewish guest as follows:

> For Ermy was beautiful (there was no getting round it) with the
> beauty of some unearthed Queen Nefertiti. She was beautiful with
> a glamour that belongs only to antiquity and racially Ermy was a
> direct blood inheritor of all the things that she, Raymonde, was at-
> tuned to. Egypt, the Syrian desert. Raymonde sensed around the
> brow of the tall Jewess (almost visibly) a band of dark exquisite wine-
> purple hyacinths. She was shocked by a sudden transference of all
> her values. Ermy was not of to-day, not even of yesterday, but of
> always and forever.   (H.D. 1968: 126)

Twenty-five years later, after another, more terrible war, H.D. would
write a major poetic lamentation primarily in the voice of another
desert-ed woman: *Helen in Egypt*. In this masterpiece of palimpsestic
thinking, she staged Helen's response to Achilles' anger as a hysterical
"racial conversion" within the context of maternity (Edmunds 1994:
120). After Achilles blames Helen for the death of his legions, his "children," she becomes "what his accusations made me, / Isis, forever with
that Child, / the Hawk Horus" (H.D. 1961: 23).

Although Helen's is the dominant consciousness in *Helen in Egypt*,
several other characters also speak: her three lovers, Achilles, Paris, and
Theseus, as well as the eidolon of Thetis. Indeed, many critics, including Ostriker, have read the poem as a psychic journey, within a psy-
chotherapeutic context, in which Helen recovers and works through
traumatic communal memories engendered in time of war. As Eileen
Gregory has written, claiming Euripidean tragedy as a subtext and
stressing its communal aspect: "*Helen in Egypt* may be understood as an
extended and greatly amplified choros sequence, in H.D.'s distinct invention of that form" (1997: 222). Helen is presented to us as the paradigmatic surviving woman. Moreover, as Adalaide Morris has pointed
out, H.D.'s extraordinary use of sound in this poem is itself a style of
thought. In Morris's words, sound here is "a mode of primary attention, an orientation, a concentration" connected "more to the Mother/
Daughter dyad than to Father . . . a preoedipal ghostland or dreamland,
at once sensuous and dematerialized, erotic and disembodied" (1997:
45, 47). These readings remind us that mourning as a communal enter-

prise has garnered extensive attention as a female discourse, perhaps because of the intensity of maternal loss. As Maeera Shreiber has written, "Throughout antiquity, in both Greek and Middle Eastern culture, the lament as a standard feature of ritual life belonged largely to the women who gathered to lead the community in the rites of grief" (quoted in Prins and Shreiber 1997: 303).

In the aftermath of war, the linked journeys of Helen and Achilles take place within the context of profound philosophical questioning about the relation of illusion to reality, of dream to waking, of memory to desire, of man and woman to God. Such questions also pervade Ostriker's book-length poem, *The Nakedness of the Fathers: Biblical Visions and Revisions* (1994). As innovative as H.D.'s in its mixture of genres (prose narrative, lyric poetry, autobiography, quotation from scripture and other writers), it, too, is the culmination of a lifetime study of ancient texts. Although I cannot do justice to its full scope here, I want to point out some of its confluences with H.D. around the themes of motherhood and morality and to suggest some differences. These differences enable Ostriker to move from lamentation encoded in myth, H.D.'s sense of art as covert resistance to the atrocities of history, to a sense of art as overt protest, in and of history.

First, more overtly than H.D. in *Helen in Egypt*, Ostriker begins with a mother's perspective. Citing H.D. as a model, she says her biblical (re)visions began when she asked some questions about the Book of Job. Specifically, how would Job's wife feel "about having the ten children who had been casually slain in order to test her husband's devotion to God, replaced by ten new children?" (Ostriker 1994: xi). This question leads her to engage in a feminist version of the Jewish tradition of *midrash* (probing, searching); that is, "the eliciting from biblical verses meanings beyond the literal . . . according to their contemporary relevance" (Seltzer 1980: 267). She organizes her book around this feminist agenda, interleaving biblical interpretation with autobiography and poetry. After an introductory section, "Entering the Tents," Ostriker proceeds through sections titled "As in Myth: The Garden," "Myth into Legend: The Fathers I," "Legend into History: The Fathers II," and finally, "Though She Delay: The Return of the Mothers." Like H.D. in *Tribute to Freud*, Ostriker engages in a daring revision of "the family romance," a revision centered on the development of female identity (instead of male) and the insight that the "power of the dream is the power of the biological family" (1994: 117). Like H.D., in "The Fathers I" she demystifies the biblical patriarchs, connecting them with her own ancestors: *"Father Abraham is neither king, general, prophet, or priest, but an obscure shepherd whose newly circumcised loins produce in old age a particular seed, representing a particular idea"* (Ostriker 1994: 50). Like H.D., this connection makes possible a recognition that the patriarchal religious impulse, God-the-Father, covers up the Goddess, suppresses the mother. However, at the end of this section, Ostriker's plot differs from H.D.'s when "The Sisters," Leah and Rachel, refuse to compete for men's approval by bearing more children whose deaths they then obediently lament. Instead, Rachel alone steals her father's "household idols," and the poet employs the story of Joseph to write an "Interpretation of Dreams" that will result in a more radical symbolization of the divine:

> Nonetheless the coat of many colors materializes at the moment of loss. A symbol of something else. A symbol of *symbolism.* The material object evoking the maternal subject: matter for pride and arrogance on the part of the naively exhibitionist child, matter for mutter on the part of his jealous brothers, patchwork of Israel's sensuous love for Rachel-Joseph, fabric for another kind of story, a new velvet moment.   (Ostriker 1994: 114)

At the end of the book this more radical symbolization culminates in a daring, "absurd" vision of the male deity. He is in "Intensive Care," laboring to give birth to the memory of the goddess he has earlier swallowed, and this vision of him is followed by a prayer for the presence in the world of the Shekhinah (God's female aspect) in which everyone participates:

> He is trying to remember something, to remember something weighty but shapeless, something he swallowed, back *there*, as he calls it. Back *there*. He almost has it. Like a sort of fish. Like a minnow thrashing its tail in the midst of a whale. But presently the agony comes on him, seizes him, an iridescent foam roaring up the beach.   (Ostriker 1994: 250)

> Shekhinah shine your face on us
>
> Shekhinah turn your countenance
>
> To us and give us peace.   (Ostriker 1994: 254)

Of course, in addressing the end of Ostriker's book, I have omitted its longest section, which holds more examples of her differences from H.D. In "Legend into History," Ostriker begins with a meditation on Moses' childhood within ancient Egyptian culture. Feminized but over-refined in its embodiment of timelessness, this culture is built upon slavery, the crudest form of social injustice. Legend becomes Judeo-Christian history when Moses nurses his people through a project of liberation from this static worldview. Midrashim upon many biblical characters and events follow: Miriam, Aaron, Joshua, Ruth, Hannah, David, the covenant at Sinai, the Sabbath. The section concludes with "The Wisdom of Solomon" dramatized as a comic "summit" between Solomon and Sheba, who talk while making love. Solomon is wise, suggests Ostriker, because he is ready to take Sheba's advice and permit women "to worship the goddesses of their choice upon the high places" (Ostriker 1994: 214). In fact, Solomon's preference for vitality over the rule of preordained law is central to Ostriker's midrashic method here, which is open and ongoing in substance as well as style. For midrash, according to Hartman and Budick, is "a life in literature or in scripture that is experienced in the shuttle space between the interpreter and the text" (1986: xi). That life, expressed in the moving autobiographical passages that recall specifics of family history, leads us to Ostriker's main difference from H.D.

In her midrash on Job, subtitled "A Meditation on Justice," Ostriker reminds us of that pivotal question she asked in the preface: "How would Job's wife feel about having the ten children who had been casually slain in order to test her husband's devotion to God, replaced by ten new children?" (Ostriker 1994: xi). Her answer, an extrapolation from the one line Job's wife speaks in the traditional story *("Curse God and die")*, is a rejection of the folktale frame of that story, "where Job gets everything back and is richer than before" (Ostriker 1994: 234). It is an angry rejection from the viewpoint of a woman "whose killed children remain under the ground where she cannot touch them again" of any formulaic assumption of God's justice (Ostriker 1994: 235). Indeed, thought about the plight of Job's wife leads Ostriker to a series of auto-biographical memories that conclude with the realization that *"without rage, love is helpless"* (1994: 238). She concludes that women aren't yet angry enough, that maybe when we demand justice of God, he will respond: "After all, he is merely the laws of physics, the magnificent laws of physics, and then the adorable laws of biology. And finally, circuit by ticking circuit through the neural nets, the exquisite laws of conscience" (Ostriker 1994: 239).

Inconsolable grief and rage at the loss of specific human children; in this midrash Ostriker is far from the sublime world of H.D.'s "Winter Love." In H.D.'s late poem, an elderly Helen, engaged in anamnesis, acknowledges her loss: "*l'île blanche* is *l'île noir*" (1972: 112). But this acknowledgment is the prelude to the birth of a mysterious poem-child "Euphorion," "Espérance," who "lives in the hope of something that will be, // the past made perfect" (H.D. 1972: 112). Similarly, in "Hermetic Definition," H.D. employs the childbirth metaphor to dramatize a poetic triumph over death: "the writing was the un-born, / the conception" (1972: 54). It is not that H.D. does not understand the laws of physics, or of biology, or of conscience. Rather, her persistent hermeticism has to do partly with temperament and education, that is, with her roots in the romantic heritage of literary modernism. Partly it reflects the indelible effect upon her of the two world wars through which she lived. The exaltation she expresses here, as in other examples of sublime discourse, "arises from terror, terror beheld and resisted" (Terence Des Pres, quoted in Wilson 1991: 39). It is an expression of fictive self-empowerment that camouflages deeper feelings of social powerlessness (Wilson 1991: 211). Innovative in its use of female experience, specifically motherhood, H.D.'s late work nevertheless reflects a belief in a predetermined cosmic order for which she yearns. In her words, "unaware, Spirit announces the Presence; / shivering overtakes us, / as of old, Samuel" (H.D. 1973: 3). Like apocalyptic prophets before her, H.D. transfers the concept of a cyclical pattern inaccessible to human understanding to "God's providential plan for history" (Seltzer 1980: 161). Even in "Hermetic Definition," where direct references to personal and contemporary history indicate a philosophical change, at the end she dresses herself in "nun-grey" to proclaim: "Night brings the Day" (H.D. 1972: 55). Were it not for the terseness of this final assertion, her recourse to the sublime would suggest complacency.

In contrast, Ostriker's midrash about Job is prefaced with two epigraphs, the first from the biblical character himself, who prays to God from his ash heap, the second from Paul Celan, who speaks bitterly, ironically, angrily. Considering the ashes of the Holocaust, Celan decries God's absence:

Blessed art thou, No-one.
For thy sake we
will bloom.
Towards
thee.   (1986: 231)

In fact, there are many references to the deaths of Jews in the Holocaust in *The Nakedness of the Fathers* and throughout Ostriker's work. However, perhaps her most powerful poem on this subject, "The Eighth and the Thirteenth," is from *The Crack in Everything* (1996). The numbers in the poem's title refer to two symphonies by Dmitri Shostakovich about the atrocities of World War II. "Music about the worst / Horror history offers," Ostriker writes (1996: 29).

Part of the composer's "War Triptych," Shostakovich's Eighth Symphony reflects "the Russian ethos of 1943 . . . a numb sorrow mixed with anger . . . life revolved around the ever-present threat of death and destruction" (Blokker 1979: 95). His Thirteenth Symphony, composed in 1962, contains a setting for Yevtushenko's poem "Babi Yar" about the thousands of Jews massacred outside of Kiev in 1941 whose traces were later covered up by Soviet authorities. Both Yevtushenko's poem and the symphony, scored for voices and orchestra, have a dual function of memorial and protest. As the composer explained in 1968, "Soviet music is a weapon in the ideological battle [against government repression]. Artists cannot stand as indifferent observers in this struggle" (Blokker 1979: 133). In her poem's tribute to these symphonies, Ostriker shares this view of the dual social functions of art. She also shares the composer's intensity, directness, and method of incorporating other voices. In one long verse column, uninterrupted until near the end, she blends her voice with the sound of these symphonies, with two substantial quotations from the composer's memoir, and with a line quoted from a sister poet, Marina Tsvetaeva. Together with these others, she makes a claim for art that transforms pathos into ethos. She substitutes an ethics of human relationship within history for one that mystifies the divine.[4]

This aspect of Ostriker's work, which extends the moral imperative of motherhood, acquires specificity when it is read in the context of Emmanuel Levinas's account of " 'responsibility for the Other' as 'the primal and fundamental structure of subjectivity' " (quoted in Prins and Shreiber 1997: 313). In *Ethics and Infinity*, Levinas explains: " 'I under-

stand responsibility as responsibility for the Other, thus as responsibility for what is not my deed, or for what does not even matter to me;
or which precisely does matter to me, is met by me as face—the "face"
meaning the fully vulnerable presence of the Other'" (quoted in Prins
and Shreiber 1997: 313). Certainly Shostakovich exemplified this view
in his life as a composer. A Christian, he faced ignominy and risked
death in his opposition to the tyranny of Stalin. Moreover, in the Thirteenth Symphony, as well as in other works, he clearly identified himself
with the Jewish dead against Soviet authority and world indifference, as
did Tsvetaeva, who ultimately committed suicide. In the course of her
poem, Ostriker gathers strength from the words of both of them.

> *Art destroys silence. I know that many will not agree with me
> and will point out other, more noble aims of art. They'll
> talk about beauty, grace, and other high qualities. But you
> won't catch me with that bait. . . .*
>
> *Most of my symphonies are tombstones,* said Shostakovich.[5]
>
> *All poets are Jews,* said Tsvetaeva.   (1996: 31)

At the beginning, however, Ostriker is in a grimmer mood. Listening
to public radio "in solitude" at night while sipping a glass of wine, she
drinks the "somber" Eighth Symphony "to the vile lees" (1996: 29). As
the composer draws out the "minor thirds, the brass tumbles overhead,"
mixing in her mind with pictures of human indifference to destruction.

> Like ravens
> Who know when meat is in the offing,
> Oboes form a ring. An avalanche
> Of iron violins.   (Ostriker 1996: 29)

The specific historical context yields a powerful, ugly image of "divine"
childbirth that contrasts sharply with H.D.'s euphoric images of hope:

> At Leningrad
> During the years of siege
> Between bombardment, hunger,
> And three subfreezing winters,
> Three million dead were born
> Out of Christ's bloody side. Like icy
> Fetuses.   (Ostriker 1996: 29)

In this image, a marvel of compression, Ostriker performs a kind of reverse Adam/Messiah typology. Here Christ does not fulfill God's promise of salvation after the fall. Instead, he is mapped onto Adam, out of whose side comes not Eve but dead babies. Thus she fuses the mystification of childbirth in Judeo-Christian religious tradition with its suppression of women, and she invests both with the pain of human history. Indeed, for Ostriker, as for Shostakovich, the assault on theodicy presented in genocide and other imposed misery is best reflected in paradoxical, discordant music:

> The words *never again*
> Clashing against the words
> *Again and again*
> —That music.   (Ostriker 1996: 31)

How would H.D. have regarded Ostriker's more disillusioned poetic impetus? At the end of her life, H.D. was moving in this direction too. In *End to Torment*, her memoir of Ezra Pound, she also addresses, in retrospect, the compulsion and grandiosity of her own romantic quest in *Helen in Egypt*, which she often referred to as her "Cantos," echoing Pound. Considering the imprisonment at Pisa of her old colleague and the motives of Eliot's poetry as well, she wrote: "The prison actually of the Self was dramatized or materialized for our generation by Ezra's incarceration" (H.D. 1979: 56). After that she reduced the scope of her poetry. There is a noticeable austerity in her late music, a greater resistance in her poetic line.

How would H.D. have greeted Alicia Ostriker's accomplishment? With appreciation and applause.

NOTES

1. Alicia Ostriker, "Message from the Sleeper at Hell's Mouth" (1982: 41–47). Ostriker includes a note summarizing Apuleius's tale.

2. Alicia Ostriker discusses H.D.'s poetics in her essay "No Rule of Procedure: The Open Poetics of H.D.," reprinted in Friedman and DuPlessis (1990: 336–51).

3. For a fuller discussion of H.D.'s poem, see Twitchell-Waas (1996: 203–27).

4. Ostriker expresses this view more explicitly in this book in the poem "The Book of Life."

5. Ostriker quotes from *Testimony: The Memoirs of Dmitri Shostakovich* as related to and edited by Solomon Volkov (Shostakovich 1979: 123, 129).

H.D.: A Joining

ROBERT KELLY

This revision is dedicated to Norman Holmes Pearson:

Of course I was there
but never met the man
never met me
she met us both
in the differences of death

defining me.

Sometimes there is a special concentration of thought, of energy to speak, when I am in a place that is not my place. To be apart from where I am. To be in the lap of, shadow of, someone other. That special intensity is what I felt in Norman Holmes Pearson's office one day in 1966. I was in New Haven at the invitation of the scholar and critic P. Adams Sitney and had been duly installed as poet in residence at Yale's Calhoun College. And here was a spring morning given to me and I was free to explore H.D.'s books, notebooks, typescripts. Mostly the typescripts got me, the works she offered to us as finished.

At the time this poem or sequence of notations was published as a little book soon afterward, there was no way for people to read the bulk of H.D.'s truest, fullest, latest work. *Helen in Egypt* had been published by Grove Press, but the concluding book of the cycle, *Winter Love*, was still unpublished, just like *Vale Ave* and *Sagesse*, while the War Trilogy poems were long out of print.[1] Yet it is precisely those texts that we think of first when we think of who H.D. was, and what she did, and what she is.

So I sat in the office of Pearson, her old friend who had done so much to keep her work in sight and make sure the ripe work got to be known. I was there through his kindness and courtesy, but I was not there as an act of piety or out of any sort of industrious scholarship. I was there just to read. To read the poems of this writer I had already begun to realize was one of the great ones of our time—and by our time I suppose I mean the stretch from George III to George Bush and beyond. If ever an American writer unselfconsciously connected our national striving to language, our word-dance, with the whole Western literary tradition—lightly, lightly!—it was H.D.

So when I sat down to read her words, I was expecting nothing but literature.

I know differently now. Something happens when we read, something that comes from someone. It is not "communication"—that shibboleth of fuzzy feeling. Even less is it some sort of "communication" in the old Spiritualist sense or the contemporary channeling sense. Instead, it is a presence, a sense of life—like the fierce sense of life *and* order I have felt when standing in an ancient Roman amphitheater or in front of a Cézanne.

I know that people come to me through their words and that's a general thing, they do and they do. But she was the first, the first one who stood there in the room beside and above me, just like (it of course only now occurs to me) the nurse, the muse. Wanting something of me she can't specify and I can't deliver. Like any poet, *I do what it can*—I do what language can. Not for poets is the proud boast of a painter like van Eyck, who describes his gesture into the world as wielding his own power—he paints "ALS IXH XAN," "as I can."

Who could the poets be talking to if not us, the ones who read? The ones who hear?

And at that time, of course, I was one of the few living beings who was privileged to be reading that work of hers; I was alone in the office. Norman Holmes Pearson had left out her manuscripts and his greetings; his secretary in the other room had gotten me settled and gone her way.

We do only what language lets us do, or a little bit more.

But when we're done with what it lets us do, the text that's left from all our work wields more meaning than we meant. And there it lies, long after its First Person (if we can dignify the writer so) is gone. So half a dozen years after H.D.'s death I'm reading her late work, loving her late work, in the office of her friend. Of course she could find me.

And I was looking only for the work, the work I felt (feel even more strongly now) our current commonwealth of letters had real need for. To talk that straight, to let the talk, parlando, rise subtly, and then gravitate into music. Fall into music. That is how her best work seems to me: the War Trilogy, and *Helen in Egypt, Winter Love, Vale Ave.*

We have a great need now for the honest humanity of what she does. As García Lorca took refuge in the tree and the bird and the moon, things that are (as far as we know) permanent, H.D. took refuge in the permanence of feelings: not that a feeling ever lasts, far from it: its very flight is its glory, the essence of the bright void in which we live and in which from time to time forever glints of feeling flicker, hurt or love us, and then disperse. What is permanent is that feelings continue to arise; H.D. more than any poet I know was faithful to their sensate and particular arisings.

It did not matter how her lover loved her yesterday. This is the beach of now, these are the rocks of now wet with this immediate spray of longing. That's what the poem has to deal with: these moments.

The sheer protean nature of the beloved in H.D., almost absurd in His (Her) many names—like the great summoning of maybes in section 20 of "The Flowering of the Rod"—argues more strongly, if we needed it, that these are not "narrative poems." They are Long Songs. However many lines they may wield, they are extended lyrics, addressing and attending the momentary and fugitive (hence eternal) upwelling of *what it is to dwell with feelings in the world.*

And if the greatest poetry is that which faithfully, ardently attends to the nature of Mind itself, then H.D. moves toward that greatness in sturdy determination to hear herself feel (if I can put it that way) and hear all the way to the end.

So what is it, this "poem" of mine that I am here reprinting, revised, thirty years after? It is a poem, yes, of a sort, not a pastiche of H.D., but surely its musics and sense of order are both calqued on her prosody. What I was learning then, and trying to give now, is a use of poetry. Poetry too has uses, and this poem means to investigate, consider, discern, respond—which are precisely the four aspects of what once we knew as criticism, before that lovely art of wandering through texts got lost in absolutes. Someday Robert Duncan's *H.D. Book*, his critical summa, may be published complete and start to restore the luster of that sensuous discipline of reading and of following the text wherever it leads.[2] Perhaps the critic should stop trying to ape the judge and the prophet and instead take counsel from the lover, such a lover as Poliphilo in the *Hypnerotomachia*, whose virtue lay in following his beloved, Polia, wherever she chose to walk.

Till then, we try with poems to seize the day, show the way, build the bridge, mock the proud, kiss the bride.

August 1997

H.D.: A Joining

PART I. TAKING NOTE

4:06 P.M. 29 April 66 reading H.D. manuscripts in the office of Norman Holmes Pearson at Yale:

Hermetic Definition (1960–61)

part one, Red Rose & a Beggar
   15 pages, 18 sections

part two, Grove of Academe
   18 sections

part three, Star of Day
   8 sections

Each part of the poem, over its title,
has the canceled title
   Notre-Dame d'Amour,

and over that, unobliterated,
Star of Day—

(on the second sheet, the third piece is
first titled *Requiem*, then that name is canceled)

———————————

The third typescript of *Sagesse* is in the font of my own typewriter.

———————————

I feel your presence
   the svelte body of your rhythm
caresses me,
   I read you

_____

(But now there is more. Above me and to my right a Being is present,
not the rhythm of an artifact but the live insistence of a person, a person
nowhere visible in the still indoor air.)

_____

Star of your true Angel,
upright,
                let my music
sustain your caresses

                as I would once
in the overspecific alchemy of time
have found your old body frightening
                and loved your blonde girlhood,
caught in the hermetic hour
                the closed desire, to touch
the small of your back, anneal it smooth
into the gloss enamel of our final works.

_____

(I have to be clear about it, I am trying to ignore the woman's presence.
It is the work that matters, I insist. She agrees, restlessly, I try again to
attend the Work.)

_____

Sagesse: first typed copy 1957

                weeks after Pentecost
    stillness
                vectoring
                        summer-still.

_____

little furry seal on Pearson's cabinet
feathery nose and bead black eye
warmth of the room, no opening

_____

"Let the child sleep, let the world sleep,
few can endure Teut, Agad, Hana, Sila,

the names you share with God,
Grande Mer . . . few can endure"   *Sagesse*, section 23

_____

& from *Hermetic Definition*, part one, section 5:

"Venice—Venus?
this must be my stance,
my station; though you brushed aside

my verse,
I can't get away from it,
I've tried to;

true, it was 'fascinating . . .
if you can stand its preciousness,'
you wrote of what I wrote;

why must I write?
you would not care for this,
but She draws the veil aside,

unbinds my eyes,
commands
write, write or die."

———

(Now on the table were *The Mystery*, by Delia Alton, where Delia Alton
is crossed out and "H.D." put in, and *Pilate's Wife*, another novel.[3] But
in the transcript of *Hermetic Definitions*, part one, section 5, H.D. had
originally typed, after *She* (thus glossing it): *(Venice-Venus)*, but then that
parenthesis is deleted by hand. *She* must be the ultimate origin of our
capacity, the *muse* or *nurse* Robert Duncan calls her in his poem after
reading this same poem. This same woman.)

PART II. STANDING UNDER

1.
But *Our Lady of Love*
to whom the words were given,

her name is taken off the typescript,
not carved on the plinth of

what is Our Lady of Love's
stone—agate, lapis, Zuñi chrysocolla,

a stone with the sky in it
flecked with sun, plinth of

the statue where another
womanly presence stands?

2.
When I sat down to read your poems
a possession

rose in me from my fingertips
in a room full of serious books,

from the table with your lost novels.
Read my poems, I heard you say,

*I have been waiting for you two
years already, because of the way*

*you love women, love to talk with women,
love to hunger at their quiet flesh,*

*are gentle at their unmothering breasts.
You are almost reverent, and at least*

(this was *Ama*, the Sterile Mother, speaking)
at least you take possession.

I was so busy hearing
I started to write my own poem[4]

when poem is: *hearing, I make.*
I make hearing. You said *I hear you,*

*but read my wisdoms, palestinian
and true, true as my longing,*

true as my fear.

3.
Once was a woman who was your poet,
had an unconscious skin that told me

Touch me. I understood her skin's cry
but I did not want to touch her

and she did not want me,
it was not I who sauntered

phallic and girlish through her dream.
But her skin called out

and we would not listen. Later we lived
in the same house, we would not touch,

and I knew, now, in April of this new
lustrum, how much I failed you

by such refusals. The woman touch
of interchanged delight and shared

implosion, joy of it, that had nothing
to do with you. *Touch me*, your skin

uttered, *touch me*, your poems
cried from your old friend's desk.

4.
"What I spent, I had; what I saved
was lost." That's what the Irish say

to appease the hunger lets them keep
nothing, touch after touch.

Sagesse, your poem where the voices blend
at the cutting blade of the *mind*,

almost bodiless, a perfected
music. I stand

beneath and am watered by Aima,
the Fertile Mother, who is $\alpha\iota\mu\alpha$[5]

your blood, spent and saved
in these poems, your blood

rises in me, I have an erection
in fake Gothic in a breathless room

touching your poems. So much
I have touched women, loved

their flesh and seen *eternal* in it.
Why not hers all those six years,

six weeks in the same house,
why not yours? Joby reads to me [6]

from *Hermetic Definition*, I answer
with *Sagesse*, my hands

hold your typescripts, I want
flesh. Your blood. I love you.

5.
So she married someone else.
Always marrying someone else,

you blonde women, you soft-thighed
dimple-backed, your heads

full of perfected musics and girlhood
longings. She wrote a poem

For R.K., because he is a powerful man.
Too powerful to touch her,

do I betray you even now,
even then in Pearson's office, writing

my own poem with Joby's pen,
conscious of general longings, are mine less

than yours, do they go on year after year
to an age with no wisdom, all turned music?

6.
But that is what we do, not touch,
we give of the music and touch

whoever we can. Your sex was secret,
only the yearnings—I want to use

those sloppy soporific words: yearning,
longing—were public.

I keep talking, your insistences
are in me, last night at a friend's house

(and that poor old man, no ordinary
evening ever in New Haven,

locking the windows of his house
to keep out what comes as the night)

7.
but last night, at a young friend's house,
I sat and listened to Ives's songs,

slack poetry of the master musician,
wishing the tenor would stop and the pianos

assert their wisdom, I mean what Ives
was good for. Your poems

inhabiting my mind, all the untouched women,
you talk to me though I betray you,

writing my own poems while yours lay there
in the sun, then reading them, never

touching the woman, then later, later,
Our Lady of Love.

Or are they my poems?
Which of us can own

a single thing, let
alone a word, a name, a poem?

You suppressed the title, I look
all evening at the beautiful

girlfriend of my friend, grace
of her simple body, then open the Larousse

and find her portrait, Sainte Madeleine
presenting a donor, soft sensuous

focused face, the eyes averted at last
to the flesh, by the Master of Moulins,

Madeleine the whore. This girl whose chastity
makes a sound like my hand

stroking terra-cotta, a smooth friction,
a knowing what she feels like,

every curve and belly of the urn,
without the interventions of the hand.

8.
So you called the poem *Hermetic
Definitions*, or *Definition*—both are written,

that is, you enclose the poem in yourself,
take it away from Our Lady of Love

for whom all words are public,
incapable of being saved. Locked

in your life, the private torment
of your yearnings, *pothos*,

pathos, to feel at all
is to give way to yearning,

you wanted death to open the poem,
give it back to the—always

waiting outside—people
(Ives's "the masses, the masses"),

give it to those who could understand it
and "stand its preciousness," the poem,

but could not touch you.
You married death for his power,

you never knew whether he was
man or woman, you sought

angelic names and ancient numbers,
I love you, my flesh rises

into the event, I come here summoned
(tired, putting it off, petulant,

wanting a shower, simple, someone in bed)
summoned by your insistence

to take possession of what I see.
You take possession of me.

I think of the face of my friend's friend
painted by the Master of Moulins,

her face delicate, intent, speaking,
spoken by the Master of Kind.

9.
She married another man, took him
for his mad energies, because he possessed,

was weak and fearful enough
to be powerful. Weak enough to possess.

Because I love to talk with women,
be close with them and study

the auguries of their bodies,
you came to me, you let your works

open before me so I could touch you,
so that I could take

here even the shape of your stanzas,
possess them, trusting my breath,

trusting what you give me as my own,
to open, touch this new body,

as you, fulfilled of longings,
opened your sense of the work, your arms

wide to death, whose true name
you crossed out,

who was not a man, was
Notre-Dame d'Amour

and not shy of possession.   New Haven, 1966

NOTES

I have revised this essay and included a new introduction and commentary. The first edition was designed and printed by Graham Mackintosh in San Francisco in August 1967 and was published by John Martin of the Black Sparrow Press, the first of many books of mine they would publish over the next thirty years. The edition was of 125 copies—and I haven't seen an actual copy in years.

1. By a strange coincidence, the Grove edition of *Helen in Egypt* had been type-set by my second wife's father, Bernard Belinky, the last monotype printer on Long Island, shortly before he had to give up his Salisbury Press, and all the wealth of type and ornaments and casting machinery were scrapped. His daughter, my second wife, was named Helen, which enriched the connection.

2. Duncan's *H.D. Book*, the critical and discursive aspect of his life work, was first made visible for me and many people in the extraordinary collection of excerpts from it that Cid Corman published in the second series of *Origin* as "The Day Book"—one of the greatest repertories of critical insight and poetics I've ever read.

3. As far as I can tell, even now in 1997 these remain unpublished. *The Mystery* was of special interest to me since it spoke of the Moravians in America and one of their early hearths near where I live, Shekomeko in upstate New York.

4. Writing is listening. I know that now, and this was one of the days when I first began to learn it was so.

5. The theme here is kabbalistic. Ama is the Sterile Mother—the name suggests the sea, which, as Homer knew, yields no harvest. Aima is the Fertile Mother—the creative *yod* or *i* has entered the word, the masculine principle whereby the Mother is made both potent and fecund—the same *yod* that Sarai gave up for the feminine *h* to become Sarah, the obedient and subordinate, hence passively fertile, wife of Abraham. My poem connects the Fertile Woman with that lost *h* of the utterly feminine and discovers that she becomes 'αιμα, *haima*, Greek for "blood."

6. This is my first wife, Joan Elizabeth Lasker, 1931–89. It was she who guided my inchoate energies—I was eighteen when we met, nineteen when we married—toward the work and life of a poet. Here she is, as usual, showing me the good stuff.

Sex, H.D., and Robert Kelly

JANE AUGUSTINE

In his essay in this volume, Robert Kelly revisits his poem of 1966, "A Joining," an homage to H.D., and meditates on it to reveal its deepening significance for the present world of poetry. It was written, he tells us, in response to his reading H.D.'s manuscripts in Norman Holmes Pearson's office at Yale—or, rather, to his experience of her mystical presence in the room with him as her words came alive. Part 1, "Taking Note," opens with the actual mundane notes he wrote on the spot. Present tense, urgent, random, they quickly reveal his sexual, passionate, lust-laden experience of the woman poet's words— of her, actually, an almost-physical voice speaking to him. She is so strong a living presence, a Being, that he reacts sexually—he has an erection, as he later confesses. On the spot, spontaneously, through the power of her language, he made a powerful connection with one of H.D.'s most profound yet often unacknowledged themes, her desire for a pure and redeemed physical sexuality, sexual union inseparable from divine love.

American puritan culture doesn't like this idea; sex belongs to the fallen Adam, to the body region between piss and shit. Therefore both H.D. and Kelly dangerously violate public taboos. Old women shouldn't even feel lust like H.D.'s, let alone declare it in a poem, and young male poets, who might be expected to declare their perennial lust, shouldn't talk about their erections. It's too raw. But H.D.'s words forge a sacred alliance between body and mind. They show eros— sexual love and longing—as transcendently pure, a divine endowment, God-given. In H.D.'s thought, sex is the "Word made flesh" of Saint John's Gospel, the creative Word of God.

While Kelly was reading *Sagesse* and *Winter Love*, H.D.'s words of erotic longing "became flesh" for him. He saw fully what readers of H.D. have not often seen: she is not interested in abstract sublimated sex or any spiritualized or elevated substitute for the physical act. She wants body-to-body and says so in "Red Rose and a Beggar," using the ancient metaphor and fixed symbol for female genitalia: the rose. "The reddest rose unfolds," Kelly read repeatedly, hearing the human voice of the old woman confessing her sexual arousal and desire to sleep with the young, amber-eyed, African-American journalist, Lionel Durand. It's heat, it will burn her to cinders, it's torment, she writes, wondering if it will ever end.

Kelly understood that H.D. was preoccupied with body-to-body sex as a mystical experience, not as a literary invention, romanticization, or airy-fairy dream for the future but as an immediate autobiographical fact. Her 1934 novella, *Nights*, purportedly based on an affair in 1931, describes the heroine's struggle on each of twelve nights to achieve orgasm, conceptualized as being identical with being rapt into the supreme ecstasy of union with God, the highest Good, the creative force in the universe. She wants to be like the Virgin Mary, who, embraced by deity, brought supreme salvation into the world. From another mythic point of view, she wants to be Isis united with her brother Osiris in one spiritual whole, differentiated by gender but inseparable and co-equal in power.

Since for H.D. sexual desire signals a cosmic sacred impulse to union, the man to whom she was attracted seemed a divinely designated partner in a sublime eternal pattern, at least potentially one with whom the primal androgyny, male and female in one being, might be restored. The failure of Durand to respond and connect with her echoed similar earlier failures, particularly of Peter Rodeck, the Man on the Boat, and Lord Dowding, both of whom she perceived as participants with her in her supernormal experiences. In section 5 of "Red Rose and a Beggar" she quotes a sneer at the "preciousness" of her writing in the review that she mistakenly thought had been written by Durand. His rejection of her words meant rejection of her personally, and she was deeply hurt.

Her pain affects Kelly and leads him into a series of meditative explorations through which he reaches an understanding of the sanctified sexuality of H.D.'s ideal. That sanctity is what he discovered in her, or, rather, it is what she awakened in him. In revisiting this poem thirty years later he revised a few words—not many—from the original 1966 version. His changes in wording reveal a sharpened reverence for the sacred power of deep love-longing and its rich inherent dignity. Basically, it is sex that engenders the "fierce sense of life *and* order" that he found in H.D. and proclaims rightly to be essential—of the essence—to our humanity.

This sexual response to H.D. as a Being present with him in the room is inseparable from language: "the svelte body of your rhythm / caresses me, *I read you*." In ordinary parlance, "reading" people means understanding them beyond the actual words spoken, getting the true meaning through interpretation of undertones, nuances, or bodily nonverbal signals. The "you" so addressed then manifests as a "Being . . . the live insistence of a person" whom he invokes to aid his poem: "let my music / sustain your caresses."

Word caress is physical caress; a sexual fantasy comes over him. The old woman's body nearby is clearly "seen," and he thinks how as a young man he would have "found your old body frightening" but would have loved and wanted to sleep with the beautiful young woman she was. In 1966 instead of "frightening" he said bluntly "horrible," a raw response, crudely worded. His present language eliminates the crudity and adds a recognition: a young man's revulsion, revisited, contains the fear of aging as well. He has an added sense of her suffering—now he too knows more about sexual feeling in old age.

Even back in 1966 he noted H.D.'s triple pun on "Grande Mer" as one of "the names you share with God"—that is, the Great Mother ("grande mère"). But as spelled here, it translates as "Great Sea," symbolically the fertile female unconscious mind, "below," "undersea," the source of heightened awareness and "supernormal" inner life, such as the "jellyfish" experience recorded in *Notes on Thought and Vision*. In addition, H.D. is a grandmother (*grand-mère*), a double role expressed in section 7 by identification of the ancient goddess Cybele with Saint Anne and her daughter, the Virgin Mary, as manifestations of the divine feminine principle. The grandmother also appears behind another image, the *sombre mère stérile*, darkness, the woman past childbearing temporally but eternally integral with the *brillante mère féconde*, the creative energy of maternal love inseparable from Venus, erotic love.

Next in his note-taking process, Kelly copied out in full section 5 of *Hermetic Definition*, beginning "Venice—Venus?" and ending with the command given to H.D. by that "She," Venus-Isis: "write, write or die." To fulfill this command was H.D.'s lifelong vow. This passage is revelatory for the understanding of Kelly's affinities with H.D.'s artistic vocation and her idiosyncratic view of language power, a view akin to the theosophical view that "thoughts are things."

For H.D.—and for Kelly as he reads her words that conjure the presence of the living woman—words are "things." They are thoughts transformed into an indescribable yet real "thing-ness" or "substance," the seed of Being itself that resides in the word spoken. Therefore words that sound alike—"Venice, Venus"—have affinity of meaning through that sound, although no formal linguist would be likely to agree. The sound sends out vibrations, energy that is fecund power, the female power of giving birth to Being.

H.D. here names that power Venus but then simply "She." "She," the goddess figure, has "many names," prominent among them Isis. "This Isis takes many forms," H.D. says in the last line of "H.D. by Delia Alton." Isis in theosophical tradition represents knowledge; it is she who draws aside the veil between life and death, between time and eternity. Kelly too feels commanded to "write, write or die," as if adhering to a religious vocation. His richly varied and prodigious output—more than fifty books of poetry—is evidence of his commitment. But even more, now, his increasingly meditational inwardness and awareness of intertwined love and death speak of the direction in which he was to move from that day in 1966 when the visit of his incarnate muse gave him an erection.

The intricate minglings of physical sexuality and language-passion aroused by H.D. are developed by Kelly in part 2 of "A Joining," with its title combining the phallic and the submissive, "Standing Under." He is "standing under" her spell, having undergone "possession," a state that arrived from outside of himself. Similarly, H.D. felt possessed by a "gift," the legacy from her Moravian maternal ancestors, grandmother and great-grandmother endowed with "second sight." She brings the "gift" to Kelly through his reading of her that induces her to appear. She comes because "you love women, love to talk with women" and, he said in 1966, "love to caress their thighs & asses." In 1997 he changed this line to: "love to hunger at their quiet flesh," another revision that smoothes over rough wording but retains the physical sexual sense to enhance H.D.'s ideal of the perfect union of spiritual and erotic love.

His sexual response to H.D.'s revelation of hers brings back to Kelly the memory of a woman he hadn't slept with, even though her "unconscious skin" said *touch me*. Now her "fierce sense of life," her chief attribute, makes him feel that he failed H.D. herself by not acting on the sexual attraction. His meditations become more sensually concrete, progressing through the five senses. First he sees (that is, he reads), then hears a voice, then feels the tactile sensation of desire to touch skin, and finally a whole-body upsurge of blood in his erection.

He sees almost mystically H.D.'s poems as her blood—"written in blood," "your blood spent and saved." The language is loaded with sexual and reproductive connotations. To "spend" is Victorian pornography's expression for ejaculation of semen. A woman's blood is "saved" in the lining of the uterus each month in case an ovum is fertilized; if it is not, the blood is "spent" or discharged. Blood, the life fluid, brings to his mind the kabbalistic theme of Aima, the Fertile Mother, through the Greek word for blood, transliterated *haima*.

Kelly's footnote glossing this passage reveals a complicated kabbalistic etymology analogous to H.D.'s "spiritual etymologies" that abound in *Trilogy* and *Hermetic Definition*. H.D. links words' meanings through their sound-similarity, which sometimes may result from a true linguistic etymology but often does not. Examples in *Trilogy* (H.D. 1973) in "The Walls Do Not Fall" are the Christian prayer ending "Amen" linked with the Egyptian god Amen-Ra (secs. 21, 24), Osiris-Sirius-"O Sire, is . . ." (secs. 40–42), and the final lines "haven, heaven."

In "Tribute to the Angels" H.D. uses the etymological method to redeem erotic love. Section 11 lists negative associations to Venus's name, "venery" and "venereous" connoting impurity and lasciviousness, a true etymology. To these is added a kind of etymology linking sexual love with witchcraft and poison. The long *e* of "Venus" is like the shriek—onomatopoetic word—of the mandrake "when foul witches pull / its stem at midnight."

In section 12 H.D. tries to counteract these denigrations and restore Venus's status as "holiest one," that is, as sacred Love, by linking the name "Venus" to "venerate" and "venerator." Linguistic science does not support her theory, but for H.D. word-sound similarities are the true basis of connected meanings; that is, the music of words, their vibrations sent out into the universe, constitute their "substance," a kind of essence that constitutes their power and reality.

The sound-link of "Venice-Venus" expands this theme in the passage from *Hermetic Definition* copied by Kelly. Because Durand is African-American, H.D. associates him with Othello, "the Moor of Venice." Her own attraction to him therefore resembles Desdemona's love for the hero whose suffering and integrity attracted her. Although Durand might have had similarly worthy qualities, no good outcome is in store. H.D.'s sexual longings can never be satisfied. The words describing her desire in turn arouse Kelly's longings, exciting his sensibility, which, like hers, responds to words as physical entities in their musicality. In this poem they generate a foundational synesthesia that creates the visceral blood-sense of H.D.'s inner realities. He grips the pages themselves, wishing they were the body of a woman. The woman poet's "body of words" brings back the physical sense of the woman he didn't touch, who married somebody else, and of his then-wife, Joby, whose pen he uses to write his poem in an androgynously symbolic gesture.

His longing leads him to ponder the phrase H.D. crossed out as the potential title of her poem, *Notre-Dame d'Amour*, Our Lady of Love. That Lady, partly H.D. herself, young and blonde as he describes her, has entered his mind, and another sexual fantasy rises. As H.D. valorized erotic love in *Trilogy*, Kelly too sees unified sacred and sensuous love as he looks at his friend's beautiful girlfriend. Later he sees her face replicated in a painting of Saint Madeleine. "Madeleine the whore" was redeemed by her faith in Jesus; she is the pure model of redeemed sexuality. The live woman and the work of art blend in "chastity" that makes a "sound" like his hand stroking a terra-cotta vase. But because of art—poetic language—the stroke shifts to spiritual knowledge "without intervention of the hand." The implication of this view is that poetry has a transcendent power to "touch," in both the tactile and psychological senses of the word, and so to convey knowledge paradoxically beyond words.

H.D.'s word-methods have evidently permeated Kelly's sensibility, as if they were the water—or blood?—of the Fertile Mother under which he stood. Her "spiritual etymologies" are echoed in lines that Kelly newly added to section 8 of "A Joining":

> Locked
>
> in your life, the private torment
> of your yearnings, *pothos*,
>
> *pathos*, to feel at all
> is to give way to yearning.

The similar-sounding Greek words *pothos* and *pathos* have emotionally adjacent meanings, "yearning" and "suffering." He added them to stress the important point that governed H.D.'s spirituality: it is humanly vital to have feelings, to recognize and to explore them in their fundamental dignity and creative power, even those feelings that lead into the complexities of sex. Perhaps especially those.

When Kelly explains his erection by saying, "So much / I have touched women, loved / their flesh and seen *eternal* in it," he allies himself with the symbolic means H.D. uses to reclaim and valorize the feminine principle, particularly the representation of erotic love through the many "names you share with God, / *Grande Mer*." In *Trilogy* the feminine principle is "Our Lady universally" (H.D. 1973: 102), the Virgin Mary, Venus-Annael, Anna, Hannah or Grace, the Bona Dea and Santa Sophia, as H.D. told Norman Holmes Pearson in a letter quoted in his introduction to the New Directions edition.

As with her reclamation of Venus through the etymological method, in section 8 of "Tribute to the Angels" H.D. analogously transforms her past bitter experience—or any woman's—into transcendent love and power. The word-change takes place through the metaphor of an alchemical ritual that converts base metal to "gold." The "base metal" here is "a word most bitter, *marah*, / a word bitterer still, *mar*," which is placed in a crucible over flame until "*marah-mar* are melted / . . . change and alter, / mer, mere, mère, mater, Maia, Mary, Star of the Sea, / Mother."

"Tribute to the Angels" brings the Virgin Mary, Star of the Sea, the primal feminine unconscious through many manifestations. She is Astarte, Aphrodite, Isis, Venus—one to be venerated—as well as the Virgin represented in art, "Our Lady of the Goldfinch / Our Lady of the Candelabra" (sec. 29), and, in the churches named for her, Santa Maria dei Miracoli and "in Vienna / *Maria von dem Schnee*, / Our Lady of the Snow" (sec. 31). She is eternally "She," "our Lady universally," and *Notre-Dame d'Amour*, Our Lady of Love in the canceled title of *Hermetic Definition* that so caught Kelly's attention.

It is tempting to make a dangerous generalization: that almost every time Kelly uses the capitalized "She," he is referring to the nonconceptual presence of the goddess of love who came to him in his encounter with H.D.'s writing in 1966. It is safer to point out a case in which her influence on him through her "spiritual etymologies" is strongly apparent, the poem titled "The Names" in his 1978 collection *The Convections*.

This poem begins on an evening when snow is falling. He sees his beloved united with himself in the "Work" (capital *W*) of poetry, "and this work is She." She is evidently his wife, Helen, but also Grace, as described in "the old texts," and "Maria von dem Schnee, / says H.D., Santa Maria de' Miracoli / one of those women":

> And who are those women? . . . Maria, Mariam, Miriamne, Maria Prophetissa, Maria of Egypt, Black Virgin of the Egyptians called Gypsies/Yiftos/Tzigane/Romany/Tinkers, Black Virgin of the Old Language . . . the old language embedded in all living languages, the grid before flesh to which flesh and speech are compatibly and confunctively obedient.   (Kelly 1978)

Kelly's "old language" is H.D.'s unconscious, the site both of female pre-Oedipal sexuality, the erotic and the maternal fused, which is also the eternal creative principle through which the Word is "made flesh."

The mutual language of these two poets is a unified language of the names of the powers that actually rule human life. H.D.'s endeavor to reclaim sexuality by means of poetry is one of the uses of poetry that Kelly espouses. It is "the honest humanity of what she does," for which he praises her. In "The Names" he adopts her method to join with her reclamation. It is a coda to that day in 1966 when she appeared to him and in fact never disappeared:

> Such a matter it is to call out names, Isis, Mary, Helen,
>   Aphrodite,
>   names of mothers
> and unmothers, gay girls of male chauvinist cultures,
> Ashera, Astarte, Ashtoreth,
> her parts of shame distributed
> as the vowels of her name.
>   For every breath
>   a shame,
>   for every shame
>   a mother of God.
>
>   A name.
>   Her parts
>   are arts
>   & still sustain us.   (Kelly 1978)

From "Perdita's Father"

SHARON DOUBIAGO

*Robert Duncan speaks over and over of the Eternal Persons of the
Dream. Or . . . Eternal Persons of the Poem. They live, act and react
within the poem. They appear in the poetry of many writers'
individual consciousness, they seem to have a life of their own that
continues in an unbroken thread as they variously surface or remain in the deep pools of literature.*

Judith Roche, "Myrrh: A Study of Persona in H.D.'s *Trilogy*"

The following excerpts are from a journal I kept in 1986—
March through November—as I completed *South America Mi Hija* and
prepared for the H.D. centennial conferences.[1] "Perdita's Father" is
part literary criticism, part autobiographical account of H.D. in my life
and, by way of her, Robert Duncan, D. H. Lawrence, Wallace Berman,
my father, husbands, lovers, and other "soul mates" or "Eternal Persons," and part common daybook. It was mostly written in 1986 during
the month of her one hundredth birthday; the heart of it, "The Reddest
Rose Unfolds," was completed on September 10, her actual birthday. It
is an attempted sorting of the seeds, through the filter of H.D., of my
then current relationship to a sculptor (of bronze) whom I was about to
marry. In it several other life events and themes are woven together: the
slow, painful dying of my father from prostate cancer and the theme of
the diseased or missing phallus are central and partly why I chose the
title "Perdita's Father." Also, I was grappling with Dorothy Dinnerstein's theories of gender in the completing of *South America Mi Hija*,
and I was rereading *Helen in Egypt* for the first time since I was eighteen.
I discovered in H.D.'s poem an understanding of gender similar to the
one I had just come to in the quest-completion of *Hija*, that is, a feminist

interpretation of Freud's Oedipus complex: that war originates in the
mother-son relationship (as it exists in patriarchy). And I was considering the question, Did my first reading of *Helen* influence my writing
twenty-six years later? "Perdita's Father" also includes essays on H.D.'s
"The Flowering of the Rod" and D. H. Lawrence's *The Escaped Cock*.
In writing these essays I was amazed again to see how their views of
the Holy Family in patriarchy correspond with the ways I'd worked it
out in *Hija*. (Even now I am perhaps most struck by the deep affinity
I share with these two writers on the issue of gender.) And finally, it
contains still another grappling, this one directly with the controversy
around the Robinson biography, particularly its revelations of the importance of Lawrence in H.D.'s life and work. As always, there is the
ongoing exploratory investigation of my own path from early experi-
mental/avant-garde/language writing to a more generous opening to
the reader, to myself, and to the story; my difficult, mystical, and ecstatic life in the King's English.

"Perdita's Father" is most simply a narration of the chronological
storyline of the "coincidental" appearances of H.D. and others connected to H.D. (and themes and events) at important junctures of my
life—for the most part not the result of serious literary study or endeavor but as persons and real events I experienced as starters, as seeds,
as "transmitters" that enabled me to overcome internal and external
hostilities to my writing. H.D. has seemed less an influence on me and
more an Eternal Person, in Robert Duncan's meaning. The "coincidences" or "correspondences" (Duncan's word)—I think of Vaclav
Havel's Czech term *nohoda* here—do seem amazing; none of them were
consciously sought.[2] It was not hearing Duncan read the Psyche poem
("A Poem Beginning with a Line by Pindar") at my first poetry reading
that "called" me to make Psyche a major motif in my work. My early
resistance to colonial Classical literature was fierce, maybe innate—by
1966 already an articulated credo. I have no recollection of Psyche that
day (just a moth disturbing Duncan's reading light); I didn't know what
he was talking about. Eight years went by before I read Eric Neumann's
Amor and Psyche and for the first time experienced deep personal recognition of a myth. In that time I had encountered countless characters
in literature with whom I did not "connect" psychically, who were not
Eternal Persons for me. To discover years later that Psyche was there
that day "disturbing the light" seems still another "coincidence."

As if she were calling me. I think of the adjective the Buddhists have for "coincidence": *auspicious.*

Whenever I gather up the seeds of the H.D. story strewn everywhere in my path, I'm stunned with a sort of urgency to investigate, to go back into this story consciously: *how much am I denying, not letting in?* But apprehensive too because it has seemed precisely the accidental mercurial quality that's always been the key. This is why I set aside the time around her hundredth birthday to pursue *my* H.D. Book. To see what would happen, to see if I might discover something if I flew directly into her light.

As it happened, my love and I spent the week of October 4–10, 1986, alone on the high desert of southeastern Oregon, a haunting and disturbing time. This was when I finally reread *Helen in Egypt.* I read it hiking alone on the sides of strange mountains, in muddy hot springs, in his van and tent. We were to marry the following Sunday in Plush, but at the last minute, as we rose out of the desert, he backed out. We did finally marry, on October 18, at his insistence and after vehement apologies. It wasn't until later that I discovered that October 18 was the date of the Aldingtons' marriage, 1986 the seventy-third anniversary of the marriage that was to become in H.D.'s life of such legal importance and issue and of literary significance forever after.

Summing it up here it would seem a small coincidence. At the time, in the psychic everlasting throes of the story I was living, which I may write someday, it was *auspicious.*

The Eternal Persons of the Poem: *"Who is it that goes there?"* [3]

Hilda Doolittle

(September 10, 1986. *For my son Daniel Doubiago.*)

H.D.
+
D.H.

The Escaped Cock. My Personal History. The One Story. The Eternal Persons of the Dream. Isis in Search of Her Love's Severed and Lost Member. Her First Published Poem Was "Priapus." Something happened. The name was changed to protect the innocent. "I will never see you again." The Helen situation in all women. The Man in the Boat, the clitoris. "In me (the worm) clearly." Mrs. Doolittle called her daughter Sister. Osiris is Ra, the setting sun, the escaped cock. Ramona/Ramon. Ray as in light. Mon, Monde as in world. My wedding night. Finding his penis is a metaphor for finding the fathers. For finding Perdita's father. Mine. We all are. Lost. The scattered body of my beloved. Ramona, lost now seven years. What did H.D. know at the end of her life? Poetry is not a commodity, a thing of literature and culture. Poetry is an instrument of the process of spirit, of the World's Mind. In Egypt the penis was called an eye. To cut if off was to put out the light, Ra, the set-ting sun. They want to put out the son. Castrated by his brother, Set. Set, the Principle of Evil. Amen. Amun-Ra is Egyptian right brain for Ramon. "He is the world's father." "Amun-Ra, Amen-Aries the Ram." Ramona, the World's Mother. Ma. Ma + Ra. "The actuality of the present, its bearing on the past, their bearing on the future." Ezra Pound was called Ra when he was a boy. "God does not weave a loose web, no." So why is his penis missing in the first myth of Patriarchy?[4] What does it mean that the Male is castrated, that She wanders the world, all of history, in search, and never finds it?

They want to put out the sun.[5]

While on the one hand, H.D.'s Notes [on Thought and Vision] con-cerns the conjoined male and female elite; on the other, female ways of knowing through the female body are privileged access points for transformative vision. Sexual energy (the love brain) and psychic understanding (the over brain) are "capable of" a special form of thought or "vision." She argues in an apocalyptic tone reminiscent of both Pound's obiter dicta and Lawrence's natural mysticism that a small elite who received these messages "could turn the whole tide of human thought." . . . Certain exceptional people . . . could func-tion as receiver/transmitters, especially for ancient material (both Greek and Christian—statues, images, texts). And lovers, who are initiates through the physical body to a spiritual Eros, constitute this elite. H.D. begins here to particularize what becomes a central motif of her oeuvre: the spiritual meaning of erotic passion. (DuPlessis 1986: 40)

The Reddest Rose Unfolds

> *Isis wandered the world*
> *picking up the pieces of her lover*

What she could not find
were his balls.
She had to become an artist
and sculpt them   *Hard Country*

The first poem I ever read was *Helen in Egypt* by H.D. In my memory I am eighteen and very pregnant, walking into the new library at Palomar College in San Marcos, California. I have driven down the mountains of northern San Diego County from my hometown, Ramona, twenty-five miles. My husband, whom I love very deeply, has not spoken to me since our wedding night, over a year now. I chose marriage rather than college as my best friend, Victoria Raymond, chose. I knew, as I know now, an education by marriage would be true education. I needed to be an adult. I could not tolerate the status of child/student any longer. I love my husband very deeply. Still, my marriage fails in the moment it begins. He quit talking as we said our vows. I will stay with him seven years, bear him two children,[6] search for all the ways, *O Hermes*, I can demonstrate my love, that he will not be afraid, that he will turn back to me. He will say my name.

I keep the vow. For better or for worse. But now I must become educated in the more standard way. I become a student, a married one. A mother. As a wife, as a lover, I am extremely unhappy. That is, I am now an adult.

In my memory I am always walking into that new library with my new resolve to start reading. I'll sign up for classes next semester after my baby is born. There is a display case inside the entrance with books and personal memorabilia of a poet named H.D. I remember a pair of gloves. Certainly copies of the original books. Photographs. The one that's inside her *Tribute to Freud* now. H.D. at sixty. A *Newsweek* article about her. I checked out *Helen in Egypt* and two other books by H.D. The first poem I ever read, typewritten on a sheet of paper inside that display case, was the opening poem of "Red Rose and a Beggar August 17–September 24, 1960":

> Why did you come
> to trouble my decline?
> I am old (I was old till you came):
>
> the reddest rose unfolds.   (H.D. 1972: 3)

It was strange being made intimate with an old woman. "Unseemly," "impossible." I've never forgotten those lines. I don't remember her other two books I checked out. I certainly didn't understand them. But I took a stand with *Helen in Egypt*. I read it during the nursing sessions with my son. Every word. "Being a mother put the muse inside her" (DuPlessis, "Family, Sexes, Psyche," quoted in King 1986: 85).

I didn't understand *Helen* either. It went right through me, as I would have said then. It was only willpower that got me through it. My Taurus stubbornness, though I knew nothing of the stars then. It was my desperation not to fail in my first lesson as I had failed so badly on my first night of marriage.

It is said you never escape the influence of your first poet, but I think really it's the other way around. You can go a long time without a lover, unable to respond to the many who would seduce you. I think, ultimately, you find the poet, your teacher, as you find your lover, mate, parent, spiritual twin, *the one you were meant for*, and it's not that they[7] *influence* you, that you then never escape their influence, but more that they release you to be who you are, they are a model for how you can give yourself to the world, the one in whom you can take heart, you recognize your story in theirs, they are the one who says it's okay, in fact, it's important, the way you talk . . .

I can still see the pages of that book, the way the poem is set on the page, the prose paragraphs, as if in explanation, at the top, then the poem, the frustrating line breaks, which seemed to me to be thought breaks, making it even more difficult for me, the virgin reader, to pull the meaning together, meaning that utterly escaped me, no matter how much concentration and willpower, or my translating into my own words, I put to the text. *I didn't understand!* To this day, however, I can feel the aura, the personality, the muse, the mystery, the silences, whatever, of the poet, Hilda Doolittle, as I first encountered her. I recognized her spiritual seriousness, her quest, that she was in touch with something sacred. I recognized my own quest, that you could still search even if you could no longer believe in Jesus. I was profoundly disturbed that I didn't understand her on the conscious level, couldn't grasp what it was that is sacred, that is, the Quest—couldn't understand her language, which was her direct attempt to tell me, or at least lead me. When I think of this moment in my life—so typical of the encoun-

ter of my spirit with the mystery that is the universe so that I don't really
know if this was the first reading or the last, or if it indeed continues in
the ever-living present—I think of a basic premise of the Language
Poets, that the reader is an important participant in the creation of the
text. I had that experience with my first poem, *Helen in Egypt* (as I had
had with the Bible), and though so much of my half of the experience
stemmed from ignorance or, to be more gentle with myself, innocence—I knew nothing of literary culture (except for the Bible, which
only recently I recognize as "literature") and despaired that I could ever
care about an ancient, stupid boys' war—they even hid inside a toy
horse—and so what if Helen escaped to Egypt, that place of the bul-
rushes of Moses? The only thing I could relate to in the story, as much
of it that I could grasp, was Helen's female beauty and the pain of her
terrible, lonely isolation.

> All Greece hates
> the still eyes in the white face
> . . . Greece . . .
> could love indeed the maid
> only if she were laid
> white ash amid funeral cypresses   (H.D.'s "Helen,"
>   quoted in Doubiago 1988: 1)

These are terrible lines, have terrible meaning in terms of Western
Civilization: our fate was something I knew deep inside my silent marriage, though I was unable to articulate it—that my husband hated me
for my female beauty, that he wished me dead. Ezra Pound, Doolittle's
childhood sweetheart, her second betrayer, after her father the astronomer, declared her the first Imagist, and in the same capture, denied her
her name. Besides her spiritual quest I think I recognized in Hilda Doolittle respect for me, the reader. She did not tell me what to think or
how to live. She presented her psyche, her story, her images, her mores,
her language, her meanings without complete capitulation to the rulers
and without intent to manipulate mine, which was so badly abused, indeed raped at that point, and though I didn't understand these things
she strung together along such a strange line, her poetry was a door I
could open.

Reading *Helen in Egypt* was a little like reading the Bible. Trying to understand, to put it together, the living book, the life you are living, through language.

> A major tenet of the Language school is the ideal of the "transparent signifier," the word which means a thing outside of words, grew up with capitalism and is alienating and oppressive. They seek to free the signifier from the signified, to allow it to call attention to itself, and restore the primitive strength of words.   (Frederick Pollack, "Rebirth of a Non-Tradition")[8]

I think that unless you have had the kind of experience I had with H.D., coming semi-illiterate, a virgin in terms of most of the culture, to sudden full baptismal immersion by one of the high priestesses of that culture, you can't begin to comprehend the impossibility, on the one hand, of freeing words from their signifieds or the absolute need, on the other, to do so. The whole disturbing mystery of Helen was that she referred to a story, or, rather, she was The Story I didn't know and couldn't read, though I had the book in my hands, my son at my breast, a husband traumatized for having married me—this is the story of the female at the beginning of Western Civilization.

For the next decade I proceeded to get "educated" in Western Civilization, but I never again encountered the poet H.D. I can remember in the midsixties sitting in class and pondering, *who was that woman?* Thinking: poor illiterate child that I was, I didn't know not to read the first book that came my way. But then I would remember, the aura would again engulf me, *H.D.*, *Helen*, and I would know, *no, she was not trash*. I'm not sure what she was or where her place in all this *education* is, but she's important. Alicia Ostriker has an essay entitled "Learning to Read H.D." For me, typically, it has been the other way around. After *Helen in Egypt* I had to learn to read everyone else.

The publication date for *Helen in Egypt* is 1961. My son was born September 25, 1960. 8:38 A.M. And so unless there were advance copies, I am not pregnant, in the literal sense, as I walk into Palomar Library— to save my life, to save my son's, the beginning of my search to save my husband, that is, my marriage, to find him—though the memory of reading *Helen* as I nursed bears out with the dates. Perhaps it was the date on that first poem, "Red Rose and a Beggar August 17–September 24, 1960," that has me pregnant. She finished her poem as I went into labor.

From *Hard Country*:

> Isis was condemned to pregnancy
> to give birth in no time
> and no place

From *South America Mi Hija*:

> Everyone blames the mother
> and all mothers blame themselves.

> Isis was condemned to pregnancy
> by Set, *the principle of Evil*,
> to never give birth
> to never find the genitals
> he tore from his brother, Osiris.

> All my life. All your life
> I have labored
> to birth the words.
> I have searched
> for the male,
> lost brother. lost father. lost son. lost lover.

> If she birthed, if she found him
> civilization (as we know it) would fall.
> We would understand
> gender.

> All creation myths
> are about God the Couple

> All myths of the Fall
> are of the loss
> we fall into
> Gender.

Ever since H.D. came back (consciously) into my life in 1976, when I began my epic poem, *Hard Country*, I've wondered about that display case at Palomar College. Who was it in that strange place who loved, who perhaps even knew H.D.?[9] Those gloves like missing parts of the lover's body. Now as I write this on her one hundredth birthday I think

Palomar, how my life was saved by that place, just down from Palomar Mountain and the world's largest telescope, that Giant Eye, two hundred inches. Once I understood why, in this world of incessant improvements, those two hundred inches could never be improved upon.[10] Perhaps it was the retired astronomer who taught there. Perhaps he knew the astronomers of the Doolittle family. I wanted to major in astronomy. I first saw the rings of Saturn through his telescope. I got an A in astronomy. Because he allowed nonmajors to write of the universe philosophically rather than mathematically.

The reddest rose unfolds.

The Eternal Persons of the Poem: *"Who is it that goes there?"*

Robert Duncan, Wallace Berman into the Procession

H.D.

+

R.D.

Much of this extra-curricular influence came to focus around a single poem. Along with "Wynken, Blynken and Nod," heard at the pre-literate age, and Denise Levertov's "The Shifting," read before his emergence as a major poet, it counts among the three most influential lyrics in the poet's development. Duncan still remembers the exact circumstances of Edna Keough's reading of H.D.'s "Heat" in a classroom of Bakersfield High School. "In the heat of the afternoon. Outside, the whir of sprinklers, the glare, the blur of voices. Inside that murmur, there was a place or refuge, a silence created in our attention:

> O wind, rend open the heat,
> cut apart the heat,
> rend it to tatters.

The patience of her voice, where resignation and the hope for a communion in teaching still struggled, the reaching out of her voice to engage our care, had a sad sweet lure for me. But now, as she read the poem, something changed, became more, transformed by her sense of the poet's voice, impersonating H.D." To young Robert, the poem sounded promises of a new life beyond the constrictions of Bakersfield: "All about one, one saw the process of the town's shaping unruly youth into its citizens . . . thickening the fire of the spirit into energetic figures that would be of public use. . . . But the sensual intensity in this poem of H.D.'s, like the sensual intensity in Lawrence's work, demanded some new beginning in life from my own intensity."

By impersonating H.D. in her reading, Edna Keough became his guide into a new life in which the poet, much later, was to write his monumental, still unfinished H.D. Book. (Faas 1983: 210)

> Psyche travels
> life after life, my life, station
>   after station
> to be tried.   (Duncan, "A Poem Beginning with a Line
>   by Pindar," 1993: 55)

In May 1986, hearing that he was terminally ill, I wrote to Robert Duncan from Sherwood, Oregon. I told him that H.D. saved *my* life, too. I also told him that he was the first poet I ever encountered in real life, the first poet I heard read, the poet of my first poetry reading, and that I wanted to tell him more about the connections between H.D. and himself and me and Wallace Berman.

Spring 1966: I am the mother of two small children, living southeast of Pomona, California—the unincorporated Montclair/Ontario/Chino area— driving seventy miles round trip into L.A. for night classes at Cal State. One, an American lit class with Peter Marin, who was using the Donald Allen anthology, The New American Poetry. *I see in the paper that Robert Duncan is to read at the Claremont Colleges. A single paragraph announcement on the left side of the page, lower section. In the afternoon. I recognize his name from the Allen anthology. My neighbors Ramona and Desdemona agree to watch my kids. I make my timid, painfully shy way up to that elite/elitist place that has so frowned on the likes of a creature like me the couple of times I've dared the campus.*

I am a few minutes late; you are already reading. The classroom is full, mostly of men, they line the three walls, one of windows. The young man at the door escorts me quickly to the only empty desk, at the front of the room directly in front of you, a seat I would have never taken on my own. I am so self-conscious and embarrassed by my intrusion I cannot cause more disruption by not following him. The boy is leading me around behind you. "Who is it that goes there?" A snicker ripples through the room, through me. Dying. You stop reading. Now I am sitting less than three feet in front of you. I can't tell, with your strange eye, where you are looking. This is causing me embarrassment now for both of us. Sometimes to me, sometimes through me, sometimes into me. You are telling the story of how you came to write "A Poem Beginning with a Line by Pindar," something about a moth disturbing your light. "The light foot hears you and the brightness begins." I hear with my ears words I know with my eyes; this too is disorienting. It's so different. "God-step at the margins of thought, / quick adulterous tread at the heart. . . ." I barely understand these words. "Who is it that goes there?" I don't know. A man reading poetry. Something I have never encountered before. Someone reading their own poetry to an audience. In my life it's always been women, to their diaries.

I have attempted two poems in my life—both school assignments, one, the year before in which the professor (now the poet), Gerald Locklin, gave us a line from a well-known poem and told us to write from it. I wrote about my husband, who had not spoken to me since our wedding night almost six years before. I negate that poem because I assume it's plagiarism, the first line stolen from a real poet whose name I don't remember and because it's from my real life which seems a form of cheating too, and worse, of using something so private and painful as to be sacred. The room hums with your voice, your strange song, with my lonely self-consciousness, with having been paraded, a class and gender joke, with the incessant Southern California whir of sprinklers, birds, saws, and hammer in the heat outside. You tell of a girl, the poet Diane di Prima, flagging down your taxi on a San Francisco street, jumping in beside you, telling you something so important it caused an epiphany within you. I see her doing this as vividly as if I am there. I long for the fog and hills of a city I have been in only once, as a young girl in 1951. The intensity of the whole reading goes on and on in many disturbing ways. Poet? Poetry? "My soul wailing up from blind innocence." I am rent open.

And the strange and wonderful thing: beginning February 14, 1976, and in the ten years since, it is your poem that will become the boost for me into what I'm currently working. I mean I don't seek this poem out because it was the first poem I heard read aloud by its maker. At least not consciously. This happens in the same way it happened to me in the beginning, like a moth disturbing my light. Most recently this happened with the writing of "Nuestro Che: The Monroe Doctrine" in my new book-length poem *South America Mi Hija.* I'm always stunned to discover what's in your "Poem Beginning with a Line by Pindar," stunned by how deeply it penetrates me, the psyche of my work. All the presidents of our country! *"Idiots fumbling at the bride's door."* I always forget that Psyche (that moth!) is in it! *"She saw the body of her beloved / dismembered as in waking."* The Psyche myth. I've always remembered that I discovered her in 1973 in Plainfield, Vermont, through Eric Neumann's *Amor and Psyche*. Clearly, you gave me her first, though nothing of that afternoon seemed clear then.

It was in Plainfield, Vermont, meeting Richard Grossinger and reading his *Io*, that I discovered you have a connection with H.D. Grossinger, in his mystical intensity, associated me with you because of our being native Californians. You had been there just before I arrived.

October 1972: I'm walking into the community hall at Goddard College in my first winter. Stomping the snow from my heavy boots, my heavy shawls, hat, coat. On the inner door an orange flyer. Helen in Egypt *by H.D. A Class Offered by Lindy Hough.*

I am thirty-one years old. In the eons since the birth of my son, the birth of my daughter, the deaths and resurrections, the travels back and forth across the land, the intense, constant "education," that is, Search, and my new love, M, I have never again, until this moment, encountered the poet H.D. I go to the library. Hough and her husband, Richard Grossinger, are publishing excerpts of Robert Duncan's H.D. Book *in their magazine,* Io. Helen in Egypt *is checked out so I check out* Trilogy *and* Hermetic Definition. *The volumes feel ancient in my hands, their familiarity like a burden on my back as I trudge home through the snowy woods. "Why did you come / to trouble my decline? / I am old (I was old till you came)."*

I didn't take Lindy's class. I didn't want to be a student again. But she became a friend (almost). And she was a poet. She was writing *Psyche*, a book-length poem structured like H.D.'s *Helen in Egypt*. In *Book 1* there is a portrait of me that I hated: *"A beautiful blond girl / figured in a mythic drama."* My whole life was trying to escape their casting me into their myths. But I was also moved and bemused to be in an H.D.-inspired book, my first appearance in literature!

The Hough-Grossingers brought many Black Mountain/Duncan-inspired poets to the town—maybe even a few H.D. ones. For two years, two or three times a week, I attended poetry readings.

Still I was unable to find the place, the courage, the truth in writing, in my being a poet. It finally came, indestructible, when I moved back to California, this time to the Mendocino coast. I started *Hard Country* on Valentine's Day, 1976. All that weekend and into the next week images of a car wreck flashed through me. So powerful were these images that some part of me waited to find out who had been killed. My children were gone that weekend, a rarity, to Paradise, California, so until their return the terror was for them. My nine-year "marriage" to M was first unraveling that same weekend, *death-by-car* conceivably a psychic symbol of our destruction that I would consider, then dismiss (except as the vehicle Pain was opening me to in the Cosmos), when still another of the images would rivet through me. It took six weeks to receive the news, a constant psychic vigil. By that time I was well launched on my long poem, which I called "Heartland" then because of the taboo against the heart in my education and love life and because of the day I started it (the day of Psyche's Love). It was Jack Hirschman—our friendship dates from his bringing me the news—who told me about Wallace Berman's death on his fiftieth birthday that Valentine's Day, which was also my father's sixtieth birthday. A head-on collision in Topanga Canyon as he was driving home in his old green pickup.[11]

Spring 1968: I am newly in love with M. We are living on a hillside in Highland Park, facing downtown Los Angeles. We don't know about My Lai yet, but it is happening, the screams come on the air currents across the Pacific, they are impossible not to hear, I don't understand how so many others don't hear them. The war is devastating, but the counterculture/hippie antiwar movement is on, strong. Is this before or after the assassination of Martin Luther King? I am in graduate school, having my first attacks of missing nature, heartsick for its absence in my school halls beneath the freeways. I had so hated Ramona I thought I hated Nature. I used to say that, I hate Nature. But now slowly I am falling in love with Mt. Washington, the San Gabriels, the geographical magic of the L.A. Basin, mountains, desert, sea. Nature in the city. We go for a Sunday ride to the beach, the kids in the back. We are looking for another place to live next year when I am through. We go through Topanga Canyon, sort of legendary. I haven't been here before. It is like Ramona, that flora and fauna, that gray-green sage and round granite hills I have always associated with depression. Now it's beautiful.

An Indian is sitting mute, catatonic-seeming, cross-legged and staring, leaned up against the U.S. Post Office—an unpainted wooden structure. He does not acknowledge the activities around him. His hair is straight, waist-length, deep dark brown. The headband is of those old paisley bandannas Ramona cowboys wear.

*On the community bulletin board to his right is a red flyer: JAH! POETRY
READING! A poetry reading Tuesday night by Jack Hirschman at the To-
panga Canyon Community Center.*[12] *Hirschman is Peter Marin's best friend.
He talked of him often in class, calling him "probably our greatest living poet."
I ache to go to such a thing as a poetry reading but it is not something that will
happen in my new life with M.*

*I approach the bulletin board to check For Rent notices. Someone asks the
Indian what the police bulletin is about. "Wouldn't know," he says, not turning
his head. "Can't read or write."*

*Rather than being the shameful confession this utterance would normally
be, it is packed with power. It reverberates out to the canyon walls, it bounces
back like God or something.*

*My son in the second grade is having trouble with reading. My mother has
always told of her brother's dyslexia. We believe it is the Cherokee in us, that
we are right-brained, from the dream and creative side. We know that left-
brained people are the powerful minority in the world that has oppressed the
rest of us, that all the ancient written languages are right-brained, written
from the right, or up from the bottom, that the "straight world," the German-
Aryan-Gutenberg-rational-logic-heartless-immovable-print ethos of Western
Civilization has alienated most people from themselves by forcing them to write
and read against the natural flow of their deep body rhythms—and alienated
them from the others, from the Earth, destroyed love, dreams, the creative, the
natural. We joke that Sequoia invented the alphabet we could and should read
and write.*

*The fact is everywhere now for me, as a result of my negative experiences
in graduate school, as a result of the lying rhetoric of the Vietnam War that
language itself can be evil. I am so far gone I am considering the possibility
that it always is. I am going mute again. This powerful man sitting here so
still, so ancient is a reminder that most civilizations, most humans have been
without books. A reminder that we don't come into this world as readers, with
language. He seems pure, uncorrupted, unprogrammed. That a man in full
adulthood—he was much older than I—could be in this life without being able
to read—well, in that one moment, in his powerful aura, I was healed of something. Or at least the door cracked opened to the rest of my life, my funny path
back to real language and words.*

(I think of Bob Kaufman here, walking North Beach all those years
with his vow of silence. When the poet stops talking the poet is still
addressing the community. If the only appropriate address is muteness,

then that is the poem: silence. Though I didn't know I was a poet yet, the poet was inside me—at that time as the stricture against using tainted language.)

When I completed graduate school my first job was as art editor for the weekly Los Angeles newspaper *Open City*, published and edited by John Bryan. After several months of covering the L.A. galleries I was once again disillusioned and angry, now with the politics of art—one glaring fact was that I could not find a single woman artist across that vast city of galleries. In my personal life it had always been women who were the artists. After covering an erotic art show in Hollywood on Valentine's Day, 1969, that, surprisingly, was excellent—there was even a woman represented: Yoko Ono!—but that was subsequently closed by the L.A. police, the art confiscated and destroyed and the gallery owner arrested, I wrote my weekly review, which ended with my resignation, in protest. Years later the writer Deena Metzger will tell me that she was the person at the front desk when I brought in my review and reproductions, that it was she who called the editor to come out and talk to me.

"Oh, I see," Bryan sighs. We are standing in the middle of the old funky print shop on Melrose. "I understand. In that case, there is a man you should visit in Topanga Canyon. His name is Wally Berman. He is the real thing, a real artist. I urge you to hold off your resignation until after you have visited with him."

February 18, 1969.[13] I pull up a steep, narrow dirt drive to Wallace Berman's cabin high on the side of the canyon, the dogs barking. I recognize him instantly. The Indian from a year ago. Though now there appears to be no Indian in him, just "a strange and compelling mixture of awareness and in-genuousness that almost defies verbalization," as a catalog will say of him. (Jung says second-generation American Jews become like Indians.) There is an enormous white boulder beside his garage-studio door on which is painted an incredibly beautiful black letter. "Aleph, the universal letter from the Kab-bala," he answers me in the Indian's tone. "I don't know what it means, but the moon comes over it now between three and four in the morning and that Indian tobacco plant has sprung up beside it." I am stunned by its inexplicable beauty. (I write over and over, "huge unbelievable white rock.") He tells me of other Kabbala letters he's printed on boulders and pebbles in the creek below. "Who knows where they are now with the floods." He says this not in loss.

He leads me into his garage studio, showing me where the rain gets in, this

being part of the process, explaining his verifax machine, an office copying ma-
chine with which he works. In the corner is the remains of one of his old assem-
blages, the Verital Panel—the haunting, sulking eyes of a woman caked in dry
mud. "It was buried in a mud slide in Beverly Glen Canyon, our place was
destroyed, everything, only those eyes peered out of the mud." He wanted to
leave it there, but another friend rescued it for him. He shows me his small
handpress; he shows me more things than I can take in. Somehow he commu-
nicates that the Aleph symbolizes the pure gesture of self, the breath of life, "the
first of the mother letters"—he actually says mother—from which derive all
other letters or language and hence all things, or at least our sense of them.

He asks me again as he did on the phone not to do the interview thing,
though I can write anything I want of my visit. This is a great relief, inter-
views are so artificial. Outside he points higher up the canyon, wants to take
me up there to another artist, George Herms. In the gesture of his hand across
the canyon slit I see the oxygen rushing up from the sea seven miles below
churning the breaths of granite, brush, and soil. He leads me up old crumbling
cement weed-clod steps to the house. "For the most part, the artists in this
exhibition are more concerned with a life-style than making works of art. . . ."
I've never been in such a house. Unpainted wood, old worn maroon velvet
divan, Oriental rugs, all natural, found, weather-beaten furnishings. The
music of Bach and Otis Redding. His wife, Shirley, the eyes from the Verital
Panel, coffee and signs of recent artists, Jack Hirschman, and a boy somewhere
in the house, up the hill. I sit on the velvet divan, looking at Semina,[14] *finger-*
ing George Herms's handprinted and illustrated publication, Haiku, *by Diane*
di Prima. And another book by di Prima, printed by Berman, Revolutionary
Letters. *Inside is the first poetry I've read about what is happening right now,*
a poetry right in the face of the war and my vow not to be a poet. He shows me
an album cover he did of Michael McClure roaring at zoo lions and the lions
roaring back. Shirley laughs that he's on the cover of the Beatles' Sergeant
Pepper's Magical Mystery Tour, *that he's in the movie* Easy Rider. *He*
keeps giving me things, his posters, photographs. He keeps giving himself,
showing, telling, offering. The sad pornographic world churns far below.

Shirley tells of his first and only exhibit in 1957 at the old Ferus Gallery.
Someone protested that it was pornographic. Wally was given the opportunity
to withdraw one item, but he refused and was arrested, spent several days in
jail. The trial lasted months, was horrible, he was convicted and fined for in-
citing lewd and lascivious passions. Most of the exhibition was destroyed by the
police. I am shown a photo of the offense. "Factum Fidei" was a large charred

cross from which hung photographs of a vulva and a penis and the words ART IS LOVE IS GOD.[15]

He has not exhibited again or made art for the public's consummation. This is when he started his verifax collages.

"This is home base," he is saying. "We'll never leave it again."

Then they are telling of their four-year departure-for-good from L.A., after Ferus, to San Francisco, in which they lived for a year in Robert Duncan's house.

"Do you know the poet Robert Duncan? We traded houses with Duncan and Jess, 1960–61."

Now I'm holding his printed words, Robert Duncan's The World's Mind. *I am beyond words but in the most powerful affirmative sense. I am holding another of his posters, Michael McClure's words, "Poetry is a muscular principle and a revolution for the body-spirit and intellect and ear. Making images and pictures, even when speaking in melody, is not enough. . . . There must be a poetry of pure beauty and energy that does not mimic but joins and exhorts reality and states the higher daily vision." This is what I have been saying in my columns and searching for in this basin of mimicking crap called art. It has broken my heart not to find it. Art must roar like a lion. McClure says, "There are no laws but living changing ones, and any system is a touch of death" (1993: 78).*

When I got home I wrote "A Revolutionary Letter Poem to Diane di Prima." I didn't mail it. Anything more than a first draft seemed dishonest to me then, and I knew it wasn't good enough, but oh it came so easy, it just flowed out, I couldn't stop it, like mud down a hill in heavy downpour. It was about my making love to M while she was making poems, celebrating and grieving both—exploring—the loss of poems within me.

The next Tuesday I drove my Wallace Berman article on which I'd struggled the whole week—*"almost defies verbalization"*—along with most of the things he'd given me for the photographer, west to Melrose. As always, I dropped them on the secretary's desk and fled. My *painful* shyness.

She called me a few days later to tell me that *Open City* had been shut down by the LAPD, their printing license revoked, because of my article and illustration from the erotic art show, the editor and maybe herself arrested and everything, but particularly my Berman material confiscated.

I just vanished then, gratefully, east into America, with my love and my children, six months living in our station wagon. Trying to find America, some sanity. When we returned to L.A. we found a two-room shack on Topanga Beach where we lived for three years. This is when I became friends (almost: my painful shyness) with Wallace. Every once in awhile he would just be at the door, me inside working on my James Joyce book. Bringing me things, like Clayton Eshleman's *Caterpillar* (a photograph on the cover of the incredible rock), Jack Hirschman's *Aur Sea*. He would tell me news of his friends, musicians, actors, poets, artists, many of them famous, but of their work, not their fame, and of his work. We would stand there in that tiny shack, the ocean pounding up the oxygen and sand particles into the room—the aether, *wherefrom fall all architectures I am* (Duncan, "The Meadow"). Wallace never saw any of my writing, not a single word, but he treated me as a writer, as an artist. Once he came to invite me to a beach a few miles north where he had printed his Kabbala letters on the rocks at the year's lowest tide, rocks that are almost always underwater. Much to my lifelong regret I didn't go with him. I was miserably uncomfortable then with anyone other than my love and my kids; I didn't know how to just be with another human who was not my lover. Having said that, this is now the important thing to say, I've said this ever since, as awkward as it is: Wallace Berman never came on to me. Not in the slightest way. Not once, not ever, not a flicker of the eye. My need for the experience of such a man—for a married man—was very great. Once he spoke a long time (for him) of having been a pimp and hustler in East L.A. in his youth. Something about questions of inhumanity, of getting the cruelty, of seeing it threaten his survival as an artist. Of changing. ART IS LOVE IS GOD. He treated me as an artist.

During those three years on Topanga, there was an obscenity trial against the poet Deena Metzger. I don't remember details, not even whether she was found innocent or guilty, though I can see the layout of part of the poem on the front page of the *Los Angeles Times*, a simple poem, it seems, about a homeless girl in Tijuana maybe, maybe an old guy exposing himself to her, a fence between them. The *Times*'s book critic's ridicule of its being a bad poem was the obscenity I remember. I followed this case, remembering Deena Metzger not as the woman at *Open City* but as the beautiful young woman dressed in a black leather miniskirt who hosted a big reading by Anaïs Nin in 1968 on Wilshire

Boulevard, my second reading after yours.[16] Only writing this do I begin to see "the story" as it must have happened. As we well knew with M, the LAPD has a policy of vendettas. *"Once you have a record . . . "* they never let you go. Only now do I see that the editor, John Bryan, probably knew when he sent me to Berman what was coming down, the erotic art show already confiscated, someone reminding him of the Ferus Gallery bust, his *Open City* taking a stand. Losing everything.

I know you have written of Wallace Berman, but I have not found it yet.[17] I am searching for this.

I never had a mentor, I couldn't trust anyone in such a position of power, but H.D.'s *Helen in Egypt* was the first poem I ever read. You were the first poet I ever heard/saw read. Psyche was the first myth I ever related to, felt inside so deeply I knew my archetype. Wallace Berman was the first male artist who treated me with respect, as another artist, and in this, along with the powerful example of his life and work, the poet began to awake, Psyche from her cocoon. Jack Hirschman has become my most important poet friend. It has seemed that H.D. has led a procession of Eternal Persons, "transmitters," starting with you, into my life. Most recently, the current caboose, is the great woman and poet Judith Roche, who when we first met brought me the gift of Janice Robinson's biography of H.D.

July 1982: Thunder after thunder, returning like rhyme, she is coming across the lawn at Fort Worden with, finally, the first biography of H.D. . . . Judith—Hermes, Messenger of the Gods—brings me the missing pieces, carries forth the story that opened my poet destiny so many years before. We sit under an enormous red cedar, we are always under that tree. We bond, each the One the other has waited for: a female, literary soul mate.[18]

I want you to know, Robert Duncan, for whatever it is worth, that I will explore and revere my connection with you and H.D. through the rest of my life. I am deeply sorry not to be in San Francisco this winter and spring to hear you speak on H.D. Judith tells me that these talks are being recorded. So at least there's that.

Enclosed is my book *Hard Country*. Its first and, for the three years of its writing, sole dedication was: *To Wallace Berman, who taught me art.* Why I finally eliminated Wally from the published dedication has to do with being a woman and what the poem finally became. But Wallace Berman is the Eternal Person of *Hard Country*. The poem "Visions of a Daughter of Albion (Eleven Valentines for America, February 14,

1976)" was the poem I wrote that weekend I kept seeing the car wreck. In the Eighth Valentine, "My Story," I quote those words you put in my ear all those years ago, my first hearing a poem. Its coming to me was an epiphany as I imagine Diane coming to you in that taxi. The Ninth Valentine is "For My Husband Preparing to Flee (after H.D.)." My husband, M, the deep ecologist, who could not love. *"What can love of land give to me / that you have not?"* (H.D. 1983: 24). *"What is this place to me / if you are lost?"* (Doubiago 1982: 91).

This is simply to thank you.

> It was the struggle not to be reduced, to be neither
>   muse nor poetess.
> It is the struggle. The career of the woman poet is the
>   career of that struggle.   (DuPlessis, "Family, Sexes,
>   Psyche," quoted in King 1986: 79)

NOTES

1. The H.D. Centennial Symposium, Moravian College, Bethlehem, Pennsylvania, September 1986, and the Emily Dickinson/H.D. Dual Centennial Colloquium at San Jose State University, San Jose, California, October 1986.

2. "Coincidences" was the word used by the reporter who interviewed H.D. in 1960. This interview triggered "Hermetic Definition."

3. Robert Duncan, "A Poem Beginning with a Line by Pindar" (1993: 55).

4. The Osiris-Isis myth.

5. This italicized passage is a prose poem; subsequent italicized passages are journal entries or memories.

6. I allow this expression even now, though I never confused the conception, the bearing, the birthing, the raising of my children as being primarily a gesture *to* or *for* him. Such a thing, even then, would have struck me as misguided, tragic, evil. He and I bore two human beings out of union in our bodies.

7. I use the pronoun of my heritage. *They* is the proper one in its nonsexism, its all-inclusiveness, its beauty (compared to the awkwardness of its alternatives). *They* works definitively, poetically, spiritually. *The Mystical They. The Definitive One. They* is what I mean. (For sources, see the Bible, Shakespeare, Whitman.)

8. From an unpublished essay sent to me in 1984.

9. When a version of "The Reddest Rose Unfolds" was published in *American Voice* (spring 1990), I sent it to Palomar College Library. The following is from the response I received on June 5, 1990: "I was the librarian while you were at Palomar having been there from September 1946 to July 1977 when I retired. . . . I remember the display case in the lobby. I'm glad to hear the 'H.D.' display meant so much

to you. We never know the influence our library and books have on our students lives. . . . Cordially, Esther Nisbin Altmann."

10. The Palomar telescope, of course, has been improved upon.

11. In writing this essay I find that Berman died on February 18, 1976, "early in the morning of his fiftieth birthday—from injuries sustained in an auto accident near his Topanga Canyon home." Perhaps the accident itself occurred on the 14th, perhaps Hirschman told me "Valentine's weekend." For now I will leave this as I've always remembered it.

12. This poster was probably made by Berman, who did the cover for Hirschman's *Black Aleph* (1968).

13. Wallace Berman's forty-third birthday.

14. Berman's assemblage/poetry magazine, printed and published 1955–64.

15. My description here is from my 1969 drafts, written after the visit, from memory, possibly from photographs. Albright, who is likely to be more correct, describes it in this way: "In 'Cross,' a photograph hanging from one arm of an old wooden-beam crucifix gave a close-up view of male and female organs in intercourse" (1985: 96).

16. In a phone call on February 1, 1999, Metzger referred to this four-year ordeal as "an academic freedom case," also as a witch hunt. She was fired in June 1969 for "evident unfitness to teach" by the California Community College Board, three seats of which were held by the John Birch Society.

17. *Wallace Berman Retrospective*, by Robert Duncan and David Meltzer.

18. See my introduction to the poems of Judith Roche.

"The mother is the muse H.D. said": Re-Membering the Reader in H.D.'s *Helen in Egypt* and Sharon Doubiago's Early Long Poems

KATHLEEN CROWN

> *The mother is the Muse, the Creator, and in my case especially, since my mother's name is Helen.*   H.D., *End to Torment*

> *The reader is the Muse! . . . The Lover who dictates the Word, the Lover to whom the word is dictated.*   Sharon Doubiago, *The Book of Seeing with One's Own Eyes*

The richly veined network of connections among the writings of H.D. and Sharon Doubiago will not fit easily into either of the two paradigms available for such textual connectedness: the familiar model of literary influence or a more abstract and impersonal matrix of intertextuality. When Doubiago started work on her first book of poems, *Hard Country* (begun in 1976 and published in 1982), it had been fifteen years since she had read H.D.'s epic sequence *Helen in Egypt* (1961). She had come to H.D.'s long poem with no literary training—in an autobiographical short story, she reports that "I didnt understand a word of it but I didnt let that stop me."[1] During the years in which she completed her second book-length poem, *South America Mi Hija* (1986), Doubiago was deeply engaged with H.D.'s life story and writing, discovering significant parallels between her experiences and those of H.D. But she did not reread *Helen in Egypt* until after she completed work on *South America Mi Hija*. Thus H.D.'s epic poem cannot be said to "influence" Doubiago's two book-length poems in the usual sense.

Despite this lack of direct influence, Sharon Doubiago is clearly engaged with *Helen in Egypt* in *Hard Country* and *South America Mi Hija*—the three long poems are woven together in a tight web of corresponding myths, codes, desires, and coincidences. The presiding myth in all three poems is that of Isis, the Egyptian mother goddess, who is doomed to search out and bind together the dispersed limbs of her brother and lover, Osiris. Both H.D. and Doubiago revise the myth so that Isis seeks not only to restore the missing limbs of her male companion but to reintegrate her own fragmented body and self. Identifying our culture's rejection of the mother as the cause of a psychic wounding that manifests itself as human violence and war, both poets argue that only remembering the lost or forgotten mother—the restoration of her dual status as questing artist and inspiring muse, as writer and reader, as the one who speaks and the one who must be addressed—can prevent further cultural devastation and begin the process of healing a traumatized national psyche. In undertaking this quest, these poems work against the forces of dis-memory: just as H.D.'s Helen seeks to remember things "as yet un-writ in the scrolls of history" (*HE* 52), Doubiago works "against the father's amnesia" (*HC* 16).[2]

Reading Doubiago's two book-length poems through the lens of H.D.'s late epic work, this essay suggests that the women narrators' search for connection with the mother or daughter parallels Doubiago's search for literary foremothers and especially for connection with H.D., her most significant female literary precursor.[3] As Doubiago's engagement with H.D.'s work intensified, her writing shifted the structure of its address—from appealing directly to a powerful but absent father or male lover in *Hard Country* to invoking, in *South America Mi Hija*, an immediate and intense mother-daughter relationship. This change in her poems' structures of address, I suggest, is related to Doubiago's rejection of a male-oriented paradigm of conscious "influence" in favor of a maternally oriented paradigm of "inspiration," which she understands as a mutual and reciprocal relation between the poet and her literary antecedents. This new structure of address enables a psychic intimacy between poet and reader, and Doubiago builds on H.D.'s use of the mother-daughter dyad as metaphor for the creative process to imagine a new set of textual relations in the reading process, one that seeks to transform or in-form the reader by incorporating the reader's voice and desire.

> *. . . there was the voice of my own loving in the voice of the poem . . .*
> Robert Duncan, *The H.D. Book*

In H.D.'s *Helen in Egypt*, Doubiago found a powerful theory of poetic creation and literary transmission. But this relationship will not fit into the paradigm of influence in which a younger poet falls under the sway of a "stronger" precursor, with the chief interactions consisting of conscious borrowing and deliberate revision. Doubiago describes her first reading of *Helen in Egypt* as follows: "I was profoundly disturbed that I didn't understand her [H.D.] on the conscious level, couldn't grasp what it was that is sacred, that is, the Quest—couldn't understand her language, which was her direct attempt to tell me, or at least lead me" (1986: 6). If the model of influence will not account for this textual relationship, neither will the abstract and impersonal model of "intertextuality," in which an endless array of texts is linked by a shifting set of relations detached from the poet's lived reality and autobiography. Doubiago insists on the bodily, confessional, and autobiographical nature of her encounter with H.D.'s writing. She figures the textual interactions between herself and H.D. as passionate, maternal, erotic, and ecstatic, even when they are highly dependent on chance and coincidence:

> so I went in labor to the library with the determination to start reading and found on display a poet named HD. . . . now I understand she had just died . . . I checked out all her books and read them cover to cover every painful grueling mysterious word of *Helen of Egypt* while I gave birth to my son and began to nurse him O patience above its pouring out of me pregnant as big as he is.   (Doubiago 1988: 263)

Here the reading of *Helen in Egypt* becomes a kind of labor—painful, grueling, and mysterious—as well as a kind of lactation, in which she nurses and is nursed into the vocation of poet and writer.[4] In this autobiographical short story, Doubiago describes her initial encounter with H.D.'s writing in the context of her relationship with her own mother:

> I never saw [Mama's] influence on me as a writer because when I look at her she always directs my attention to Daddy but shes the one who told me the stories and encouraged me always and shes even a writer shes written me a letter every week at least since I left home the mother is the muse HD said when I was huge and pregnant and so dangerously unhappy I didn't know what muse is.   (1988: 262)

Although this short story suggests a mother-daughter intertextual dynamic between H.D. and Doubiago, it is by no means clear which poet is the mother and which the daughter. The conjunction of these two careers, then, suggests a literary mother-daughter relationship in which the boundaries between both figures are blurred; theirs is a circular relation that operates by dream-logic rather than a linear genealogy. The literary daughter gives birth to a recently deceased but powerful mother figure who in turn initiates the young woman artist's poetic development.

When asked recently about the influences on her work, Doubiago responded that "'influenced' seems the wrong word, fundamentally," and she claimed instead to "take *inspiration* from just about anyone" (Goodman 1997: 17, my emphasis). Rejecting the concept of conscious choice inherent in the model of influence and the abstractness inherent in the model of intertextuality, Doubiago replaces both with an older, even anachronistic discourse of "inspiration," most often connected to the muse as a female divinity (1988: 263).[5] One of the forms that this muse takes in all three poems is that of Isis. Even before she wrote *Helen in Egypt*, H.D. had reinterpreted the Isis myth to understand the mother goddess as both artist and muse. According to mythic conventions, the role of Isis was confined to reproducing the male lover, mourning his loss, or giving birth to his son—she was "condemned to pregnancy" (*HE* 24) or "forever with that Child" (*SAMH* 238). For H.D., the task of Isis is to re-member and give life not merely to Osiris but to her own fragmented and disassociated self:[6]

> As the Eternal Lover has been scattered or disassociated, so she [Isis], in her search for him . . . She knows that to keep him, she must lose him . . . She can not know that she knows this, until she has progressively retraced her steps, redeemed *not so much the fragments of Osiris, as of his sister, twin or double, the drowned or submerged Isis* . . . This Isis takes many forms, as does Osiris.   (H.D. 1986: 4–5, my emphasis)

For Doubiago, H.D. was herself a kind of "submerged Isis," a literary foremother whose life story and dispersed body of work—largely unpublished, out-of-print, and untaught—must be gathered together and rethreaded. It was not until many years after her first reading of *Helen in Egypt*, however, that Doubiago was able to articulate her sense of painful gaps in literary history that denied the work of women writers. As she felt the absence of these voices more acutely, she began to understand the repression of female literary voices as an example of a larger cultural attempt to repress the speaking and desiring feminine subject:

I was so starved for the female in myth and literature to work inside
words the critics wouldnt read what a real woman has to say theyd
treat her like Williams did that womans letter in Patterson or HD
a sort of embarrassing curiosity too close to what they've heard all
their lives and have banned together to ignore their mothers and sisters and lovers and daughters and wives.   (Doubiago 1988: 227)

The task of Isis becomes the searching out of "the female in myth and
literature" and the piecing together of a literary tradition that would
acknowledge the work of women writers. Thus the revision of the Isis
myth offered both H.D. and Doubiago a way of redefining the poet's
relation to the dead, to the male lover/brother/son, to the mother/sis-
ter/daughter, to literary precursors (male and female), and to her own
body of writing.[7] This new Isis myth also renegotiates the poet's relationship to her reader. To redefine Isis as an "artist"—to say, as H.D.
does, that "the mother is the Muse, the Creator" (1979: 41)—makes
room for the *reader* to occupy this creative space. *Helen in Egypt* is striking in its refusal to differentiate writer from reader and reader from the
text. As an epic poem, it is surprisingly able to share authority with and
even to incorporate the reader, who by weaving together meaning becomes a kind of Isis. Although H.D. did not make these connections
explicit until the end of her life, they are the matrix from which even
Doubiago's earliest work proceeds.

> *the invincible armour*
> *melted him quite away,*
> *till he knew his mother;*
> *but he challenged her, beat her back*   H.D., *Helen in Egypt*

> *O, husband, we were almost*
> *great*
> *but in me, you did not learn*
> *to be a mother*   Sharon Doubiago, *Hard Country*

H.D.'s *Helen in Egypt* set a powerful precedent for Doubiago's *Hard Country* by speaking in the voice of a beautiful woman who
has been blamed for the devastation of the country she loves, by transforming her into an active decoder and critic of her culture, and by
creating an epic form that, while speaking of national catastrophe and
"public scandal," could also account for "the million personal things"

(*HE* 300). Rather than justifying the nation, H.D.'s markedly interrogative poem questions national subjectivity, it invites challenge and interpretation by including the voice of a critical reader, and it circles through time rather than marching forward to a manifest national destiny.

The structural and thematic parallels between *Helen in Egypt* and *Hard Country* are manifold. In H.D.'s poem, the speaker is the beautiful, hated Helen, and the national catastrophe is the Trojan War. Doubiago's protagonist, "Sharon," is also a former beauty queen—a California "Blondie"—while the most immediate national crisis is the Vietnam War.[8] Just as Helen "travels" through psychic space to ancient Egyptian temples of Isis, Sharon wanders across the land of the United States as an "American Isis" who attempts to reconnect her male lovers with the mothers they have lost or forgotten. Both poems restage an epic drama of nation making with the woman as protagonist and agent. "I would renew the Quest," insists Helen, and Doubiago's narrator, Sharon, stakes a similar claim: "From now on / I will act. / From now on / he must understand" (*HC* 85). Both women narrators live in a culture that despises the women of which it makes sexual spectacles: Helen is "cursed by Greece" (*HE* 16), just as Sharon is told, "*You are a woman / a violation / to your country*" (*HC* 54).

Both epic protagonists challenge the powerful cultural forces that, in assigning iconic status to women, silence them as readers and writers. Although she is not formally instructed in hieroglyphic script, Helen attains a kind of visionary literacy and utterance that provokes Achilles to seize her throat in rage. Sharon writes, even though the voice of the "*One*" tells her: "*We killed everything / for you. We forbid you / to write of this*" (*HC* 129). If the woman of beauty serves in our culture as sign, spectacle, or script, H.D. and Doubiago transform her into a woman who interprets and reads her self *as writing*. "I am instructed," claims Helen as she decodes the vulture hieroglyph and thus invokes Isis. "I know the script" (*HE* 13). According to Rachel Blau DuPlessis, "The poem allows icon to become critic, yet remain icon; object to become subject, yet remain object; interpreted to become interpreter, yet remain interpreted" (DuPlessis 1986: 109). *Helen in Egypt* and *Hard Country* are both poems that make us aware of their narrators as readers, drawing attention to the many operations that readers, writers, and texts undergo. It is only as a "reader" or listener, for example, that Sharon can serve as witness to the stories of the dispossessed, moving as she does "into the body-time / the story / of Others" (*HC* 9). In the closing poem of *Hard Country*, Sharon opens a book, trying to read the words for answers, but behind

> the livid hieroglyphs a woman
> I don't see is on the horizon of the desert, screaming.
> She tears her body against the blue hills, throws
> the pieces to the coyotes who surround her.   (*HC* 255)

Behind the legible script is another illegible and marginal voice of an invisible woman; Sharon's goal is to learn how to read it or hear it, how to bring it into articulation.

In H.D.'s writing, Doubiago may have found confirmation of her own emerging feminist analysis of the connections between the oppression of women and the mechanisms of war. Both poets criticize a masculinist war culture founded on the repression of the active feminine principle; as Donna Hollenberg argues, H.D. connects a "warrior ethos" with the "patriarchal family drama": "She sees that just as the masculine sex role requires the son to repress connection with his mother in a patriarchy, so the warrior must devalue eros and the woman's world to survive on the battlefield. The result is an unacknowledged inner schism that manifests itself violently" (1991: 187).[9] Doubiago connects the "war over the land" with the "war over the women" (*HC* 40), writing that "when you come into me / it is the body of America you enter, / her dark unwritten stories" (*HC* 89). Here, specifically, *Hard Country* connects gender oppression with the bombing of Vietnam, the genocidal war against Native Americans, and the destruction of the environment. This feminist analysis views men and women as equally implicated in the repression of the mother: "I am as guilty as he," writes Doubiago, "betrayer of the Body, the Earth" and one of those who "gathered on the shore / to watch her drown" (*HC* 256). In *Helen in Egypt*, Thetis warns that women too can adopt masculinist violence in attempting to reconstruct society, insisting that "no sword, no dagger, no spear / in a woman's hands // can make wrong, right" (*HE* 101).

In both poems, the erotically charged female body that is desired, feared, and reviled by masculinist culture becomes a site of political struggle as well as of resistance. In Homeric epic, of course, women's bodies are the stage for national dramas—the rape or seduction of Helen, the sacrifice of Iphigenia, and the revenge of Clytemnestra all have ramifications for the status of the nation. In *Hard Country*, Doubiago makes explicitly anatomical connections between men's violence against women (here embodied in the medical establishment) and the United States' attempt to colonize weaker nations: "your uterus has been punctured. invaded" (*HC* 33). She further connects the assault on women's bodies with our violence toward the earth: "your uterus," she writes, referring to the land, "fills with politics" (*HC* 42). In response to this violence, both Doubiago and H.D. assert the primacy of the female sexual organs as metaphors for a powerfully transformative cultural force. *Helen in Egypt* offers carefully wrought images of female creativity (e.g., unfurling lotus buds, spiral shells, pearls, and winding interior corridors) that often describe the poem itself as an erotic point of contact between poet and reader, while *Hard Country* celebrates the vagrant and exuberant sexuality of a desiring and desirable woman. Both poets insist on the authority of the womb as a transformative force capable of both birth and death. In emphasizing the female genitals and reproductive organs in the context of the Isis myth, with its traditional focus on the need to restore the missing male members, both poets combat a cultural prejudice that would mark female sexuality as lacking or insufficient. In conventional psychoanalytic constructs, such burnished beauties as Isis, Helen, and Sharon could only *stand in* for the missing phallus, never possessing it for themselves.[10] But just as H.D. transports Helen out of Troy, Doubiago writes Sharon out of this passive role and into the role of artist. In these poems, masculinity's social castration is no longer a threatened loss but a traumatic psychic reality that only the female artist can heal:

> Isis wandered the world
> picking up the pieces of her lover.
> What she could not find
> were his balls.
> She had to become an artist
> and sculpt them.   (*HC* 90)

Envisioning Isis as a woman artist who actively complements the male Osiris, both *Helen in Egypt* and *Hard Country* set forth an ideal male-female relationship modeled on the brother-sister equality of the lovers Isis and Osiris. This "complementary heterosexual relationship," as Lynn Keller terms it in a discussion of *Hard Country*, relies on an androgynous ideal of psychic bisexuality (1997: 33). Both poems suggest that only by revealing to the son his repressed love for the mother can the narrators achieve the idealized androgynous relationship they desire and with it an end to violence and war. H.D. revises the Homeric epic so that the warrior Achilles renounces his place in the command structure of war—*"the purely masculine 'iron-ring'"*—by connecting erotically and spiritually with Helen and thus with Thetis (or Isis), his mother (*HE* 55). To help Achilles make this connection, Helen must realize that she herself is a version of the Egyptian Great Mother, even though she thereby brings on herself the hatred and anger of Achilles. In that eternally violent moment on the Egyptian beach, Achilles attacks Helen because she elicits a memory of his forgotten but powerful mother, Thetis: "he knew his mother; // but he challenged her, beat her back" (*HE* 271). But the attack becomes an embrace, and in the end Achilles is able to connect with his mother, "to break his heart / and the world for a token, a memory forgotten" (*HE* 315). This idealized merging of the two lovers (Achilles and Helen as Isis and Osiris) results in the lover/child Paris, an androgynous figure who is *"incarnate / Helen-Achilles"* (*HE* 224).

Lynn Keller's reading of *Hard Country* shows how Doubiago idealizes the androgynous twinship of Isis and Osiris, seeking a new, equal relationship between the narrator, Sharon, and her lover, Max. The poem's overtly stated goal is for the woman narrator and her male lover to occupy the androgynous position of "the human between the male and female" from which they can work together to heal a war-torn national culture (*HC* 258). But unlike Achilles in *Helen in Egypt*, the male lover to whom *Hard Country* is addressed fails to make this connection: "I learned to be a man from you," writes Doubiago. "You did not learn to be a woman from me" (*HC* 252). By the end of the narrator's quest in *Hard Country*, she has not managed to envision an end to gender asymmetry or to avert its inevitable violence (*HC* 33).

Keller argues that Sharon's quest for a new complementarity of the male and female is further exemplified in *Hard Country*'s intertextual dynamics, in which the woman poet struggles with and reforms the poetics of her (mostly male) predecessors. "Though H.D.'s long poems are also a significant example for Doubiago's writing," Keller points out, "Doubiago focuses less on that empowering female precedent than on seeking a satisfying relation with the male poets 'behind her'" (1997: 62).[11] Because such male poets as Walt Whitman, James Joyce, D. H. Lawrence, Charles Olson, and Robert Duncan are central to Doubiago's poetic development, it is not surprising that most critical discussions of "influences" on Doubiago's work place her writing in the context of men's precedent texts and male-dominated traditions.[12] Keller, for example, considers *Hard Country* in relation to Olson's *Maximus*, arguing that Doubiago creates an ambitious "woman's epic" that "complements" the male-dominated epic tradition by incorporating feminine values and perspectives.

Doubiago herself has called Olson her "first conscious inspiration" and "the first poet I could understand on the rational level, not just the psychic level" (Goodman 1997: 23).[13] Charles Olson is, however, neither "father" nor "mentor" for Doubiago, who projects her "American Isis" of Ramona, California, on no smaller scale than his "Maximus" of Gloucester. As Keller points out, Doubiago claims equality with Olson just as Sharon does with her lover, Max, although this model of intertextual connection requires potentially problematic assumptions, including "a belief in an ideal of textual and personal androgyny and a belief in the value of heterosexuality (the coming together of male and female individuals in a sexual, and emotional, unit)" (1997: 27). Even if the poet Doubiago can reform "Olson's poetics and thematics," as Keller suggests, her narrator "cannot in life reform her lovers' attitudes" (1997: 31). Sharon may be able to translate "the futile dialogue with her male lovers into a larger dialogue with her country," as Jenny Goodman argues (1997: 4), but the address to the male lover in *Hard Country* remains failed and incomplete, with the female narrator grieving deeply over her lover's inability to connect.

Doubiago suggests that *Hard Country* is addressed to "the traditional Muse": "I address the cosmic male spirit before he's crippled, made impotent. I address the male who can read. You might even say I address God" (Goodman 1997: 36). The muse, of course, is traditionally female; for Doubiago, however, the gender of the muse depends on the reader that we imagine. Defining the muse this way, she points out that poets have traditionally imagined their readers as male. In thus addressing this male muse in *Hard Country*, Doubiago submerges her narrator's simultaneous quest for connection with the lost mother or sister. Thus

Sharon does not ask with the same directness and insistence as Helen, "where is she, / my sister" (*HE* 78), although this woman-centered search will emerge with special intensity in *South America Mi Hija*. *Hard Country* remains focused on the absent father, as the book's opening line ("My father leaves us in the car") and epigraph (about a little girl's terror at her "Papa's" disappearance) suggest. Yet there are many moving statements in *Hard Country* about the lost connections between mother and daughter across generations of women: "my mother / my orphan / country," writes Doubiago (*HC* 202). Although Sharon claims that "everything I write is a poem to my mother," she concludes, less optimistically, that "my mother is a poem I will never write" (*HC* 109).

> I am half-way to that Lover. . .   H.D., *Helen in Egypt*
>
> I will always be on the equator
> with my daughter. . .   Sharon Doubiago,
>   *South America Mi Hija*

In *South America Mi Hija*, Doubiago writes the poem that she could not imagine writing in *Hard Country*.[14] Whereas *Hard Country* had emphasized disconnection between mother and daughter, *South America Mi Hija* insists on connectedness and restoration of that relationship, including vital literary connections between Doubiago and her female literary forebears. Published ten years after her first book, *South America Mi Hija* includes a critique of *Hard Country*'s poetics and politics: "All my life . . . I have searched / for the male. / lost brother. lost father. lost son. lost lover," Doubiago writes (*SAMH* 239). While *Hard Country* had noted "the mother's betrayal" in turning her sons and daughters over to a violent world, the speaker in *South America Mi Hija* holds herself more personally accountable for the failure to reach out to her own teenage daughter, lamenting that "I have handed you over // a virgin // to the patriarchy" (*SAMH* 244). The distance traveled between Doubiago's two epics is evident in the opening epigraph to *South America Mi Hija*, which rejects androgyny as a strategy for healing gender oppression: "The female void cannot be cured by a conjunction with the male, but rather by an internal conjunction, by an integration of its own parts, by a remembering or a putting back together of the mother-daughter body" (Hall 1980: 68). Without giving up the dream of twin-like companionship between men and women that motivated *Hard*

Country, Doubiago develops a model of intertextuality in which the restoration of the "submerged or drowned" mother takes center stage, eclipsing the search for equality with a male lover/precursor. In this volume, Doubiago forcefully connects her political goal of reconstructing a damaged society with her literary project of reconstructing a lost female poetic tradition and with her personal project of reconnecting with her fifteen-year-old daughter, Shawn, with whom she travels to South America.

The key difference between Doubiago's two book-length poems is their very different structures of address, a difference with profound implications for Doubiago's theory of intertextuality and her poem's relationship to the reader. In *South America Mi Hija*, the speaker in the poem addresses herself for the most part to her daughter instead of to the male lover (the title itself addresses "my daughter"), and Doubiago exchanges the pronounced heterosexual script of *Hard Country* for a thoroughly female-centered or matrisexual script. Whereas *Hard Country* sought to realign the male and female principles, with the woman poet addressing herself to the male lover and hoping to reassemble his lost parts, *South America Mi Hija* emphasizes instead the reintegration of the mother-daughter body. In this poem, the body that is fragmented and buried across the land is no longer that of the brother, Osiris, but that of the mother, Isis, whose cultural dis-membering is responsible for destructive gender relations and for larger oppressive structures of violence and war. Just as H.D.'s Helen travels to Leuké (*l'île blanche*), the island kingdom of the matriarchal goddess Isis or Aphrodite, Doubiago's narrator travels to Machu Picchu, a "city of women" (*SAMH* 225).

At the same time that Doubiago moves outside the borders of culturally sanctioned modes of poetic address, her narrator steps beyond the borders of the United States, traveling to Machu Picchu, the mountain city where the Virgins of the Sun took refuge after the sacking of Cuzco, the "American city of Sappho, Isle of Lesbos" (*SAMH* 208). H.D. had similarly transported her epic narrator to the ruined temples of a reportedly matriarchal religion. This move to "elsewhere"—the imagining of self in new locations—apparently enables a new structure of address. Each geographical shift that the narrators make serves also as a temporal shift and a corresponding shift in consciousness. Whereas H.D.'s Helen is, at the beginning of the epic, a disassociated subject (literally "beside herself" in Troy and in Egypt), Doubiago's narrators are seldom "called away" into trancelike states of "willed possession" (see Stewart 1995), although they too encounter plural ghosts on the battlefields of the nation. Helen presents the paradox of an "ecstatic subject"; her quest is precisely to wake up from the trance and heal the schism in consciousness. H.D.'s work insists that only by entering fully into psychic states of disassociation and ecstasy can Helen access her buried traumatic memories. Doubiago, on the other hand, is wary of such states: "I feel my skeptical caution in this realm to be greater than my openness . . . I am not called away" (1986: 2). Whereas H.D. did not want to "mix the dimensions" by publishing the "earth-bound" *Winter Love* in the same volume as *Helen in Egypt* (see her November 19, 1960, letter to Norman Holmes Pearson in Hollenberg 1997: 284), such mixing is exactly Doubiago's aim. Thus refusing transcendence, Sharon moves nonetheless out of place—into the place and body-time of others—and also allows her narrator to be *inhabited* by those others. The move to "elsewhere," for both H.D. and Doubiago, also gestures toward the poem's attempt to incorporate the one who is "outside" and other—the addressee, whether daughter, mother, or the musing reader.

"*Mi hija*," writes Doubiago, or "*mija*," a word that blurs boundaries between the maternal pronoun and the daughter so that both occupy the same word-space. Both H.D. and Doubiago insist on psychic intimacy between mother and daughter. Helen addresses herself directly to the mother, invoking Thetis or Isis, "*re-living her own story . . . in terms of that of her twin-sister*" (*HE* 74). Rachel Blau DuPlessis compellingly describes how H.D. in *Helen in Egypt* moves beyond the male-female desire of Isis for Osiris "to another, matching desire: of Isis for Isis": "The feminine quest for the Lover is not the more prominent; H.D. places the heterosexual, culturally powerful script in a new context, one formed by the reconstruction of Isis in two forms. First, as the sister-mirror; and second as the Great Mother" (1986: 104). In *South America Mi Hija*, Doubiago reconstructs Isis in an additional third form, that of the daughter, the "new Eve," although in addressing herself to the daughter ("*the core of the mother*"), Sharon addresses the mother as well: "My daughter is my mother," she writes (*SAMH* 218, 101).

The theory of gender psychology proposed by *South America Mi Hija* bears strong parallels to H.D.'s critique of the Oedipal family in *Helen in Egypt.* Remarking on the strong affinities between the two works, Doubiago wonders, "Did my first reading of *Helen* influence my writing twenty-six years later?" [15] As DuPlessis points out, *Helen in Egypt* antici-pates Dorothy Dinnerstein's hypothesis in her 1976 work of psychol-ogy, *The Mermaid and the Minotaur: Sexual Arrangements and Human Malaise*, a book that Doubiago acknowledges as a direct inspiration, summarizing it as follows:

> the hatred of the mother is the hatred of nature, which is the hatred
> of our mortality. Patriarchies are the universal psychological reaction
> of the child—male and female—to the mother. If fathers were the
> primary caregivers, the early ego reaction would be against them and
> the psychic longing would be for the female, for the feminine, which
> the world desperately needs to survive.   (Goodman 1997: 30)

Like H.D.'s *Helen in Egypt*, Doubiago's poem argues that "*the rejection of the mother / is the origin of war*" (*SAMH* 268). Her main object of cri-tique is no longer the deafness of the male lover or culture but the in-sidious Oedipal construction of the family, in which "the ego's rebel-lion, male *and* female, / from the mother" results in violence (*SAMH* 235). Arguing that this model of the family results in cultural forces that destroy the possibility of intimacy or communication between mother and daughter, Doubiago follows H.D.'s precedent in turning to the mother-daughter myth of Demeter and Persephone to mount a full-scale reinterpretation of the gender dynamics theorized in the Oedipal and Osirian myths.

Both poets revise the Oedipal myth in a similar way—by merging the myth of Isis with the story of Demeter and Persephone/Koré and the associated rituals of Eleusis, in which the mother grieves for and recovers her stolen daughter. When Helen is summoned "home" to Leuké by Thetis, for example, H.D. informs us that "in Egypt / we are in Eleusis / Helen is Persephone" (*HE* 218). One important step in this reinterpretation is to assert the primacy of a maternal deity: "She is stronger than God," writes H.D. (*HE* 63). Doubiago indicts our cul-ture's "Fear of the First God / Female" (*SAMH* 194). Stressing further Demeter's association with the earth, the narrator's address to the mother becomes the address of one body of land to another: "the love poem of North America / to South America" (*SAMH* 149). Doubiago hopes to reimagine the Oedipal story by excavating the pre-Oedipal semiotic realm (suggested by the ruined temples of archaic matriarchal religions at Egypt or Machu Picchu), thereby opening a road for connecting not only with the son but, even more importantly, with the daughter. Doubiago explores this pre-Oedipal state in a multilingual poem, blending Quechua, Spanish, and English, that draws attention to potential multivocality and to the "lost languages" in which mothers might have been able to speak to their daughters.

In emphasizing the maternal function so strongly, H.D. and Doubiago do not espouse an ahistorical or essentialist view of the mother's role as completely empowering or morally superior. For the women narrators in these poems, the role of mother is, at times, unchosen (something to which one is "doomed" or "condemned") or refused (as in the poems about abortion in *Hard Country*). When she momentarily becomes Thetis, Achilles' mother, Helen laments, "I became what his accusation made me" (*HE* 24). It is a burden that Helen's mentor and guide, Theseus, would lay upon her, insisting that "you are Demeter," and that Helen would refuse, saying "I am only a daughter" (*HE* 157, 203). Neither poet ignores what Hollenberg describes as "the historical incompatibility between procreation and intellectual pursuit" or the potential for "psychic fragmentation" in the bodily experience of pregnancy or childbirth (1997: 5). Nor does the mother necessarily occupy an ethical position. Doubiago points out in *Hard Country* that the mother betrays her son by turning him over to become a soldier and betrays her daughter as she "hands her over, a bloodstained spoil of war, / to the father" (*HC* 256). She rejects the idea that women are somehow more strongly linked to transformative "natural" processes — she desires, instead, to expose essentializing gender binaries not only as culturally constructed but as lying at the very root of destructive tendencies in modern culture: "*the war / is gender*," she writes (*SAMH* 233).

Although *Helen in Egypt* and *South America Mi Hija* offer powerful critiques of gender dynamics within the family, neither imagines an alternative to the psychoanalytic paradigm of the family—to the Holy Trinity of mother-father-child. Although both poems challenge patriarchal conventions and what DuPlessis has called "romantic thralldom" (1979b), they remain caught up in a family paradigm in which heterosexual romance predominates. Desire in these poems may be fundamentally matrisexual, but it is easily convertible at almost any point into heterosexual desire. The result for H.D.'s *Helen in Egypt* is

"an overwhelming engagement/engorgement with heterosexual desire," according to DuPlessis (1986: 116), while Catherine Stimpson
points out that Doubiago's *South America Mi Hija* "asserts a profound
causal relation between sex and gender" and has an "ahistorical and essentialist commitment to heterosexuality" (1993: 264–65).

Despite this commitment to an idealized heterosexual desire, Doubiago's narrator moves away from a posture of mourning the absent
male companion or of piecing him together. In the powerful epilogue
to *South America Mi Hija*, Sharon arrives at Machu Picchu, where she
touches the stones of the city and receives a vision of "The Return of
the Goddess." She sees

> *fathers returning to the children*
> *so our ego turning from the parent*
> *is not universally turning*
> *from the woman*
>
> . . . .
>
> *I touch the stone and see*
> *the world break open.*   (*SAMH* 282)

The return of the mother goddess is also the return of female literary
antecedents, and we hear in these lines an allusion to Muriel Rukeyser's
well-known assertion that "the world would split open" if a woman told
the truth about her life.[16] The hard phallic stone of Machu Picchu, incorporated into the female psyche by means of the poet's touch, breaks
open into a uterine world whose transformative power makes possible
the closing lines of the poem, in which the visionary poet imagines

> *the male*
> *bonded to the mother*
>
> *to the sister*
>
> *to the daughter*
>
> *to woman*
>
> *to Earth*
>
> mi hija.   (*SAMH* 284)

In addressing herself to the daughter, Doubiago realizes that *"the
daughter is the core of the mother"* (*SAMH* 218). The relationship—which
has ramifications for the dialogue between poet and reader—is one of
tenderness, intimacy, listening, and mutuality:

Your body came out of mine.
Our mouths are identical twins.
Labia minora, labia majora.
Yours is about to speak, mine demurely shuts.
    (*SAMH* 220)

How does the Message reach me?
do thoughts fly like the Word
of the goddess? a whisper—

(my own thought or the thought of another?)
                              H.D., *Helen in Egypt*

In the opening canto of *Helen in Egypt*, H.D. writes that "there is no veil between us / only space and leisure // and long corridors of lotus-bud" (2). If we read these lines as the poet's address to the reader, so that the "long corridors" of "lotus flower unfurled, with reed of the papyrus" are figures for H.D.'s own long poem, they suggest new relations among writer, reader, and text. Rather than establishing a controlling narrator who will parcel out the epic story to a passive reader, H.D. imagines an intimate, leisurely, spacious, and even timeless relation between the readers who will unfurl the papyrus/book or lotus/poem and the writer who "*herself is the writing*" (*HE* 23). The connections among the reader, the poet, and the book are direct, sensuous, and unveiled, perhaps even unmediated by the "Muse," who becomes simply "She who draws the veil aside" (H.D. 1972: 7). In one sense, this veil is time—that which divides writer and reader, past and present. The situation of reading is that of the rent veil when as readers we are ushered into the "time-less time" of the Egyptian temple and of the written page (*HE* 73). By emphasizing Helen's role as decoder and interpreter and by incorporating the reader fully into the body of her text by means of the critical and interpretive voice in the prose interludes, H.D. manages to bring the reader fully "inside" the poem.

Doubiago's work strives for a similar dynamic between reader and writer, one that emphasizes mutuality, reciprocity, and even physical intimacy:

The reader is the Muse. The Muse! I'd never understood the concept of the Muse before. I'd always gotten confused in the issue of its gender. Now I saw, very clearly, my real confusion stemmed from

my denial of the reader . . . *The reader is the Muse . . . The Lover who*
dictates the Word, the Lover to whom the word is dictated.   (1988: 128)

Doubiago writes that she was drawn to H.D.'s work—and especially to
Helen in Egypt—because it invites and accepts the reader in this way: "I
recognized in Hilda Doolittle respect for me, the reader" (1990: 59).
Of H.D.'s long poems, *Helen in Egypt* most resolutely refuses to differentiate between the one who writes, the one who reads, and the one
who is read. It was after writing this poem that H.D. asserted that "the
mother is the Muse, the Creator," a statement that itself blurs the
boundaries between the subject of the poem and its object, demanding
a fluid sense of poetic agency. In a footnote Doubiago claims she titled
her book *South America Mi Hija* "with deference": "My meaning is *not*
from traditional cultural imperialism, nor is it from traditional parental
presumption" (*SAMH* 285). Taking H.D.'s gendered model of poetic
inspiration in *Helen in Egypt* as a starting point for her own evolving
theories of textual connection, Doubiago presents her long poems as
potential sites for "alchemical exchange" (see Crown 1998), in which
the reader participates as *"mi compadrazga"* in the creation of the text
(*SAMH* 191). Poet and reader, like mother and daughter, are equal
presences in the poem, inhabiting one another without violence. Thus
the following lines from *South America Mi Hija* refer not only to Doubiago's intimate relationship with her daughter but to her respectful
ventriloquizing of the repressed voices of her culture, her intertextual
dynamics with her literary foremother, H.D., and her intimate cama-
raderie with the reader: "you, Soul of the Other / born out of me / you
the inside of the outside" (145).

NOTES

1. Sharon Doubiago, "Joyce" (1988: 263).

2. Titles of the following books by H.D. and Doubiago have been abbreviated
throughout the essay as follows: *HE, Helen in Egypt; HC, Hard Country; SAMH,
South America Mi Hija.*

3. In making this connection, I follow a suggestion made by Lynn Keller in her
work on the intertextual dynamic between Doubiago and Charles Olson: "An essay
parallel to this one," writes Keller, "might compare the narrator's relation to the
mothers with Doubiago's relation to her most significant female literary predecessor, H.D." (1997: 314).

4. In the very first lines by H.D. that Doubiago read (the opening lines of *Her-*

metic Definition displayed in the glass case), H.D. gestures to her own body and to the reader's entry into the poet's *physical* and psychic space: "Why did you come / to trouble my decline? / I am old (I was old till you came)." Although the poem's speaker adopts the posture of an old woman who does not want to be troubled by the visiting "you," the structure of the poem—based on the nine-month gestation period—would seem to acknowledge the young woman reader and her pregnancy, suggesting that the young reader has regenerated (or given birth to) the older woman writer.

5. Many readers share this response to H.D.'s very long and difficult epic sequences—they feel they can "grasp" their sense even without the literary training and background in classics that might seem necessary. As Alicia Ostriker puts it, quoting *Helen in Egypt*, "the secret is no secret" (*HE* 303): "A student of mine reading the late H.D. told the class that it was the strangest thing: she didn't understand a word of what was going on, and yet she felt the poem had happened to her, somehow, was about something in her own life that she had forgotten. Others at the table nodded . . . although we cannot read H.D.'s late poetry rationally, we can read it with, as it were, our own dream-lives, our own 'secret' knowledge of ourselves" (1983: 31).

6. Doubiago may have encountered H.D.'s ideas in published excerpts from *The H.D. Book*, Robert Duncan's revisionist account of literary modernism that places women poets at its center. His daybook (which inspired Doubiago's "own H.D. book") opens with a theory of "inspiration" derived directly from H.D.: "Back of the Muses, so the old teaching goes, is Mnemosyne, Mother of the Muses. Freud, too, teaches that Art has something to do with restoring, re-membering, the Mother . . . Poetry is the Mother of those who have created their own mothers" (Duncan 1967: 27–28).

7. By pointing out these convergences, I do not mean to suggest that Doubiago finds nothing to critique or reject in the work of H.D. and Duncan. By the time of writing *Hard Country*, for example, Doubiago could not find a usable model in Duncan and H.D.'s opaque, difficult, and esoteric revisions of the modernist aesthetic, having moved beyond her early interest in radically experimental poetry to a direct and accessible style that she felt was more accountable to the working-class community in which she had her roots.

8. This essay will now use "Doubiago" to refer to the author of *Hard Country* and *South America Mi Hija* and "Sharon" to refer to the narrator in both poems. "Sharon" also appears in Doubiago's *Book of Seeing with One's Own Eyes*.

9. The most detailed discussion of the childbirth metaphor in H.D.'s poetics is Donna Hollenberg's *H.D.: The Poetics of Childbirth and Creativity* (1991). Many of Hollenberg's insights about H.D.'s poetics are helpful in thinking about Doubiago's work—in particular, her reading of *Winter Love*, the "coda" to *Helen in Egypt*, as displaying Helen's ambivalence about the "act of nursing this poem child" (1991: 177).

10. Cynthia Hogue describes this dynamic in *Helen in Egypt*: "[H.D.] insists that readers inside and outside the text examine how relation to the symbolic phallus constructs gender difference (in the masculine imaginary conflation of phallus/pe-

nis, women can 'be' the phallus that men 'have'), and how the threat of its fantasized 'loss' destabilizes masculinity" (1995: 119).

11. Despite the striking set of correspondences between the two epic plots, a reader looking at *Hard Country* would find only a few mentions of H.D.'s work, including a poem inspired by H.D.'s early poem "The Islands" and a passage about Ezra Pound's mother from H.D.'s *End to Torment*. There is no mention at all of *Helen in Egypt*.

12. See Goodman (1998). In her essay on Doubiago's negotiations with the epic conventions established in Walt Whitman's *Song of Myself*, Goodman notes that Olson's *Maximus Poems* and William Carlos Williams's *Paterson* are Doubiago's "chief modernist models."

13. Even so, Doubiago hints that there may be maternal underpinnings to this overwhelmingly masculinist influence, connecting Olson to her mother by emphasizing the geography, land, and place: "Black Mountain," she told Jenny Goodman in an interview (1997: 23), "is a place in North Carolina, which is where my mother is from."

14. "Do you think that in *South America* you were trying in a way to write that poem, 'My Mother Is a Poem I'll Never Write'? I mean, *South America* was to the daughter, but it was all about what the mother didn't say to you" (Goodman 1997: 32).

15. Doubiago writes that "H.D. came back into my life in 1976, when I began my epic poem, *Hard Country*" (1986: 9). The connection to *Helen in Egypt*, however, remained under the surface, although by the early 1970s Doubiago had read *Trilogy* and *Hermetic Definition*. During the years between the writing of *Hard Country* and *South America Mi Hija*, Doubiago's involvement with H.D.'s writing intensified. From March to November 1986, when she was completing *South America Mi Hija*, she kept a journal, or daybook, called "Perdita's Father."

16. Muriel Rukeyser, in "Käthe Kollwitz" from *The Speed of Darkness*: "What would happen if one woman told the truth about her life? / The world would split open" (1994: 217). As Catherine Stimpson points out in her review of *South America Mi Hija*, Doubiago's book directly acknowledges its connection to the work of poets Muriel Rukeyser, Adrienne Rich, Susan Griffin, and Carolyn Forché.

A Gift of Song: My Encounter with H.D.

FRANCES JAFFER

Months after I had returned from a Mediterranean cruise, my parents asked me, "What did you enjoy most about the trip?" Without hesitation I said, "The Parthenon."

It was my eleventh birthday in March 1932. While our ship was docked in Piraeus, I climbed the Acropolis to the Parthenon in the company of the handsome German cruise director with whom I was secretly in love. He was being transferred to another ship, and I was in tears. The Parthenon was awesome—its pale marble had a lyrical austerity that dominated the Acropolis. My father, a structural engineer, had relentlessly taught his one daughter about architecture and religion. Though in tears, I was happy to recognize that the Parthenon's columns were Doric and that I had actually absorbed what my father had taught me. That March day I had my first mystical experience, what I would now call a spreading sense of spirit that manifested itself as a premonition of my father's death later that year. Walking under Homer's sky, we came upon two Greek children, younger than I—perhaps six or seven years old—who seemed to be waiting to be photographed. They stood with their backs to a fence, and I watched the photograph happen. The boy's green jacket and the girl's red dress signified something both knowable and unknowable, an opening into the real world of time and loss. In the instant of the photograph of these two Greek children (me and not me), I felt the touch of sorrow that subtly colors our experience of Art. What to an eleven year old was a stirring, even ecstatic experience became one of the determining moments of my life.

Decades later, when I discovered H.D.'s poems on the dirty floor of a San Francisco bookstore, I thought, "Again, Greece." It was as though H.D. had been waiting. I had found a poetry that opened and deepened the world for me in a way that felt akin to that instant at the Parthenon years ago.

I began to read poems seriously in my early fifties when I decided that it was time to make up for not having had a formal literary education. I read intensely in order to come to some understanding of what the canon was. Reading extensively in the major anthologies, I was sickened when I discovered the almost universal neglect, even absence, of women as writers of any significance or as truly human actors in the poems of men. There was hardly a poem in the anthologies that was not dismissive of women in one form or another. Although I had no political agenda, lesbian or otherwise, I was extremely depressed by what I was reading. These were the poems women are regularly handed and asked to identify with. I decided then that for a long time I would read only poems by women; after all, my literary education was mine to create. I wanted to know what women had written, but we were told that it wasn't very good, that the poetry women write has always been irrelevant, that it wasn't Art. But as Carolyn Kizer insists in "Pro-Femina," "We are the custodians of the world's best kept secret: / merely the private lives of one half of humanity" (1965: 40). I wanted the lives of that excluded half in a poetry free of misogynist attitudes. And I found in H.D. what I had been looking for.

The first poem I read in H.D.'s *Selected Poems* was "The Helmsman." In it, I heard a music that still delights me:

O be swift—
we have always known you wanted us.

. . . .

We forgot—we worshipped,
we parted green from green,
we sought further thickets,
we dipped our ankles
through leaf-mould and earth,
and wood and wood-bank enchanted us—

. . . .

We were enchanted with the fields,
the tufts of coarse grass

in the shorter grass—
we loved all this.

But now, our boat climbs—hesitates—drops—
climbs—hesitates—crawls back—
climbs—hesitates—
O be swift—
we have always known you wanted us.   (1988: 7)

It was a new song that held me, intense at times and urgent but also tenderly erotic. The insistence of rhythm and its hesitation, its constant variation and repetition, seemed at once freely active and constrained. There was a double mood, persistent and self-questioning. And the ambivalence toward violent resolution was both subject of the poem and a characteristic of its voice. In "Hermes of the Ways," H.D. embraces this irresolution, affirming its value:

Hermes, Hermes,
the great sea foamed,
gnashed its teeth about me;
but you have waited,
where sea-grass tangles with
shore-grass.   (1988: 13)

Here, before the sea, H.D. invokes a god "of the triple path-ways" who alone has waited for her. But he himself is "dubious," a vacillator, unsettled. "Facing three ways," one of which is death, Hermes is a god of change. In this poem, H.D. affirms life in all its contradiction, for she risks embracing a god of inconstancy, a constant in a world of violent upheavals.

Reflecting on my first readings of these poems, I recall my delight in having found a woman writer for whom there was violence in every landscape and whose reality was not a "sheltered garden" with "border on border of sheltered pinks" ("Sheltered Garden"). And so I entered her garden with its reeds "slashed and torn / but doubly rich" ("Sea Lily"). "Sea Rose," one of H.D.'s ecstatic flower poems that bears witness to the rough, dark side of beauty, begins by invoking "Rose / harsh rose, marred with stint of petals, / meagre flower." Here, the cliché of poetic beauty is "caught . . . stunted . . . flung . . . acrid" and "hardened" as H.D. searches for a new kind of beauty that will compromise neither strength nor life. Again, in "Orchard," the lyrical voice pleads to be free of the object of its desire. Beauty will never be a source of comfort, and this poem is a prayer to "spare us from loveliness." H.D.'s experience of beauty seemed very different from that of men for whom danger meant the beauty of women rather than the beauty of nature. Here was no Belle Dame sans Merci.

Discovering these poems was a turning point for me. I was fifty, just diagnosed with cancer and beginning to write. And I had found a great poet.

It was 1976. For the first time in seventeen years of marriage I had taken a trip by myself: a week in Palm Springs, where I could write and swim. I was sitting in the sun thumbing through an anthology I had picked up to take along with me, *The Voice That Is Great within Us* (Carruth 1970). I was looking for poems I liked and admired written by women.

To say that H.D.'s "Eurydice" changed my life may sound hyperbolic, but it is not an exaggeration. I found myself shaking with angry pleasure. Here was a volcanic poem, an angry poem that dealt passionately with the difficult reality of women's lives. The language, too, exceeded the limits prescribed by the feminist poems of literal statement I had until then considered appropriate models:

> so for your arrogance
> and your ruthlessness
> I am swept back
> where dead lichens drip
> dead cinders upon moss of ash;   (H.D. 1988: 36)

In the early years of feminism, stating the facts of women's lives was considered artistically sufficient. But here was a poem untamed by the mold. I read "Eurydice" out loud to myself many times. And with the song came the powerful reversal, Eurydice's defiance. Her loss of the upper world of light becomes a triumphant discovery and embrace of herself:

> Against the black
> I have more fervor
> than you in all the splendour of that place,

against the blackness
and the stark grey
I have more light;   (H.D. 1988: 39)

No longer did the story belong to the man, nor was the woman a possession. This remarkable poem—written before 1920, long before the second wave of feminism—strengthened me in my fragile feminist identity.

I was a middle-aged housewife struggling to give myself permission to write when I discovered H.D.'s version of Sappho's "Fragment Thirty-six":

I know not what to do,
my mind is reft:
is song's gift best?
is love's gift loveliest?

.   .   .   .

My mind is quite divided,
my minds hesitate,
so perfect matched,
I know not what to do:
each strives with each
as two white wrestlers
standing for a match,
ready to turn and clutch
yet never shake muscle nor nerve nor tendon.
    (1983: 65)

I too was torn between the demands of art and the demands of love. Echoing my own struggle, H.D.'s extrapolation of the fragment acknowledged and honored my difficulty. I was truly encouraged.

As I continued to read I was surprised by the flatness of many of the poems in *Red Roses for Bronze*; this master could stumble. But in the late, great epic works, I rediscovered her music, though in a radically different form. The early poems were purely lyrical with varying line lengths and irregular stanzas. In *Trilogy*, her flexible two-line stanzas sustain a narrative voice that ranges from the early lyricism to ordinary speech. Any number of passages might illustrate how this form is able to accommodate these extremes. In section 32 of "The Walls Do Not Fall," for example, H.D. summarizes all the objections that might be raised against her, then answers them in a flying affirmation of possibility:

> Depth of sub-conscious spews forth
> too many incongruent monsters
>
> and fixed indigestible matter
> such as shell, pearl; imagery
>
> done to death; perilous ascent,
> ridiculous descent; rhyme, jingle,
>
> overworked assonance, nonsense,
> juxtapositions of words for words' sake
>
> .   .   .   .
> you find all this?
>
> .   .   .   .   .   .
> separated from the wandering stars
> and the habits of the lordly fixed ones,
>
> we noted that even the erratic burnt-out comet
> has its peculiar orbit.   (1983: 534)

H.D. was almost sixty years old and writing at the peak of her powers. But even after this great epic work, she continued to write strong poems throughout a long life. In fact, she wrote some of her most beautiful and revealing series of poems in the last years of her life, "Winter Love," for example. Many older women might find this series of poems embarrassing because the erotic life of old people is taboo. But H.D. had the courage to declare her vulnerability.

> How could I love again, ever?
> repetition, repetition, Achilles, Paris, Menelaus?
> But you are right, you are right,
>
> there is something left over,
> the first unsatisfied desire—
> the first time, that first kiss,
>
> the rough stones of a wall,
> the fragrance of honey-flowers, the bees,
> and how I would have fallen but for a voice,
>
> .   .   .   .

Helen, Helen, come home;
there was a Helen before there was a War,
but who remembers her?   (1972: 90–91)

Upon reading these poems, I thought to myself that not many women would take this risk, and I was deeply moved and inspired.

Enthusiasm for H.D.'s work led me to a widening circle of feminist poets. Reading periodicals like *Signs* and *Feminist Studies*, I found frequent references to H.D. Across the country I made contact with fellow enthusiasts. In my local community my goal was to introduce her to as many women as possible, and I proceeded aggressively. I gave readings of H.D.'s poems and lectured. To my delight, an "H.D. Network" developed.

All the while, of course, with growing freedom and energy, I was writing my own poems. At that time I had to deal with the knowledge that I had cancer. Suddenly, one afternoon, a poem came to me, quickly, the way some poems do. In the middle of a long, serious poem about the cancer, a piece inspired by H.D.'s language and image appeared:

Oh the tomb, delicate sea shell, H.D. said
the temple or the tomb, but there are
the waves holding the moon, the flicker

that holds light, the space
between columns where shape
dances, bright fog sings—

the ride undersea, the leap
spraying the world pink, the sun
swings on the sea

I won't sit still   (1981: 9)

I felt this was the most lyrical poem I had written. I was ecstatic because I had been able to write a poem whose song I loved and because it was so affirmative. It seemed to signify a connection between H.D. and myself as poets.

My introduction to H.D. opened me not only to the work of a great poet but to the realization that much of what we know as modernism was perhaps inaugurated and sustained by an entire milieu of women, long neglected originators on the left bank of Paris and in London. When H.D.'s work was revered, as it was by Pound, it was admired as he defined it, not as she herself would come to understand it. She would, of course, eventually abandon Pound's narrow requirements in order to become her own poet. This, of course, is the subject of much of her autobiographical prose.

I have dealt almost exclusively with the poetry, but I don't want to overlook her unpredictable and beautiful work in prose. *HERmione, Palimpsest*, and *Bid Me to Live* all excited and surprised me. With considerable effort, I had to learn to read *HERmione*. Initially, I was afraid of it. I thought she was too crazy, and I was put off by her use of the objective case: "I am the word . . . the word was with God . . . I am the word . . . HER. Hermione Gart hugged HER to Hermione Gart. I am HER. The thing was necessary. It was necessary to hug this thing to herself. It was a weight holding her down, keeping her down. Her own name was ballast to her lightheadedness" (H.D. 1981: 33). But as I taught myself to read it, I was struck by its intended psychological and literary effect. It was beautiful desperation. I was eventually captivated by this perfect rendering of a young woman's struggle to hold on to her subjectivity. And although *Bid Me to Live* is more conventional than *HERmione*, it bears the imprint of a remarkable sensibility exploring the creative self.

Ever since my first visit to the Acropolis, I'd been drawn to the Greek myths. I was fascinated by the irresponsibility of the Olympians, their high jinks, their peculiar morality, their beauty and drama. For me they signaled a continuous sensuous awareness of the cosmos and its unmanageable authority. H.D.'s obsession with them enhanced my own.

For many years I had been hoping to get back to Greece. The truth is, I had become fixated on the goddess Athena. I had found an image of her that astounded me, a photo of a statue of the goddess without her military headdress. She was softly beautiful and sweet-faced, more maternal than I had ever imagined. This statue was only about four inches high, but that was enough. I knew I had to go to Greece and find this goddess. Waking from a dream one morning, I had a prophetic vision. I heard a woman sternly ordering me to go to Greece. And in this dream there was a Woman in a boat. A baby was beside her and a green snake sweetly swimming. From the top of a hill, the goddess shone a great beacon into the night. She would protect the baby, she was Athena leading me back to Greece with H.D.

In Greece again, on Patmos, the small white buildings looked like toys and marked the turns on hillsides. And there were the powerful icons. I found a picture postcard captioned "Virgin Almighty and Guiding" and began my search for this Christian vision of the virgin goddess. A breathless woman in high heels and a black skirt came tripping down the stony path from the twelfth-century monastery. Gleefully she said, "Tomorrow is Ascension Day! It's a great day for the Virgin!" I followed a little boy who took me to the woman who cared for the church that housed the icon I was seeking. Years later I would recall this quest in a poem:

The Ikon
stares from the shadows at the back,

I know her! Zeus' motherless Daughter. She
holds an angry Child.   (1981: 14)

When I recall writing this, the central debt to H.D. is clear, and I am moved by the recollection. It was she who inspired this religious quest, just as she helped me see Athena in the image of the Virgin. Indeed, my indebtedness goes far beyond this discovery on Patmos: H.D. sanctioned me as a fully human woman and artist open to the deep unity of experience.

In the years since my astonished discovery of "Eurydice," H.D. has gained a great following. Her collected poems have been published, books have been written about her life and her works, and it seems strange to remember the days when most women, and men, would say, "Oh, that Imagist. I haven't read much of her work." I have to admit, I miss some of the intensity of those missionary days; to be a lover of H.D.'s poems no longer excites comment. At a recent feminist literary conference, the embattled were the ones who (courageously) stood up and said, "I don't like H.D.!"

I didn't feel it was necessary to argue. H.D.'s reputation is relatively secure. Disagreements are merely interesting. And every time I open a page to one of her poems, I'm transported again by her song.

Again She Says Try To:
Frances Jaffer and H.D.

KIM VAETH

William Carlos Williams has written of the eye's dual nature as "the little hole" through which the world enters. Frances Jaffer's
eye, often reluctantly, lets in a taut, mercurial, anxious, and wildly in-
subordinate landscape. But this eye is neither Williams's, nor her friend
George Oppen's, nor any modernist's eye; it is her own serious and provocative eye, perpetually uneasy about its job.

Snagged by several convergent events in midlife, namely, a cancer
diagnosis, her discovery of H.D.'s *Selected Poems*, and the swirling insur-
gence of feminist writing in the San Francisco Bay Area, Jaffer began
her own writing life in the 1970s when she was in her fifties and became
one of the founding editors of the magazine *HOW(ever)*. With each of
her three books—*Any Time Now, She Talks to Herself in the Language
of an Educated Woman*, and *ALTERNATE Endings*—Jaffer takes more
chances in pursuit of a new poetics; these necessitate an active engagement with the demands of syntax in order to allow the relentless inter-
ruptions of the mind into her work. Thus does Jaffer render the switch-
backs of her own mind that rise from the deep and surface before
submerging again. The effect is one of extending or elongating the
poem through the unexpected reach of its sound and syntax, as in these
stanzas from separate poems in *ALTERNATE Endings*:

> Westering. The where and the do-not-move
>   palpate sod. And her breasts
>   burst and the nattering
>   fields. Yestering.   (1985: 72)

and this:

Cut the top off it, look, gray matter, Old Bag, Lady
be good, Music hath, Music bath, Singing in the flood.

Lady be God.   (1985: 66)

These lines gather the American speech and music that Jaffer turns
to and is nurtured by, that set her on a different linguistic path from
H.D., whose line "mère, mere, mater, Maia, Mary / Star of the Sea, /
Mother" (1973: 8) invokes a spiritual, religious tone—almost a chant.
By contrast, Jaffer's work delivers the pleasures of the unhabitual, of
syncopation. Indeed, jazz and the blues are the source for so much of
Jaffer's play with sound and movement; "Lady Be Good" is a perfect
instance of one of her literal references to a jazz rendition with her subversive improvisation on the phrase to "Lady be God." And "Music
hath, Music bath" is her own sardonic comment on "Music has charms
to soothe a savage breast"—her own dark joke on herself.

Jaffer has grasped that thought can make a sound in the ear that is
immediately recognizable and, further, that sound and syntax carry
their own meanings and echoes. In her reach for a language that will
render what her real eye sees, Jaffer subverts traditional syntax, in part
by building her lines with unusual words and peculiar off rhymes and
by extending her line just a word or two beyond the ear's expectation
(or by compressing it), dropping an article, pulling back on a phrase's
expected finish or flourish, and, in this, further implicating her reader's
reliance on a more usual rhythm or sentiment. While her formal intentions are both playful and suspicious, she is nowhere more immersed
in the qualities and possible meanings of sound as she is in the work
achieved in *ALTERNATE Endings*, where sound and syntax are Jaffer's
delighted vehicle, as in

> caught in quirks particles radiate
>   waves being true
>
> she sees in her loss not roses she tries
>   to say shadows not as we are   (1985: 23)

or these lines:

> How the scientist tries
> to remain real

Fan-belts
lasers and their spawn and Words

　　　Milky Way
　　　Ursa Major How Lovely

　we think
　　　　and the Ark rips
　　　　　　　on the peaks
Heave
Ho
　　　　　　Hearties　(1985: 28)

Jaffer's poetic practice often evolves from an unfolding of questions. Indeed, she studied science avidly, and her analytic mind always drew her to philosophic questions and readings, notably the pre-Socratics. Heraclitus, who presented the idea that out of flux comes harmony, appears in the first stanza of the first poem "If All the World Went Up" in *ALTERNATE Endings*. A reader becomes immediately absorbed by the rarest of intelligences—jaunty, prickly, and argumentative—while held, displaced really, in suspension. Again and again the poet invites the reader to contemplate a feminist version of Negative Capability whereby doubts and uncertainties have an equal footing with what Keats called an "irritable reaching after fact and reason" (1739; see Keats 1968). The presence of both doubt and reason are necessary mandates.

Jaffer's poems complicate as well as argue for the state of precariousness that she most deeply feels and desires to explore—about being a mother, a daughter, and a wife, about having and surviving cancer, about being a poet. One of the conjunctions that exists between Jaffer and H.D. is the awareness that each poet culled from death's nearness. The compression of adverse, out-of-control events—acute illness and war—brought each poet into the fire-circle of her writing life.

In much of her work, Jaffer contends with the perpetual disruption of self that illness bestows. Where is the integrated self when the body is under the siege of chemotherapy? When Heraclitus considered whether or not it is the same stream when we step into it twice, he questioned the nature of continuity. Jaffer's underlying question is what self appears to take the place of the integrated self when illness arrives, or, as she poses in a series of searing questions at the end of the prose poem "Who Would Dance Around in Circles,"

What would happen to me if I were REALLY well? Would everyone stop
loving me? . . . How to know in my deep bones that sympathy is not love?
Gratitude is not love? Envy is not love? Pity is not love? Sex is not love?
Staying alive is love. (1981: 35)

Jaffer questions both what the essential self is and whether being ill has
interrupted what others perceive and cherish.

Contending with illness, particularly one that is life threatening, is
an insistent kernel around which Jaffer's poems shape themselves, layer
by layer, stubbornly and often with great resistance. As with H.D.'s
mollusk trope in *Trilogy*, illness, for Jaffer, is the grain of sand that transforms the organism as it is itself transformed into the "pearl-of-great-
price," ultimately becoming that which is cherished not as a piece of
wealth but as a means of new insight, albeit not in the way hoped for.

Thus the integrity that was initially believed to be lost is ultimately
regained through the transformation wrought by being ill. For Jaffer,
this shift manifests in the poet's work as an urgency to utter a (new) self,
one that can fight with her earlier beliefs, one whose considerable intellect can now hone its edge against more difficult surfaces and disparities
of male/female relationships—inclinations that Jaffer shares with H.D.

In "The Walls Do Not Fall," both the worm and the word have the
innate power to hatch the butterfly, one of H.D.'s most vibrant metaphors for the decoding of spiritual knowledge. The critic Jeannine
Johnson believes that in *Trilogy* H.D. does not "minimize the all too
real material ruin surrounding her and her writing. *Trilogy* suggests that
we require an aesthetic lens (poetry, metaphor) through which to understand and to personalize what is so palpably close and yet so difficult
to contain in words" (1998: 120).

Perhaps this difficulty can be circumvented if the poet herself becomes the cocoon for the words themselves—wrapped cryptograms
that hold the soon-to-be-transformed worm. An insemination of the
self (DuPlessis 1990a: 33). As she allows her poems to become increasingly difficult, Jaffer establishes a correlation that seeks to honor both
the worm and the butterfly throughout their inchoate larval stages. She
deploys the idea that words can act as seeds:

> and you see the totentanz on the ridge, death
> shakes the dancers
> the words say *let me in*

you get up and write them down
(1981: 1)

Rather than distance herself from mastectomy and chemotherapy, which could silence or paralyze the most intrepid, Jaffer knits a rageful, courageous intimacy with her changed body: "The missing breast points its bony fingers / at its twin and the rigorous mind falters" (1985: 45).

Furthermore, by facing the very thing she fears, cancer in this case, she propels herself toward the source of her power and courage—her writing life, seized late and wholeheartedly:

> . . . faith
>
> won't move the wild cells outgrowing her
> life   what holds her she
>
> will not see nor what
> she holds   no widening
>
> flame spreads into night   (1985: 20)

Indeed, over the course of *ALTERNATE Endings*, Jaffer insists on the experience of fear as her subject as she insists on contemplating her own death.

> . . . Is she dying today or tomorrow
>
> yet we do weep. The dark she's in flows
> with the tide and the road
> to the next room eludes her.   (1985: 42)

and

> Dying is good-bye. The absence
> of me.
> Unthinkable.
>
> Immeasurable. My absence is
> Absence. It will not be all right.   (1985: 43)

Witnessing her own absence fixes the depth of her gaze onto the things of the world and their shadows, an act that marks the poet as it marks the reader, momentarily made aware and implicated in a death that is now shared. Jaffer never steers her poems toward solace, nor is it her intent to "light a new fire" of regeneration that H.D. yearns for in the aftermath of war's destruction (1973: 17). Jaffer's reader must therefore consider being suspended in the wreckage without the balm of hope or spiritual transformation.

In the long poem "Any Time Now" (in *She Talks to Herself in the Language of an Educated Woman*) Jaffer disrupts temporal order by conflating various illnesses from childhood to the present. Though the predominant voice of much of the poem is in the third person,

> Her Jewish mother despises
> Jews and women, adores doctors,
> loves the sick; her father
> dies early and she has been sick
> all her life   (1981: 5)

the poem takes jolting turns into the first person:

> I say what about love?
> My mother says I think you're catching cold
> Of course I love you.   (1981: 8)

When H.D.'s lines are woven into the last section of the poem, *"Oh the tomb, delicate sea shell / the temple or the tomb,"* they work as a palliative to the din of mother and daughter caught up in their ancient chant. H.D.'s words part the waters for a turning point in the poem as the most lyrical lines of the poem follow:

the flicker

> that holds light, the space
> between columns where shape
> dances, bright fog sings—
>
> the ride undersea, the leap
> spraying the world pink, the sun
> swings on the sea
>
> I won't sit still   (1981: 9)

Jaffer's inclusion of H.D. does not point the way to resolution but offers instead a guiding voice that can show her the way into and out of the family tomb so that she may be able to speak. As guide, H.D. can help her to inscribe the difficult historical narrative about how she came to be herself, *her selves*:

> Morning, is it
> a mortal flare? Laughing ourselves awake
>
> we stare, tanager, columbine, holding
> sunlight in our teeth.

The poet's complex relationship with illness is seized and re-measured: "she sticks her neck out. / It is dangerous. / She talks" (1981: 7). Though Jaffer worries in "If All the World Went Up" that she "close(s) [her] poems before they begin," here, the whole terrain of the poem seismically shifts our vision away from the tomb toward the possible temple where "sunlight" is held "in our teeth" and where the poet's voice is now located.

Invoking H.D., who stuck her neck out to Pound, Lawrence, and Freud, to name only three, Jaffer's own poem can also be seen as dangerous and thus absolutely necessary. To invite H.D. into her poem, a largely symbolic act, is to be accompanied in the struggle to become a poet, to not be reduced or silenced, to take control of her story and the chances it takes to tell it. H.D. has parted the literal waters for Jaffer and invited her to undertake her own writing life in her middle years, a commensurate act of insubordination for a bourgeois housewife and mother. H.D. holds out the permission, finally, to argue, to speak up, to talk back, to create a poetic space that will be Jaffer's alone to define.

> over here ladies and gentlemen we have Nature
> with all its not-hers
> power and grandeur
>
> > is what is MEANT
> > Who
> > Means it
> > (1985: 29)

"She Says Try," the second poem in *ALTERNATE Endings*, investigates beauty, specifically what comprises a beautiful poem; Jaffer wills herself to look at beauty undefined. "Red leaves lighting / a green hill are not poetry," though suddenly her gaze ratchets up a notch as she regards how

small selves
in the stones hide from each other, rough
brown stones cracked and edgy lying

in broken scrubby fields sometimes
have the loveliest selves . . .   (1985: 18)

Soon the poem cuts an unexpected swath through more predictable conclusions with the lines *"She is afraid / of dying and watches mist on the bay / loaf across opposite hills."* Beauty is temporarily marooned while the poet pursues her primal idea: *"how great it is to be alive with / or without beauty or a world beyond / this to think of."* Jaffer can barely conceal her ambivalence about her desire to define beauty. Even beholding it is secondary to being alive.

Though the origin of the poem seems at first to be a noble endeavor, perhaps the most famous poetic endeavor—to witness and report back on beauty—"She Says Try" accomplishes something far more interesting and complicated as it locates, by default, the otherness of beauty, that which falls between the cracks, that which is hidden.

She is afraid no beauty can pull her
back from the edges she is teetering on and
wonders if not beauty what
shadows might   (1985: 19)

The striking implication is not that Jaffer seeks the shadows but that they seek her, despite her first intention. Once the thing hunted for is relinquished, something else may then come to take its place; in Jaffer's poems, that nothing that we scarcely know usually appears, breaking up what we know or thought we expected—the mark of a true and original poet. As it turns out, Jaffer's *nothing* is busy with dense associations: the otherness of beauty, the hidden, invisible layers of subatomic physics, the tug of shadows. Here is the work of a fighter who has survived, appropriating a poetic space in which to hold precariousness with which we spin in the human and particled cosmos.

Haibun: "Draw your / Draft"

RACHEL BLAU DUPLESSIS

Her books were there on my shelf, waiting for me to attend; I had bought them, but I didn't read them. Grove and ND. The cover of *Bid Me to Live* a photo taken at a vertiginous angle. Of a blank space. Telling the book by its cover. Telling a woman's book by the cover. The surface. (But it was not blank; it was a photo of military monuments. Could I see?) The moment not heroic but compliant, with hardly an undercurrent of resistance. Just the fact that I had bought her books, there was some kind of declaration. But not reading them—another kind. The vertigo of acceding to something called "woman"—the danger of it. *Helen in Egypt* looked too "neat," too "centered." I was, instead, challenging myself with the all-over page space collage works of Williams (*Paterson*) and Pound (*The Cantos*). This date is 1965 through 1974. I have (1968) read *The H.D. Book* chapters in *Caterpillar*, in *Coyote's Journal*, in *Stony Brook*. Robert Duncan is my first path to H.D., for he made a heterodox modernism with women's work and men's intermingled, counter to any version the university or the general literate culture proposed. Getting something of that "feminine" associative build and the insouciant resistance to convention via a (gay) man. Shock, scandal, pleasure. And his essay form—the form of thinking, himself indebted to her, so that in hearing his essay with a wild alertness, I was also beginning to hear H.D. The essays I have written first occurred under the sign of Duncan's *H.D. Book*: his work and Woolf's, Rich's, and then H.D.'s tipped me into that tonality of consideration, the burst of vectored thought, the feeling analysis. I heard it first there, and then I did it, and still do.

During my Columbia Ph.D. oral examination in, was it 1966 or 1967, I spoke about Williams's *Spring and All*, a work no one (I ever knew) had read, written by a poet almost totally discounted. I also spoke critically about Dorothy Wordsworth's position as a conduit for the imagination of her brother, about the cultural meaning of the female figure in "Tintern Abbey." I had never heard anyone saying the things that were coming out of my mouth.

> Prima Donna Illusion
> the dreamed dreamer
> my silhouette, sleep, swirled like a silver streamer
> the stage is swept with shards.

At a peculiar location, tamped down, insecure. I heard the New American poetry through the Donald Allen anthology, and I listened at a place where Olson, Duncan, Creeley, and also *Caterpillar* (edited by Clayton Eshleman) existed, but I didn't search for any personal bond. On the other hand, with much personal and intellectual bonding, I connected to the Objectivists, primarily to George Oppen. Oppen and I met and engaged with each other from August 1965; I think of him and his work insistently (he died in 1984). He is central to my sense of the seriousness and scrupulousness of poetry, and he influenced my knowledge of the poetic career: exilic, nomadic, working out of a marginal place into both the leverage of marginality and sense of centrality, building himself an oeuvre in twenty-five years of intense work. These forces in poetry and poetics (all loosely emerging from Pound and Williams) met the loose professional complacencies of the university as institution, in which there were a history, a library, a site of enterprise but no real or consistent training, certainly not for women. I never went downtown, kept to a little poetry group on 100th Street. In 1968 the radical liberatory thinking of civil rights and antiwar analyses contributed to the beginnings of a feminist movement in which I was abruptly immersed to my fibers. After a first flurry of activity, I went to France for several years (1970–72) and had to invent a feminist cultural position for myself, without immediate peers or interlocutors. Isolation is a motif. There is also no doubt I was afraid of the gift.

> hooded woman, black coat
> rigid in an
> anxious walking context
> I expect her to howl
>
> falling into the well of swallowing herself

During the early period of my (particular/peculiar) poetic career (1963 forward) I was very good at inventing blockages. I was always writing the long poem. Before 1968 I had written good works: a serial poem called "The War Years," a long sequence called "Villa d'Este Staten Island," and a serial work that was really about gender, beginning "Train journey and / journey by water," yet there were no ways for me to understand in my head what my subject was telling me nor ways to move into a real poetic career. During the time I was writing my gnarled-up dissertation (on Pound and Williams, called "The Endless Poem"), I diminished to three-line, to one-line poems. The fragment is not inconsistent with the urge to seriality, of course, but this felt like the end of my poetry. I remember with great gratitude George Oppen looking at this work (and at this situation) and saying, "Well, a good one-line poem, that's not nothing." It now grieves (and almost frightens) me how many opportunities I missed, how wayward was my path, how divided I was, how underutilized (how I understood little or nothing of what I actually could do)—especially in the mid-1960s, when some of my age cohort were publishing, even with trade presses. I was the Pokey Little Puppy. Now isn't that cute. And ain't it a shame. It's good I've lived as long as I have, even so. Any work is in part shaped by luck. The luck of being here.

> How many overtures
>> you gonna write
>>> to yr only
>> OPERA
> "get on with it"

Yet still during the early and mid seventies there was more blockage or, rather, the invention of a certain structure of resistance. No easy way to say this, it seems so scrupulously—what? (certainly undercutting). The question of beauty. I just didn't want beauty in my poetry: any hint was an invitation to a slippery slope of the feminine. Beauty was too nice, too expected, too complicit with what the feminine was in poetry and by extension what the female was. The poetry of the death of the beautiful woman was the death of the woman writing. The death of the poet in the poetess. Of course, this became a subject of some of my literary criticism. I am so stubborn about this structure of feeling that, even now, I have much suspicion of the triumphant investiture of awe and blessing in female figures by culture and cultural products—from Dante to Breton and beyond. This is a serious blind spot as well as part of my critical advantage. That's why I now love Lyn Hejinian's wry, recognizing line (from section—that is, age—26 of *My Life*) "The Muses are little female fellows." It takes that whole structure of feeling and flicks it away at about the same age-time as I also confronted the situation of woman writing.

So I tried *not* to write beauty (and images, and sonority) but to write language, to write syntax. Or to compose a beauty so hard and selective as to contain its presence. This urge has analogues with early H.D., but I "got it" via the Objectivists and Pound. An unintended consequence: my poetry could not be fluid, fluent, it could only stop and start. It was so angry about rhetorics—these are the years before *Wells* (that is, before 1980) and just after. This explains why my first book was about fifteen years late. I thought—in the jargon of the time—that "I hadn't found my voice." I'd now say (other jargon?) that the positions available for me to take up as a woman writer—inside language and inside the mechanisms of poetry, and outside it in various apparatuses and institutions of culture—were unsatisfactory to me. I was writing the lyric, yet increasingly I did not want the perfection of lyric, the separation of lyric, the selectivity of lyric, the purity of lyric. This is surely a contradiction. Thus my allegiance to the Objectivist purities, because they offered some way of skepticism and quasi-refusal, some method of documentary.

> blank-bud book
> not even certain
> which way to o-
> > pen it.

In 1973–74 I wrote "Eurydice," a poem (like its companion "Medusa") out of an early feminist critique of culture—a redirection of mythopoesis: telling the "other side." That gender binarism was an important invention of the time, for it allowed us to bring women as a socially formed group up to concerted scrutiny. My sense of the potential of feminist critique was imagining the whole world differently, the reinvention of culture. There was a growing context for this thinking—an explosion of investigations and poetries. Adrienne Rich was a very important ethical and intellectual figure in this feminist effervescence. It was no accident that this work was about the opposite of the imprint of the poet-Orpheus, about the female figure who, turning away from the one whose very name is a synonym for poetry, chooses to go back underground. Only after I had completed my "Eurydice" did someone tell me about H.D.'s poem called "Eurydice." This was a talismanic moment of connection between myself and H.D. Because I had written my poem, I suddenly could read and recognize her poem and her project: it became legible. I understood that we were involved in parallel studies of the position of the female figure in culture. The intertwined turn of reading and writing, the reading of the writing created a bond between this poetic mind and my own, a spiral of recognition. Without exaggeration, one might say that moment opened my poetry as it opened my literary criticism and my essays. H.D. was enabling for my poetic career.

"I needed a woman, a poet, and a modernist and I needed her badly." (This from my "Reader, I Married Me.") H.D. was this figure.

"What, then, must a woman do with the reactionary sexual ideology of high art?" (Spivak 1980: 74).

I wanted to start modernism again, all over, from the beginning.

> "finally a woman on paper"
> "I'll paint it big"
> "with flowers on my flower"
> "I brought home the bleached bones"   (O'Keeffe)

The revision. The reassessment. The reconsideration. Had this person ever been read before? A few now read H.D. voraciously. I heard Susan Stanford Friedman talk about H.D., read S.S.F.'s first work (in 1975), bonded with her. The confrontation she postulated between H.D. and Freud—the deep intellectual and spiritual engagement and the deep resistance—resonated with my relations to (loosely) the patriarchs. Feminist thinking about literary texts vibrated with questions about myth (that is, the spiritual and ideological stories culture tells to announce, investigate, and explain itself). It resonated with questions about the nature of the poetic career for women, with ideas about production, dissemination, reception, with materialist scrutiny of the ideologies and institutions that organize the poetic career and the reception of individuals.

So first off, it's not so much the influence of H.D. on me but (don't get me wrong) my influence on H.D. (In a few years, she reciprocated.) This peculiar position is true of several other feminist critics who wrote on H.D. very early—around 1979 and for a few years after: Susan Stanford Friedman, Adalaide Morris, Lucy Freibert, myself (and with different agendas, Susan Gubar), and other feminist poets or poet critics—Alicia Ostriker, Beverly Dahlen, Adrienne Rich, and then Barbara Guest. These people in some ways worked on, worked out, and worked out of H.D. to accomplish the very, very first years of her rediscovery. We were inventing H.D. We influenced her work—how it was read, what parts of it were read, why it was interesting. We made it matter for this generation. It is astonishing to make this claim, yet it is simply true. Not arrogant; it is a statement of fact, the fact of our reading of H.D. and our engagements.

But it is odd: wasn't she there before? weren't there a few books in print? hadn't I been blind to her too, and once compliant to reject her? Later there would be criticisms and modifications of our critical work, extensions and reassessments of our work, maybe even the (un?)motivated disparagements, but our work putting H.D. forward as a twentieth-century poet of grandeur is there in its commitment and its subtlety— quite the opposite of crudeness. Yet as I've already suggested, it's not as if no one had noticed before—both Robert Duncan and Lawrence Dembo had, Vincent Quinn and Joseph Riddel had, Norman Holmes Pearson had, Denise Levertov had. And they knew the H.D. of majority. But this critical situation is the story of a conjuncture. Here were the components: feminism in general; plus an incontestably "major" woman writer (so none of us had to fight the paradigms of major/minor right away and change other imbedded mechanisms of critical recognition); with an audience ready to understand that (patriarchal) structures of recognition had blocked and filtered our vision of her career, as they had intervened and been a condition of her employment and her own self-scrutiny for many, many decades. She was a big dolphin ridden by desirous feminists who needed to find her and to be buoyed in her ocean of texts. And she was a haunting presence: we had conjured her; she had conjured us. Dux femina facti.

Levitation (leviathan)
I am smelling my own bread
rising
stepping out over air eyes, walking
over the water and into swimming—
in the present
participle.

Reading the then-unpublished *HERmione*, reading *The Gift* at the Beinecke Library where H.D.'s manuscripts were housed (in fact, eventually helping to provoke their publication as books), like a train I was riding, speeding the tracks: clacked this is good, this is good, this is really really good. Her whole work was answering questions we had just begun to formulate; we were hot with it, and in that heat H.D. emerged, like a secret, encrypted, and invisible writing that could be read when it got hot-light enough. We had sought the story of modern female cultural position, the portrait of the artist as a struggling and investigative woman. We had sought women's contributions, women's intervention in the Western cultural compact. At every moment that the bucket went down into her vast and capacious oeuvre, it came up full, full, full. That metaphor suggests that we still need the theoretical (that is, ideological) capacity to understand the matter of Mater—the "matriarchal" figure standing at the wellsprings of cultural generation. Was it Irigaray who told us about a real second sex? about the despisal of and desire for the Mother? It was also H.D., with her grand psychoanalysis of culture and society. We found a magisterial work, intense and passionate in the most nuanced turns of language, austere in its knowledge of the past, and fierce in the will to interpret modernity. Reading, teaching *Trilogy*, *Helen in Egypt*, the short poems, some of the novels as I did beginning in the mid-1970s through to now, the 1990s, one can also use the archaeological metaphors that H.D. would, perhaps, have appreciated. We had started with a shard, a scrap, a mark on a piece of stone or papyrus; we had ended by commencing a multigenerational dig at an enormous city-temple complex. We had opened (Queen Tut's) tomb.

such *avis* in dreams
do the strange-handed "draw" or "read" the lines?
ombre'd on rich riven rock

Working on mss. The trace, the feeling, the mark of her on the page. Not hero worship, the question of evidence of being. Of negotiating inside the pressure of detail. Open the boxes. Hatchlings. Open the cardboard hutch of archival acid-free boxes. I am sitting in a library staring at the white underground sculpture court of Isamu Noguchi and on the plaza outside the monuments to Yale men killed in the Great Wars. The floor was carpeted; the tables were large and solid. The chairs were elegant and capacious. A portrait of Gertrude Stein hung on the wall to the ladies' room. It was luxury, the *luxe, calme, volupté* of supported work. Open the trunk. Reading H.D. letters: gender and sexuality emerge everywhere in the deep desire to search for response, to give response: H.D. eroticizes the reader. The erotic radiance and the pleasure of finding, knowing, unveiling, being absorbed, being nourished, being taught, reading—like food—breathless. She was aware of the power and necessity of those archives. Indeed, one of the works of her later years was to arrange them, to organize them, and once again to consider her own career in one of the most brilliant essays she wrote—"H.D. by Delia Alton." She exercised Control (as all poets do). Her voracity and control.

The facts and activities of this rediscovery had a deep influence on my sense of the complexity of female cultural position and the ways one must investigate it historically, situationally, biographically. Susan Friedman and I together at Yale doing H.D. research in 1983 met Susan Howe and argued over feminist criticism; S.H. is incensed at *The Madwoman in the Attic*, especially the portrait of Dickinson; S.H. hated any notion that the female writer is a "victim." She was prescient about damaging aspects of contemporary feminism, the resistance to identifying agency, a certain sentimentality about women. *Madwoman* (I know from another position) was both a melodramatic book and a breakthrough. But I also know that the complexity of the impulses to— and the findings of—feminist criticism could not be contained in any one gesture. Indeed, there are many textures and methods that are possible once one asks gender questions of culture, including a materialist and situated notion of the poetic career: class and other social materials do matter, the particularities of gender and sexuality do matter, historical nuance does matter in production and reception. H.D. and feminism and the rush of interpretations and passionate debates about women in culture—this marked the moment in the early 1980s. What I still see is that it is crucial to maintain feminist reception (and, indeed, to reject particular, limiting, infuriating demands of any theme or style for female production). I brought to H.D., evoked in H.D. a sense of her agency and desire, of the need for poesis; I saw her complex negotiations with ambition, how she went Working on the Work of the Gift. It was, as I said, the career of that struggle.

> Demeter statue
> carrying a pig.
> Nike, very fluid.
> Kore, the thin folds.
>
> Running in a forest of papyrus
>
> how can the rose speak?
> is it "it" or is it "she"?
> so to speak—rewrite the rose.
>
> "Peut on faire des oeuvres
> qui ne soient pas 'd'art'?"   (Picabia)

After *Wells* (1980) I had begun to write "The 'History of Poetry'"—a way of harrying and leveraging the lyric tradition (this work is in *Tabula Rosa*, 1987). It became my position of angry/hungry—as per the text called "Crowbar," which was written as a fierce critique of "trobar" treatments of the female figure. After "For the Etruscans" (1979–80), my next essay (1979) was the one on H.D.—"family, sexes, psyche." And I composed the book *H.D.: The Career of That Struggle* about four kinds of authority of the woman writer. In 1986, after a significant serial poem called "Writing" (1984–85), itself linked to an early version of the essay on Williams and others called "*Pater*-daughter," I began writing *Drafts*, a long poem in autonomous "cantolike" linked sections. As we passed into 1998, it was in its twelfth year.

In the historical narrative of beginning *Drafts*, H.D. was one of the central figures of the opening along with several others: Beverly Dahlen's *A Reading* (and my 1985 essay on Dahlen in *The Pink Guitar*), my daughter Kore (arrived in 1984), and George Oppen, who had died in 1984. I finished copyediting *H.D.: The Career of That Struggle* in Nijmegen in the autumn of 1985 for publication in the next year, the cen-

tennial of H.D.'s birth, and I also began the essay "Language Acquisition" (written in 1985, as was "Otherhow"). In it there are little
chapters and textual multiplicity: theory, poem, analysis, baby babble,
documentary, even picture—the hieroglyphic of Isis. It is a work clearly
written under the simultaneous regimes of Kore's learning to talk, Kris-
tevean analysis of the pulse of poetic language, and H.D.'s essays and
her deep investigative sounds and soundings. One agenda was to examine H.D.'s midrashlike quality of continuous chains of interpretation
where there are no closure and no authoritative statement but where
the production and productivity of meanings are continuous. The interest in child language acquisition is also indebted to Mary Kelley's
"Post-Partum Document"—a conceptual work that had a lot of impact
on me and that also influenced the pre-*Drafts* serial poem "Writing."

> "pinkie"
> "tow"
> "cookie"
> are Dutch words in English we know

In 1985 and 1986 I began to imagine how to exit and encircle all that
limited me, and I saw that it was a gigantic project/prospect. The invention of a stance capacious, ready, open-throated, alert and altered,
serious. A voiced text that could play with, and beyond, all the features
of poetry that I had resisted. Sonority. Metaphor. Even beauty. I didn't
feel exiled from language but from the conventions of poetic discourses,
from the construction of what is called "poetry" by our culture, and
from my gender position within those discourses. In April 1986 I was
(finally) developing a changed relationship to the blank page.

> so that—what.
>   so that the point of this argument
> is
> To stop writing
>   "poetry" (and)
>   draft, draw
>
> Take the razor point fine tip
> & draw it all over the page
> to draw it
> makes drafts

In summer 1986, at the conference in Orono, Maine, for H.D.'s centennial, I uncharacteristically stopped listening to my fellow critics and wrote in a journal:

> put yr hand down
> on the paper & draw your
> draft for the most thirsty selfs.

The moment had begun. It continued in San Diego, after the conference on George Oppen and some study in the Archive for New Poetry where Oppen's papers were housed, for I was also working on *The Selected Letters of George Oppen*, which would be published in 1990. I sketched "Draft 1: It" (without knowing quite what it was yet) by following the instruction to

> write
>   writings
>   that.
>
> all the materials ARE   there here
> the ocean changed to lines

I worked into the page that had called me. I knew that I had begun a long poem in "cantos" but was sure of no more than that. The first two poems of *Drafts* emerged together and were separated during the summer of 1986. I knew, from all my struggles before this, that one central impulse of "Drafts" was the critique of the lyric. What I felt in July 1986 is how the critique and the temptation occur simultaneously, for I wrote "Afterimage" at the same time as writing "Draft 1: It." But "Afterimage" was (so far as I can reckon) my last simply lyric poem. Instead I was seeking the authority of the multiple. Willing to follow the track of making. And to think about the implications of the poesis as furthering. To read the writing. But a cultural project—making something of extent. Casting myself into that sea. No matter what one touches, the ongoingness of language demands more writing.[1]

No plan, no design, no schemata. Just a few procedures: placing works on the big stage of the page, making each be itself intact and autonomous but connected to themselves as they emerged. No continuous narrative. No myth as explanation. Here *Drafts* are very different from

H.D.'s long poems and quite related to Objectivist ethos and poetics. The works are influenced by Objectivist argument and propositions about reality. That the image is encountered, not found, as Oppen proposed. That *the* and *a* (said Zukofsky testily) are words worth investigating, as suggestive and as staggering in their implications as any epic or myth.

Draft. (1) current of air in an enclosed area (2) pull or traction of a load/that which is pulled/traction power (3) depth of a vessel's keel (4) heavy demand upon resources (5) document or instrument for transferring money (6) gulp, swallow, inhalation/a measured portion or dose (7) drawing of liquid from a keg (8) selection of personnel/conscription (9) drawing in of a net (10) preliminary outline or plan of a document or picture (11) a narrow line chiseled on a stone to guide the mason in leveling the surface (12) a slight taper given a die to ease the removal of a casting (13) an allowance made for loss in weight of merchandise

> full & empty
> the more marks
> the larger emptiness
>
> generative

One first idea about "Drafts" was that they pretend to be informal, "unfinished"—that is, self-questioning and processual, a rhetorical texture one might describe as a flow of interruption across a surface. Another idea was that they pretend to be real "drafts"—that is, certain lines, images, or materials can be (as if) provisionally placed at a number of different positions. Hence certain lines or phrases repeat across poems. This tactic is central and continues. Another part of the idea of "drafts" is the interest in marks or marking. I had a number of textual markers in early drafts. The instruction "CUT" that begins "Draft 3: Of" created predictable difficulties when the book *Drafts (3–14)* (1991) went to the printer.

At a certain point in this exploration of the rhetorics of "drafting" I realized that I was constructing a texture of déjà vu, a set of works that mimicked the productions and losses of memory. And that the works were my own response both to the memorializing function of poetry and to my own bad memory. "An exploration of the chaos of memory (obscured, alienated, or reduced to a range of natural references) cannot be done in the 'clarity' of a linear narrative" (Glissant 1989: 107). Bad memory. Bad dog. Bad bad memory. The poem replicates (but neither reconstructs nor represents) a space of memory.

I am no one to say. When I began *Drafts*, I thought of it as "an endless poem of no known category all about everything." My way of interpreting the no known category (which for Pound and Williams was the encyclopedic poem; the citation is Pound's) was a kind of playful heterogeneity. For instance, the poem sounds off against the "meditative derivative" while its little feet are stuck in precisely that tar. But the midrashic is extremely important as a genre: the continuous practice of examination, gloss, and reinterpretation. This draws upon H.D., upon Freud, and upon a tradition of Hebrew textuality all at once. Once the line or word or turn of phrase is stated, once the material exists as the stuff of language (and means what it claims to mean), any particle can open out to more. The generative principles of *Drafts* are repetition, recontextualization, reconsideration, returns that are not returns to the same. The "same/different" of *Helen in Egypt* is different from before, never quite the same as before. Sometimes H.D. knows this, but to claim that nothing was ever lost or that it would recur—to me that was mysticism, and I parted intellectual company with H.D. over the issue of "origins" and recovery.

The texture of commentary and gloss led me to composition by fold. At a certain point (around "Draft 19: Working Conditions" in 1993), the sheer construction of the linear repeats seemed inadequate, and I decided to make the poems fold over each other. In some sense, even a minor sense, or an allusive sense, a donor draft (such as "Draft 4: In") generates some relationship with its counterpart (in this case, "Draft 23: Findings"). The periodicity is 19. "The long poem, then, is a rereading of writings, a rewriting of readings" (Kamboureli 1991: 99).

H.D. looked at her own files. H.D. reworked elements of her life and her mythoi over and over. Studied the traces. If a photo was blurred, there was a reason. If a line was made, it could be understood and rein-

terpreted. A Freudian poetics: that there is no wasted mark, no unmo-
tivated gesture. Reading the reading was writing the writing. Not just
talking the talk but walking the walk. Not just reading the written but
writing the wrote. Not the rote. That's how it first felt, when one could
reject it—resist H.D. But it was not rote but road. Ever enough rope.
In her method was pleasure and also obsession, "obsessing," as we say,
hissing sounds like an airlock. The film was run, rerun, spliced, reshot.
Palimpsested, so that scrim-films of one picture are superimposed, un-
derposed. Taking what you are given (she was given a lot, but a lot was
taken also) and mulling it.

> Shimmer spectra of intercut;
> waves rays way
> the page is never blank

I must say her ear, her ear, her magnificent Ear, the subtle netting of
phonemes across her poems. The way a sound map of H.D. can be revelatory of subplots of sound, of pool words into which important phonemes gather and are held, of the tone-leading so phonemes and sound-
clusters track each other and are caught up, split, and engage again. The
sound—it was not "beauty" as a limit term but the language leading
itself to more language. Thus the issue of "beauty" could be encircled
and contained by the fullness of, the tremendousness of sound. This I
feel I follow and I want to follow.

There is, inter alia, in all the *Drafts* a good deal of "debris" and "fragment," and this is often provoked by a sense of twentieth-century history, including the Holocaust. Thus the poem has come to recognize in
itself a Jewishness of theme and of textuality. It is focused by Walter
Benjamin's paradoxical and painful figures but not necessarily influenced by them beforehand: the angel of history, the sense of a displacement in the storm blowing this figure backward into the future, while
the angel is still staring stunned at history and its unfixable debris. Failing memory, strange memory, lost memory, construction of memory.
Being haunted. At a further remove than many, still I am haunted by
the loss of people, the moral nightmare, the randomness, haunted by
the ability at which this century has excelled, several times, to extermi-
nate a group, by the loss of cultures of Jewishness, the loss of languages,

the loss of those who might have been. I am haunted by a sense of the ones who are not. Their shadow or the stain of them. A sense of ghosts, but ghosts who do not even declare themselves. I do recognize that this situation is something H.D. also entered. Abraham and Torok's concept of the "transgenerational phantom" may explain why someone like myself, two generations removed from direct and intimate ties to European Jewry, speaks a poetry haunted by the ghosts of ghosts.[2]

Drafts have a midrashic element: that means the generative processes of continuous rereading and marking. The poetry works by the endless elaboration of a practice of gloss, including self-gloss. The impulse to analysis and doubled, redoubled commentary. There is a good deal of "debris" and "fragment"—let's call it a creolized Jewishness. Writing (by study and certainly by authority claims) commentary adequate to the text that has been set, on which there are many prior comments. The concentration on (the concatenation of) the small—the detail of the letter. Yod. Any tiny mark. Any thing can open out to meaning and be connected to other things. The way a toddler will pick up a speck of dust. Every detail could in a particular light have meaning. Error has meaning. Slip has meaning. Anything could be glossed. Gloss generates more text. Text and gloss exist in a permanent, continuous, generative relationship. Gloss on text is more text to be glossed. One makes gloss to comment on loss, against the loss of loss, but there is always more loss. "Even the loss is lost." Preserving has its antonym. Every dot cannot open for every one, but after many years on task I could finally say: I found the opening and I wrote into it.

> Think of the tit
> The tit and the title
> and the entitlement
> think of the jot and tittle.

Drafts construct the space of memory; they also face the breast of the mother. They bring back the cut-off breast of the mother: a work of fake restoration, of impossible milk. The hidden maternal presence: the gift that is also poison ("gift" is poison in German, she says in *The Gift*) has analogues with H.D. My mother died of cancer of the breast in May 1990; ten days after, Mary Oppen died. My mother's predeath words of bemusement and anger occur in "Draft X: Letters." (And my father had already died in December 1986. His death is spoken of in "Draft 5: Gap" and "Draft 6: Midrush." Elegy, and not simply for two people, is a part of what the poem concerns.)

The poem is a letter, a stranger (a low flame on the grate in Coleridge's conversation poems). It is a folding over in time, of time at the mercy of its thinking. And the thoughtlessness of time.

> Memory is dissolved.
> "Plenty of debris.
> Plenty of smudges."
> > (W.C.W. to L.Z., in Williams 1957: 94)

"Writing is a [daily] task, and the temporal demands of the work are a part of its argument with existence. . . . The querying of language by language in time is the method" (Watten 1984: 103).

The poetics of Mass Observation (in which H.D.—astonishingly— briefly participated, writing about the coronation of George VI in 1937) became important to me as a democratic ethics of invested examination. What is it like to live through the texture of our days? What is it, like? There is always a documentary aspect to my poetics. Trying to live in historical time and give some testimony, to bear some (direct or indirect) witness. This means bringing the unspeakable into words or at the edge of words. Leaving it be mystery but now in words.

Even the tiniest mark, even down to the tiniest mark; it is "through-composed." And

> documentation of the art
> > object that is the art
> > object
> > is Duchamp

> The Large Glass cracks
> ill-packed from Brooklyn
> and it is all absorbed into itself
> trucked
> a turn, a term of its placefulness

The hero of the poem—without a hero. "Not hero, not polis, not story, but it" ("Draft 15: Little"). "It" speaks.

I cited Virgil. Cano. Arms and the man cano. "CANO, can o yes no / conno- / tations of impurities fill the fold" ("Draft I: It"). Motive for me from the very beginning. All the Can's and Can no's, and the way I used to Freudian-slip the Cantos (into Canots) while writing my dissertation. Arma virumque cano. H.D. meditates this passage in her work *Paint It Today* (1920). I felt kinship, kindship: another link among the many that set me going.

> that bilingual
> hip-hop talk
> a creature/écriture's
> langdscapeof anguage

I wanted exodus, the ex-odic, watchfulness into departures. H.D. wanted to return to plenitude, postulated as origins. I quarrel with the nonpresence. "El" and the loss of L means oss, a bony site. She builds a space in which presence can reemerge. I want (and this from J.-F. Lyotard, painfully) "the forgotten never part of memory": "a demand for a form of thinking and writing that do not 'forget the fact' of the forgotten and the unrepresentable" (*Heidegger and "the Jews,"* introduction).

I was convinced I had entered a letter and was traveling thru its uncontrollable tunnels.

This is the gift.

December 30, 1997–January 1, 1998

NOTES

Haibun is a Japanese form of journey writing: prose passages interspersed with haiku. In homage to Cid Corman's translation of Basho's *Back Roads to Far Towns*, I composed "Draft 13: Haibun" in 1991. But the mix of haikulike objects also seemed appropriate to this account. I also follow the "hermetic" encoding in H.D. that involves having an H and a D in titles that consider her. People interested in this account as a memoir of my practice might want to supplement it with "Reader, I

Married Me: A Polygamous Memoir" (DuPlessis 1993); "Otherhow" and "For the Etruscans" (in DuPlessis 1990a); "On Drafts: A Memorandum of Understanding" (DuPlessis 1996c); and "Manifests" (DuPlessis 1996b). See also my essays on H.D.: "Family, Sexes, Psyche: An Essay on H.D. and the Muse of the Woman Writer" and "Language Acquisition" (in DuPlessis 1990a). My books of poetry are available via Small Press Distribution, 1341 Seventh Street, Berkeley, CA 94710-1403.

　1. If I were to track the origins of *Drafts* justly, I would want to note that I was reading not only the modernists but certain of my contemporaries: the *HOW(ever)* cohort (Bev Dahlen, Kathleen Fraser, Frances Jaffer) and some others at various times in the early to mideighties and forward: Rae Armantrout, Michael Palmer, Robert Duncan, Ron Silliman, Susan Howe (about whom I also wrote), Bob Perelman, Robin Blaser, Charles Berenstein, Lyn Hejinian, Clayton Eshleman.

　2. See Abraham and Torok (1994), especially "Mourning *or* Melancholia: Introjection *versus* Incorporation" and "Notes on the Phantom: A Complement to Freud's Metapsychology."

Renewing the Open Engagement:
H.D. and Rachel Blau DuPlessis

BURTON HATLEN

H.D.'s influence on Rachel Blau DuPlessis? That is, I take it, the question I am here asked to address. But what about the possibility—one that she herself, in the accompanying essay, only half ironically raises—of Rachel Blau DuPlessis's influence on H.D.? "Influence," for starters, seems an inadequate word to describe what is going on here. Perhaps we might talk about an ongoing dialogue between H.D. and DuPlessis—which now becomes, as I intervene in the exchange, a trialogue. But I prefer—and have incorporated into the title of this essay—a phrase that DuPlessis uses to describe her relationship not to H.D. but to Louis Zukofsky and George Oppen. In a poem punningly titled "Midrush," number 6 in her ongoing series *Drafts*, DuPlessis declares, "Wraiths of poets, Oppen and oddly / Zukofsky / renew their open engagement with me" (1991: 18).[1] So, too, we may speak of DuPlessis's open engagement with H.D.—and because the engagement is "open" it is also reversible, for indeed DuPlessis has, as I will argue later, significantly influenced H.D.

But to understand the complexity of DuPlessis's engagement with H.D. and vice versa, it is necessary first to recognize the remarkable breadth and quality of this still relatively young writer's achievement to date. This book examines the impact of H.D. on contemporary poets, and DuPlessis certainly deserves to take her place among the other poets here included, for she has published four volumes of poetry, and these books have won the esteem of many notable poets and critics, including Susan Howe, Alicia Ostriker, Robin Blaser, Barbara Guest, Kathleen Fraser, and Peter Quartermain. She has also published what she herself calls "criticism" but what I will here refer to as "scholarly" writings to underscore the difference between these writings and what DuPlessis calls "essays." DuPlessis's scholarly writings include two books and several articles, all composed in standard academic format. But third, DuPlessis has also reinvented the essay, a form in which she feels especially at home because it invites "feelingthinking" and is always "oppositional," "forever skeptical, forever alert, forever yearning."[2]

There are some common qualities that cut across DuPlessis's writings in these three modes. In particular, she writes always as a feminist: "If I had not become a feminist," she says in her autobiographical essay, "Reader, I Married Me," "I would not have been able to write much or to think anything especially interesting in any original way. I would not have been able to create the works that came through me and go under my name" (DuPlessis 1993: 97–98). So, too, DuPlessis's engagement with H.D. cuts across her work in all three modes. Nevertheless, her decision to work simultaneously in three quite different literary modes creates some vertiginous gaps and fissures within her work, including in particular a tension between her career within the burgeoning academic discipline of women's studies and her in many ways quite distinct career as a poet.[3] I explore this tension in the first part of the essay. In the second part I address more specifically some ways in which DuPlessis's poetry enacts her open engagement with H.D.—an engagement that, as we will see, encompasses resistance as well as influence. In the final section I examine an extended sample of DuPlessis's verse in an attempt to define the character and to demonstrate the quality of her work as a poet.

I

Had she never published any poetry, and had she never ventured into the intermediate genre that she calls the essay, DuPlessis would be a major figure in academic literary studies, and especially in the world of H.D. scholarship. Her "Romantic Thralldom in H.D.," first published in 1979, four years after Susan Stanford Friedman's "Who Buried H.D.?" and one year after Susan Gubar's "The Echoing Spell of H.D.'s *Trilogy*," stands with these among the five or six essential articles on this poet; and DuPlessis's 1986 book, *H.D.: The Career of That Struggle*, remains perhaps the most useful short critical introduction to H.D.'s work. Indeed, contemporary H.D. scholarship in large measure emerged out of the vibrant collaboration between DuPlessis and Friedman that began in the late 1970s and extended through the summatory anthology *Signets: Reading H.D.*, published in 1990. But DuPlessis has not limited her scholarly publications to H.D. Her *Writing beyond the Ending: Narrative Strategies of Twentieth-Century Women Writers* includes some discussion of H.D., but it also explores a broad range of other women writers, recovering a lost classic in Olive Schreiner's *The Story of an African Farm* and developing important new perspectives on Virginia Woolf. This book, along with a series of articles on women writers published in journals during the late 1970s and early 1980s, established DuPlessis as an influential figure in the then-still-emerging discipline of women's studies, and for several years in the early 1980s she directed the women's studies program at Temple University. DuPlessis's scholarly work has won for her the kind of reputation within an international academic community that university promotion and tenure committees claim to be looking for, and she has moved up through the academic ranks to a position as full professor at a major university. That this scholarly career has been largely independent of her work as a poet is suggested by the fact that *Writing beyond the Ending*, her "big" scholarly book, the "tenure and promotion" book, devotes at least as much attention to prose fiction—a genre into which DuPlessis has, as far as I know, never ventured as a writer—as it does to poetry.[4] *Writing beyond the Ending* is in its way a passionate book: as a woman scholar, DuPlessis is deeply invested in the ways women give shape to their experiences in literature, whether prose or poetry. But as a practicing poet, she brings a kind of personal investment to writing about poetry that she does not bring to writing about fiction. The voice of *Writing beyond the Ending* is the voice not of a poet talking about her craft but of a scholar addressing issues of general concern, especially to women. And the large numbers of people who come out whenever DuPlessis gives a paper at an academic conference are attracted, I am quite sure, largely by the fame that this book, along with her book on H.D. and certain of her essays, has won for her as a women's studies scholar. Indeed, many in these audiences may be unaware that she has also had a second career as a poet.

I don't want to exaggerate the differences between DuPlessis's career as a scholar and her career as a poet. Her poetic interests have clearly affected her scholarly work. For example, she wrote her Ph.D. dissertation on two male poets, Ezra Pound and William Carlos Williams, whose modes of composition have, as we shall see, continued to influence her practice as a poet. And while most of her scholarly writing focuses on women poets and novelists, DuPlessis has also published several substantial articles on the Objectivist poet George Oppen, and she has also edited his *Selected Letters*. Furthermore, DuPlessis's major poetic project has been a long poem with no terminal point in sight titled *Drafts*. This project is anticipated both by DuPlessis's unpublished dissertation, which is titled "The Endless Poem," and by *Writing beyond the Ending*: the similarity between these titles suggests that both as scholar and as poet DuPlessis has been throughout her career concerned with how to keep going, beyond those moments that announce themselves as THE END.

DuPlessis's essays, as collected in *The Pink Guitar: Writing as Feminist Practice*, also allow her two literary personae to enter into dialogue. Many of these essays are written in a collage form modeled in part on some of H.D.'s prose works and on Robert Duncan's *H.D. Book*. This form allows DuPlessis to address the broad theoretical issue that she has engaged in her scholarly writing in a mode of discourse that remains, like her poetry, open, provisional, and disjunctive. In particular, she has used this form to explore the relationships between the issues of gender politics that have preoccupied her in her scholarly writing and the issues of "open" versus "closed" poetic form that she has been working through in her poetry.

DuPlessis has also, starting in the mid-1980s, published some very influential pieces of writing, both in the collage-essay form and in more conventional academic discourse, about such experimental women poets as Marianne Moore (in this case, DuPlessis is trying to rescue Moore from critics who have made her seem to be the one "safe" woman modernist), Mina Loy, Lorine Niedecker, Beverly Dahlen, and Susan Howe. In these essays, and in her relationship with the influential journal *HOW(ever)*, DuPlessis has been working to define a tradition of experimental writing by women: a tradition within which, clearly, she wants to place herself.

Finally and most significantly, DuPlessis has always written as a feminist, both in her poetry and in her scholarly work. Hers has always been a deeply engaged scholarship, dedicated not simply to describing the world but also to changing it by creating a space where the voices of silenced women can, however belatedly, become audible.[5] And as a poet she has defined herself as a woman, gendered both by circumstances and by conscious choice, and she has set herself the task of "rewriting stances central to the positioning of women in the anthologized history of poetry as we know it" (DuPlessis 1993: 107).

Despite these linkages between her scholarly work and her poetry, however, it seems to me significant that while her scholarly work has focused on a tradition of writing by women, her poetry has drawn on a broad range of sources and models that include many male writers—indeed, before the current generation at least, more men than women. Since the mid-1980s, DuPlessis has devoted all—or so it would appear—of her poetic energies to a numbered and dated series of poems called *Drafts*, which reached number 30 in June and July 1996. In talking about *Drafts* at the 1996 Twentieth Century Literature Conference in Louisville, DuPlessis said that her principal models were Pound and Rilke. Pound, as a model for a Jewish feminist poet? Surely we may be excused for feeling a certain cognitive dissonance at this moment. Pound the fascist, the apologist for Hitler. The same Pound whose insistence that all the women in his life play the role of icon to himself as poetic maker has been brilliantly dissected by DuPlessis herself in five pages of the collage-essay "*Pater*-daughter" (1990a: 42–47). But, yes, Pound is, I believe, the decisive model, for DuPlessis has located her own poetic project within a tradition of the polyvocal, open-ended, nonlinear long poem that originates in Pound's cantos and passes down through Zukofsky's "A" and Williams's *Paterson* to, in the generation just before DuPlessis's own, Olson's *Maximus Poems* and Duncan's *Passages* sequence.[6] DuPlessis's title explicitly evokes Pound, whose *Draft of XXX Cantos* became the foundation of all his later cantos and remained still in draft, unrevised, when the poet died. DuPlessis not only bows to Pound by calling her poems "drafts," but she also underscores the link by giving her thirtieth draft not an Arabic numeral like her other drafts but a Roman XXX, as in the title of Pound's first installment. DuPlessis's title implicitly recognizes that Pound's *Cantos* is of interest to modern poets precisely because it remains, despite Pound's intentions, "unfinished" and thus offers a model of the provisional, open-ended text.

Rilke seems, at first, a less tainted model. But would Rilke, had he lived longer, have found some way of accommodating himself to Hitler, as did Heidegger? I sometimes think so. And Rilke's behavior toward

women artists seems only marginally preferable to Pound's. Nevertheless, the *Duino Elegies* also offer a formal model that DuPlessis has
adopted for her own ends. We know that Rilke saw himself as engaged
in a kind of spiritual preparation for the *Duino Elegies*, which then came
to him in sustained bursts of inspiration, and the dates on DuPlessis's
drafts suggest that she has been cultivating a similar mode of composition. The individual drafts are about the length of one of Rilke's elegies
or of Pound's earlier cantos: from three to twenty pages, with the aver-
age around five pages. And like them, the drafts constellate themselves
into an ongoing series. Rilke's series is finite. Pound planned his to be
finite too, but it devolved into an open-ended series.

The next logical step is represented by Robert Duncan's "Passages"
series—probably also, as Lynn Keller (1997) has argued at length, a
model for DuPlessis—and by *Drafts* itself: the poetic sequence that is
planned from the start as open-ended, unfinished and unfinishable.

In addition to the influence of such classic modernists as Pound and
Rilke,[7] DuPlessis has also acknowledged a poetic debt to the Objectivists: I have already quoted her lines about her "open engagement" with
two of these poets, George Oppen and Louis Zukofsky. As a young student in the mid-1960s, DuPlessis began to correspond with Oppen and
eventually developed a close personal relationship with George and his
wife, Mary, and this relationship has profoundly shaped DuPlessis's career as a poet. Oppen's Jewish heritage, his political radicalism, his scru-
pulous moral integrity, his determination to confront the hard surfaces
of the urban scene, his commitment to a rigorously antirhetorical poetry—all these qualities drew DuPlessis to him.[8] As a poet DuPlessis
shares with Oppen a sense of the inescapable thereness of a physical
world knowable through the senses. "The self is no mystery," says Oppen, "the mystery is / That there is something for us to stand on" (1975:
143). So, too, DuPlessis finds herself

> Engulfed, each night,
> with tsunami from the vibrant void
> of sky and space,
> from the implacable emptiness, or untillable fatedness
> of all spires, cycles, works, words, worlds, and wires:
>
> Thus.
> To be so. In is.   (1997: 53)

To find oneself, prior to all choice, inescapably *in* the world, "in is"—this is the condition out of which DuPlessis speaks in all her poetry, and in this respect she stands solidly within an Objectivist lineage. Oppen, a reader of Heidegger, seeks to open his poetry to Being. Zukofsky, a student of Wittgenstein, is more interested in how the play of language creates spaces that we can inhabit for a moment but that always turn out to be transitory, contingent, so that the "is" always remains somewhere beyond. Like Zukofsky, DuPlessis relishes the play of language. Both love puns: Zukofsky once wrote a poem called "Hi Kuh" about a meeting with a cow, and at one point in *Drafts* DuPlessis offers us a gallery of "Dreamatis personae" that turn out to be, simply, words: for example, "Words ending in -ette. // Kitchenette. Dinette. / Luncheonette. Laundromat. Hopper" (1997: 75). The "-ette" words, with their reduction of women's domestic labor to the cute and trivial, elide into the "-mat" word, with its more mechanical overtones. "Hopper" is, of course, the painter, who turned the desolation of luncheonettes into an elegiac poetry. But a "hopper" is also what, not so long ago, you put your clothes in to take them to the laundromat, so we have another pun here. And maybe the poem is another kind of hopper, full of words. But aside from such potential logopoetic meanings, DuPlessis clearly just likes the sounds those words make when lined up like that—and Zukofsky would have liked them too. In particular, DuPlessis shares both with Oppen and Zukofsky (who wrote "A Poem Beginning 'The'" and then followed it with a vast epic titled simply "A") a love of the (as we can read on the same page as the "Hopper" passage)

> Little words,
>   worming into incipience.
> "The a."
>   Then, half-contrary,
> "a the."   (1997: 75)

With her Objectivist mentors, DuPlessis is convinced that the poet is simply someone who knows how to hear what these little words are saying.

DuPlessis's long-standing "open engagement" with Zukofsky also points us toward another major influence on her poetry, the work of the Language poets, all of whom have been touched in one way or another by his long shadow. As far as I know DuPlessis never published in

$L=A=N=G=U=A=G=E$, the journal that proclaimed itself in the mid-1970s as the voice of the newest avant-garde, but her writing even at that time displayed some affinities with the work of the poets grouped around that journal. Of course, all poetry is made of words and is in that sense "Language poetry." But as a group the Language poets went beyond their predecessors in deliberately making their language as opaque as possible to foreground the materiality of language and to short-circuit the reader's impulse to look "through" the words at a "real" world presumed to lie "out there." DuPlessis's poetry never seeks opacity as an end in itself, and it never resists meaning to the degree that some Language poetry does. But like the Language poets, Du-Plessis wants us to remember that in a poem we're always dealing with *words*:

> Words from before, words
> from after,
> they
> specified into my blank voice
> the. They said this this,
> this that, and glut in the wonder
> of all such singularity became the work.   (1991: 33)

Many of the drafts also center on some sort of unifying linguistic principle. Drafts 3 and 4, for example, revolve around the prepositions "of" and "in," respectively. Draft 8 reflects on the article "the." Draft 10 consists of brief epigrammatic spins on each letter of the alphabet. And draft 14 explores a range of conjunctions.[9] In "f-Words," DuPlessis says that the essay is defined by an "attentiveness of materiality, to the material world, including the matter of language" (1996a: 24). So too, her poetry returns obsessively to the "matter of language":

> Everything
> but weed slack's
> loose with melted
> writing.
> Like one wrote IMPISM right on that rude wall.

> Words come just like that, vision.   (DuPlessis 1991: 1)

Of course, an emphasis on the materiality of language is not limited to male writers. Ron Silliman's *In the American Tree*, the watershed 1986 anthology of Language poetry, includes selections from the poetry of Lyn Hejinian, Bernadette Mayer, Hannah Weiner, Carla Harryman, Tina Darragh, Susan Howe, and several other women poets; and in his introduction Silliman lists several additional women poets—including Beverly Dahlen and Kathleen Fraser along with DuPlessis herself— whom in different circumstances he might have included in the collection. This list is long enough to suggest that there is a coherent subgroup of women writers within the Language movement. Nevertheless, this movement was/is clearly male dominated. There are more than twice as many men as there are women in Silliman's anthology, and among the contributors to *The L=A=N=G=U=A=G=E Book* (Andrews and Bernstein 1984), a substantial selection of material from the influential journal of that name, men outnumber women by more than four to one. In linking herself to the Language movement, then, DuPlessis has once again subordinated issues of gender to issues of poetics.

II

But most of the poets that I have mentioned thus far, as defining the poetic tradition(s) in which DuPlessis wants to place herself, are men. Can we not also place her within a lineage of women writers? On this score H.D. plays a crucial role in DuPlessis's work. In "Reader, I Married Me," DuPlessis says—in a sentence she herself quotes in the essay included in this volume—that in 1975, at the moment when her sense of herself as a feminist was coming to its full flowering, "I needed a woman, a poet, and a modernist, and I needed her badly" (1993: 103). DuPlessis needed, indeed, a Major Woman Poet as a role model, simply because she herself was a woman, and she was (or would soon become, when the label became available) a self-identified postmodernist (so she needed a modernist as foil), and she was determined (she may deny it, but she shouldn't, for large achievements demand large ambitions) to be a Major Poet. H.D. was a poet who could plausibly be—was by the early 1980s, after DuPlessis herself, Friedman, and their compatriots had finished revising the canon—ranked with Pound and Williams, the male modernists whose formal inventions DuPlessis admired.[10] But while DuPlessis enthusiastically dedicated herself to the canonization of H.D., even as a scholar she has had some doubts about the viability of H.D. as a model for younger writers, and as a poet she has been at most a distinctly ambivalent reader of H.D.'s work. What role does H.D. play as an influence on/source of/model for DuPlessis's work as a poet? There is no simple answer to this question, for DuPlessis simultaneously (1) identifies with H.D. as a major woman writer who brought all dimensions of a woman's experience to her poetry; (2) distances herself from—although not without considerable admiration for H.D.'s struggle to confront and overcome this emotional trap—the "romantic thralldom" that DuPlessis sees as central to H.D.'s life and writing; (3) disassociates herself from H.D.'s poetics, which she (often, at least) sees as essentially lyric, symbolist, and transcendental, as opposed to her own postlyric, objectivist, and materialist poetics; and (4) at certain other moments engages in a deliberate "misreading" (in the Bloomian sense—a "creative" misreading, a misreading that opens up new dimensions of the text so read) of H.D.'s writings, or at least some of them, to claim her as a direct ancestor for an open, processual poetics. In this section of my essay, I address in turn each of these dimensions of DuPlessis's complex and ambiguous response to H.D.

First, then, H.D. as a model of the woman writer. We can understand why DuPlessis needed a model of a major woman poet, but why H.D.? For at least a decade prior to 1975, DuPlessis had been reading Virginia Woolf and Doris Lessing, crucial makers of the consciousness of the 1960s generation, but they were British and prose writers, while DuPlessis was an American and wanted to write poetry. Why not Marianne Moore? Here was a canonical poet, admired by Pound and Williams and Eliot, who was indisputably both a modernist (on this score the Millays and the Teasdales were already excluded) and an American. I am speculating here, but to DuPlessis in 1975 it may have seemed that Moore had made too many compromises with propriety in her efforts to win a place in the canon. The tricornered hat, the poems about Roy Campanella, the lists of names for new Ford cars—these were hard to get past. Where, in particular, was Moore's sexuality? For the former Rachel Blau, child of the 1960s, determined to enter into possession of her own sexuality, this was undoubtedly a crucial question.[11] In Moore, the sexuality was there somewhere, but it was hard to pin down, whereas H.D.'s language is saturated with her polymorphous sexuality. As DuPlessis says in the essay printed in this book, for the reader of H.D. "gender and sexuality emerge everywhere in the deep desire to search for response, to give response: H.D. eroticizes the reader." For the "poetess," of course, "feelings" always came first, and many of H.D.'s early readers apparently read her as another "poetess." [12] But the feelings at work in H.D.'s writing are, as the poet herself intermittently recognized, dangerously subversive, calling into question all established gender hierarchies. H.D.'s bisexuality and her potentially scandalous relationship with Bryher positioned her beyond the boundaries of respectable society, and she welcomed this marginality; with no need or desire to win the acclaim of the reading public, she was able to make of her writing an ongoing experiment in the search for illumination. Yet at the same time, H.D. claims for herself and her writing a world-historical role: she could and did see herself as the prophet of a syncretic religious consciousness that might redeem the world from war. By the 1970s, a new generation of feminist was ready to acknowledge and celebrate H.D.'s sexuality, including—often especially—her Lesbianism; to identify with her self-chosen marginality as perhaps the only position that allows a woman writer to preserve her integrity; and to see her apocalyptic sensibility as anticipating the various social and spiritual transformations erupting out of the 1960s. And in the discovery—or indeed, as she herself rightly claims in these pages, the invention—of this "new" H.D., DuPlessis played a major role.

From H.D. DuPlessis gained, I think, a sense that all dimensions of her experience as a thinking/feeling woman could find a place within her poetry. How much of this confidence came from H.D. and how much from Lessing or Woolf is hard to say. But in the fifty pages or so of poems from The "History of Poetry" included in Tabula Rosa, we can see her working her way beyond the lyric mode of Wells and on through the tangles of patriarchal discourse, and in Drafts she speaks to us in the voice of a woman fully alive in the now of the poem as it moves through time. The "History of Poetry" poems are "feminist" in ways that the Drafts usually are not. These poems of the early 1980s give us a world gendered distinctly female:

> Tender pain
> flat milk
> a chest for holding women's things.
> Under the flesh-pink moon
> I keep my hand cupped.   (DuPlessis 1987b: 3)

At times the world evoked in these poems is richly sensuous, pulsing with life:

> Sweet the push push out of the cell
>
> mint watery by waysides
> soft-leafed basil
> tipped by bushy bracts
>
> cusps of the moon.
>
> Under the fingernails
> dirt, flour, yeast
>
> crusts of the sun.   (DuPlessis 1987b: 4–5)

Yet the voice speaking in these poems is, as DuPlessis declares at a key moment, both hungry and angry:

> Milk of the culture's teeming
>   HU
> gushes at my A NGRY weaning.   (DuPlessis 1987b: 25)

And several of these poems angrily or sorrowfully confront the male inclination to grind the "psyche-elf" beneath the boot heel:

> no voice, no lute, no pipe, no lucent fans,
> no more the essential elements' distinction
> delicate within a solemn perfect insect
> able to spin a being from itself.   (DuPlessis 1987b: 38)

Only intermittently are these poems specifically "H.D.ish," but one such moment comes here, in these lines from a poem called "Moth: 'Ode to Psyche,'" as DuPlessis, echoing the famous section 6 of "The Walls Do Not Fall," identifies with a lowly worm—which, however, contains within itself the power to become the psyche-moth and fly up toward the light. Gender issues are less insistent in *Drafts*, but rarely a page goes by in which we are not reminded that the voice(s) here speaking is/are gendered female.[13] Hunger is still an issue, and there is a sense that the production and consumption of food are, in some both wonderful and terrible way, woman's work:

> In eating, I skim the sticky flats called
> "Plenty." It is a strange site.

Have some! can offer
nice engineering
in pretty packages of crackling;
in quaffs of flavored water
a strange, estranged air.

What is enough?
If I eat for the hungry, there are many.
If I buy the coupon'd food,
I crunch sugar and pee salt.

Everything o so "good" and E-Z

to eat for the dead, for the dying,
to keep them in my belly, fetally, or fecally.   (DuPlessis
    1991: 45)

And the speaking subject in these poems is constituted not only by her
hunger but also still, sometimes, by her anger:

I resisted initiations
        into "virile pieties,"
            which were everywhere, nevertheless.

But the rage of the mother
        is an unsolved problem
            in language.   (DuPlessis 1997: 23)

The sensuality and the hunger and the anger, the loyalty to the mother
and the impulse to raise up the dead—all these motifs in DuPlessis's
poetry echo, at least in a loose way, certain strains in the writings
of H.D.

Yet while H.D. offered a model of a major poet writing out of her
full experience as a woman, there is also considerable evidence to suggest that DuPlessis has been an ambivalent and resistant reader of
H.D.'s work. This resistance works on two levels, psychological and poetic. In her scholarly writings on H.D., DuPlessis presents a sharply
critical analysis of a recurrent psychological pattern in the poet's work.
DuPlessis calls this pattern "romantic thralldom," and the label itself
suggests that she sees this pattern as deeply pathological:

Romantic thralldom is an all-encompassing, totally defining love between unequals. The lover has the power of conferring self-worth

and purpose upon the loved one. Such love is possessive, and while those enthralled feel it completes and even transforms them, they are also enslaved. . . . Viewed from a critical, feminist perspective, the sense of completion or transformation that often accompanies thralldom in love has the high price of obliteration and paralysis, for the entranced self is entirely defined by another. I do not need to emphasize that this kind of love is socially learned and that it is central in our culture.

Female thralldom occurs with startling, even dismal frequency throughout H.D.'s published and unpublished works. In particular, H.D. was vulnerable to the power of what she terms the "héros fatal," a man whom she saw as her spiritual similar, an artist, a healer, a psychic. Again and again this figure that she conspired to create betrayed her; again and again she was reduced to fragments from which her identity had once more to be painfully reconstructed. . . . Whatever personal and sexual arrangements she made could not obliterate the culturally reinforced plot of thralldom.   (1979b: 179)

As these sentences make clear, DuPlessis's goal as an H.D. scholar has been not to create another modernist cultural icon to counterbalance those icons that we call T. S. Eliot and Ezra Pound, etc., but rather to learn what she/we can from the example of H.D. And the H.D. that here emerges seems to be not so much a model of the self-defining woman as an object lesson in the "dismal" (this word sets the tone of the whole passage) consequences of a failure to break out of the social roles offered women in a patriarchal culture. As this essay develops, DuPlessis proposes that H.D.'s later writings, especially *Helen in Egypt*, construct an imaginative vision of "reparenting," through which the "wounded woman is saved by taking the form of a child, subsumed under a caring mother or father" (1979b: 200); this reparenting in turn makes possible a conception of the "sufficient family" centered on the "mother and child, flanked by father and brother" (1979b: 202). In imagining an alternative to romantic thralldom, DuPlessis's H.D. has defined "the relationships that would have to be transformed in order for a new kind of male-female sexual and spiritual relation to exist; that is, to end romantic thralldom" (1979b: 203). On the imaginative plane, then, H.D. becomes an ally in the political struggles in which DuPlessis herself is engaged. But as we see in H.D.'s feelings toward Lionel Durand during the last year of her life, she remained to the end trapped

within the psychology of romantic thralldom, and on this score Du-
Plessis is clearly *not* asking us to see H.D. as a role model for women.

DuPlessis also in a variety of ways disassociates herself from H.D.'s
poetics. In the essay published in this volume, DuPlessis says, speaking
of *Drafts*, "no plan, no design, no schemata. Just a few procedures. . . .
No continuous narrative. No myth as explanation. Here *Drafts* are very
different from H.D.'s long poems and quite related to Objectivist ethos
and poetics." By implication at least, DuPlessis here sees H.D.'s long
poems as grounded in a "plan," a "design," a "schemata," and as invoking "myth as explanation." In sum, she reads H.D. as essentially a symbolist, and she is, like most of the poets and critics within the Objectivist
tradition that she has claimed as her own, deeply suspicious of the symbolist impulse. It is no accident that neither Hugh Kenner nor Marjorie
Perloff, the two critics who have done more than anyone else to create
the vocabulary we need to talk about this "alternative" tradition, show
any interest whatsoever in H.D. For them, H.D. belongs not with
Pound and Williams and Moore and the Objectivists but somewhere
else, perhaps with the "poetesses" like Millay and Teasdale (but maybe
these writers too deserve another look!), perhaps with James Gould
Fletcher and other belated symbolists.[14] As we shall see, DuPlessis wants
to rescue H.D. from these dustbins of literary history, but she also accepts the assumption, common among both pro- and anti-H.D. fac-
tions, that a symbolist hunger for the transcendent and the eternal is
the driving force of H.D.'s poetry: "her hermetic textual assumptions
unveil a nature in which is revealed the feminine/maternal psyche, the
metamorphosis and resurrection at the core of 'real' reality, a substra-
tum beneath interpretation, only capable of being hidden or revealed,
but not susceptible to change" (DuPlessis 1986: 16). DuPlessis sees
H.D.'s "symbolist rediscovery of an Historical ancient verity" as effect-
ing "a major cultural displacement by insistently making the matriarchal female power of the mother-goddess figures dominant" (1986: 16).
But in her writings since the mid-1980s, DuPlessis has become increasingly suspicious of transhistorical and archetypal rhetorics, even when
mobilized for feminist purposes. In "Manifests" she forthrightly declares, "to write poetry with a gender critique in mind one must attempt
to withdraw from these universal narratives. Resist the transhistorical.
Reject special spiritual access ascribed to one group. Suspect Oedipal
theories or family narratives of poetic power. Disclaim any theory that

ascribes full subjectivity to one gender (etc.) only" (1996b: 41). Du-
Plessis isn't talking specifically about H.D. here, but the critique would
seem to apply to this poet's hunger for a "real" reality, beyond all
change. And in another recent essay, "Corpses of Poesy," this critique
of H.D. becomes explicit. DuPlessis has repeatedly associated what she
calls "lyric" with a verbal dynamic that locates women in the object
position as the (silent, passive) focus of the adoring male's gaze, and
she has described her poetic goal as finding some way around the lyric
as poetic norm.[15] In the "Corpses" essay, DuPlessis specifically sees
H.D.'s verse—some of it anyway—as characterized by "a perfection of
mellifluous lyrical markers" (1994: 86), and she contrasts such poetry
with the harsher, more satirical poetic modes of Mina Loy and Marianne Moore—so by this point the old Moore/H.D. polarity seems to
have reversed! As a poet, H.D. beyond question pursued "beauty," and
DuPlessis wants no part of "beauty," which she can see only as a trap.

Yet our story does not end here, for DuPlessis also at times sees
H.D., more often in her prose than in her poetry, as a pioneer in developing the open, disjunctive, "processual" modes of writing that she herself has pursued. In *H.D.: The Career of That Struggle*, DuPlessis detects
some of these qualities in H.D.'s "palimpsestic" prose writing of the
1920s and 1930s, including *Palimpsest* itself:

> *Palimpsest* may suggest the metonymic chain, a series of tellings of
> something with no one ever having final dominance, an evocation of
> plurality and multiplicity, lack of finality. This suggests the porous-
> ness of H.D.'s style, its unauthoritarian, constantly exploratory qual-
> ity, despite this firm appeal to a final truth, saved from the embar-
> rassments of authority precisely by being perpetually hidden as well
> as being exactly different from what dominant culture offers. The
> word palimpsest textualises mind, history, reality. To understand is
> to read, decode, translate, but there is always something not fully
> decipherable.   (1986: 56)

However, the text in which DuPlessis most fully describes this "other"
H.D. is "Language Acquisition" (in DuPlessis 1990a: 83–109). The argument of this essay turns on Kristeva's distinction between the semiotic and the symbolic. In the semiotic, language becomes labile/labial,
pure sound and play, returning us to the heterogeneity of the body and
to the chora that is always, Kristeva herself says, the lost mother—but

there is, DuPlessis herself adds, "No pure semiotic; (except in psycho-sis)" (DuPlessis 1990a: 87). In the symbolic, the flow of the semiotic gives way to "meaning, sign, and the signified object" (Kristeva 1980: 134). "For H.D.," says DuPlessis, "the semiotic is safest when it can be interwoven with a symbolic (interpretive) function so fluid and polyva-lent that it almost annexes itself to the semiotic; the semiotic is there-fore safest, most satisfying when it is not glossalalia, not syntactic rup-ture, not invective/obscenity (Celine-Pound), but when it is expressed as signs" (DuPlessis 1990a: 88). So the semiotic in H.D. reaches toward the security of the symbolic; but the symbolic also tries to return to the (maternal) fluidity of the semiotic. This seems a potentially fruitful way to read H.D., and DuPlessis herself identifies certain texts in which the interplay between the symbolic and the semiotic achieves a fully satis-fying dynamic: *Tribute to Freud, The Gift, Compassionate Friendship, End to Torment* (DuPlessis 1990a: 98; see also 1986: 85). All these texts fall into the category of what DuPlessis calls the essay: "H.D. found a key medium when she found (re-founded) the essay, because she makes it the medium of endless interpretation, intellectually bold. She makes it palimpsest, she makes it plenitude" (DuPlessis 1990a: 98).[16] In these texts, then, DuPlessis finds an H.D. that she can happily adopt as a model, an H.D. whose ways of working with language are fully com-patible with the process-centered poetics that DuPlessis herself had learned from Pound, Williams, and the Objectivists.

Her sense of H.D. as, if a symbolist, nevertheless a resistant and re-luctant one,[17] a symbolist open to the pull of the semiotic, allows Du-Plessis to make use for her own antisymbolist ends some specific poetic devices pioneered by H.D., and I would like to look briefly at one of these devices, the metamorphosing of words. In *Trilogy*, H.D. becomes fascinated by the auditory relationships among words and by the way such relationships can lead us back toward some lost originary meaning. One well-known example is her recovery of the lost Mother within the Hebrew word for bitter, *marah*, in section 8 of "Tribute to the Angels":

> Now polish the crucible
> and in the bowl distill
>
> a word most bitter, *marah*,
> a word bitterer still, *mar*,

sea, brine, breaker, seducer,
giver of life, giver of tears;

Now polish the crucible
and set the jet of flame

under, till marah-mar
are melted, fuse and join

and change and alter,
mer, mere, mère, mater, Maia, Mary,

Star of the Sea,
Mother.   (H.D. 1973: 71)[18]

Similarly, in section 40 of "The Walls Do Not Fall," Osiris becomes "O-sir-is" and "O-sire-is" and then the star Sirius—at which point, although H.D. does not make this connection explicitly, the categorical proposition seems to turn into a prayer, as "sire" becomes a verb: "O sire us." But then, in section 43, the sound of Osiris elides into the whine of the falling bombs:

> *there is zrr-hiss, I*
> *lightning in a not-known,*
>
> *unregistered dimension;*
> *we are powerless.*   (H.D. 1973: 58)

Writing about this verbal device in *H.D.: The Career of That Struggle,* DuPlessis interprets H.D.'s goals as essentially archetypal:

> The ability poetically to deconstruct words, as in the set of Osiris phonemes . . . leads to spiritual, even mystical knowledge of the One. . . . The process of decoding reiterates the Osirian fragmenta-tion. To achieve the Isisan rejuvenation, one must look hard at/for the scattered "members" (syllables, associations) and understand the meanings offered by the fragmentation. Finally, such phonemic pun-ning gives access to the language "inside" the language, suggestively occult; suggestively female.   (1986: 91–92)

DuPlessis herself isn't interested in "mystical knowledge of the one" or in occult meanings, even "suggestively female" ones. Nevertheless, she is willing to adopt the technique, and in her hands it becomes a way of opening up the text to potentially infinite metonymic play. A striking example is "Crowbar," from *The "History of Poetry"*:

lay dee	hist!story
l'idée	mystery
lay dés	My hyster y (DuPlessis 1987b: 21)

There is a bit of *Finnegans Wake* here in that "hist!story." And the "dés" (French "dice") buried in "ladies" triggers thoughts of Mallarmé, who shows up a few lines later in this same poem: "all MherY duplicity of gesture / a throw of the ring not / abolishing" (DuPlessis 1987b: 21). So H.D. marries Mallarmé, just as, in a similar verbal Reconstruction at the beginning of this poem, she had married Zukofsky:

> Snow on o-
> pen
> yellow for-
> sythia
>
> Sno
> won
> open force
> scythe
> ya   (DuPlessis 1987b: 11)

The delicate Imagist lyric is suddenly transformed into an allegory of rape as the syllables are pried apart.

Despite her uneasiness about H.D.'s symbolist proclivities, then, DuPlessis finds a good deal in the older poet's work that she can use; and in the process she does, as she herself claims in the essay published in this book, exert an important influence on H.D.—perhaps we might even say that she *invents* an H.D. that remains, in unexpected ways, usable for us. By this point it should be apparent that I am deeply sympathetic with DuPlessis's poetics. Like most of my contemporaries, I experienced a certain frisson when I first encountered the archetype of the Great Mother. In common with, I suspect, DuPlessis herself,[19] I made Her acquaintance in the pages of Erich Neumann's *The Great Mother*, and so I knew what I was seeing when, in section 25 of "Tribute to the Angels," the Lady knocks and enters. Yet it is too late in history to recover the primal unity of the One concealed behind the many, even if

we gender the One female: the attempt breeds fascism, as the troubling
life story of Jung himself suggests. Ours is, for better or for worse, the
Time of Difference (*Différance*), and we need a poetry that can embrace
Difference. (And Difference, tiresome stories like the reports out of
Cambodia and Bosnia and Iraq remind us, can breed Indifference, so
poetry still has an ethical task too.) DuPlessis's poetry offers us a vibrant
model of a poetry of heterogeneity, the lived moment, history as something we are actually *in*. And she has taken some important steps to
show how H.D. can help us to create a Poetry of Difference. On this
point I'd like to place her beside Robert Duncan, who seems to me,
simply, right about everything—and I think DuPlessis admires him almost as much as I do. Duncan insisted that to create the poetry of our
time, we must resist the temptation to choose between Pound and Williams, on the one hand (and it is no longer so hard to put these two
together—Marjorie Perloff has shown us how), or H.D., on the other;
that, rather, we must find some way of thinking Pound and Williams
and H.D. all in the same thought, which is still not so easy to do.[20] But
in her poetic praxis, DuPlessis has done exactly that. Nor can we recover Pound and Williams as poetic models unless we frankly confront
the fascism of Pound and the sexism of both these poets, so in this
respect DuPlessis's criticism (see especially "*Pater*-daughter" in Du-
Plessis 1990a: 41–67) has served an important poetic purpose. But I
would want to go a little further than DuPlessis herself in reinventing
H.D. for our time. Yes, H.D.'s verbal Reconstructions are intended to
recover a lost archetypal truth. But in practice these Reconstructions
also place us firmly within the materiality of language, and in this respect—like the sheer momentum of language in *The Cantos*, or like the
flood of water over the waterfalls in *Paterson*—they impel us beyond the
author's intentions into the flux of history. For H.D. too the act of writing was an act of discovery, a venture forward into the unknown. As she
says in the great concluding lines of "The Walls Do Not Fall,"

> *we know no rule*
> *of procedure,*
>
> *we are voyagers, discoverers*
> *of the not-known,*
>
> *the unrecorded;*
> *we have no map;*

> *possibly we will reach haven,*
> *heaven.*   (H.D. 1973: 59)

Possibly we will get there. But what thread do we have to lead us, except the rhymes of the words we speak?

III

In view of her long and deep engagement with an array of male writers, it is not surprising that DuPlessis's poetry, as she herself has acknowledged, does not fit comfortably into the dominant current models of a "women's tradition" of writing: "My poetry does not resemble hegemonic feminist or women's poetry or mainstream poetries in its form or its poetics. I draw on avant-garde traditions in written and visual texts, always working with metonymic exposition and the possibilities of collage. Virtually unpublished throughout the 1970s, I said 'I was too feminist for the objectivists, and too objectivist for the feminists'" (1993: 107). In *Stealing the Language*, Alicia Ostriker argues, "When a woman poet today says 'I,' she is likely to mean herself, as intensely as her imagination and her verbal skills permit, much as Wordsworth or Keats did . . . , before Eliot's 'extinction of personality' became the mandatory twentieth-century initiation ritual for young American poets, and before the death of the author became a popular critical fiction" (1986b: 12). And indeed, if we take Adrienne Rich as the exemplary figure among contemporary women poets, Ostriker's assessment seems accurate. Creating the subjectivity (or subjecthood?) effaced by patriarchy, telling us the good and bad news of what it is like to be this woman speaking—such would appear to be the poetic project not only of Rich but of, for starters, Sylvia Plath, Anne Sexton, Sharon Olds, and most other recent women poets who have achieved canonical status. But DuPlessis has read enough contemporary continental theory to be wary of any claims concerning the ontological priority of the "I."[21] All pronouns, including "I," are, she suggests, functions of a grammar that "speaks us," and rather than seeking to re/discover some primal authenticity of selfhood she is more interested in trying to disrupt those social "sentences" in which we find ourselves embedded:

> Write poetries. Write writings, write readings, write
> drafts. Write several selves to dissolve the bounded idea
> of the self

who is "I" who is "you"
who is "he" is "she"
fleeting shifts of position, social changes implying a
millennia of practice. To disturb the practice.
(DuPlessis 1990a: 149)

But perhaps this kind of writing as interruption/disruption, this "labial" writing that issues from the semiotic rather than the symbolic order, this writing that destabilizes all traditional structures of authority, including the authorial "I," is itself distinctively "feminine"? Indeed, the kind of writing that DuPlessis wants seems very similar to what Cixous calls *écriture féminine*, and DuPlessis herself sees an open, disjunctive mode of writing as uniquely suited to a feminist project. But in the last analysis she is willing to call such writing "feminine" only in a provisional sense: "I should . . . want to substitute untranscendent, situated materiality as a source for thought and mainly forget about the word feminine for this concept, all thought being so situated, so invested (in-f-ested). The issue is finding and tracking interests, not denying them" (DuPlessis 1996a: 36–37).

The draft form in which DuPlessis has been writing for over a decade now is uniquely suited to her poetic goals, as it incorporates into the flow of discourse the random one-thing-after-anotherness of daily life, and the eruption into that life of History, and the writer's experience of facing again the blank page and strewing it with words, and, always, the moment by moment rediscovery of a world that is insistently *there*, beyond our will and intentionality. All the drafts are dated, and the poems are arranged in chronological order. In this respect the series represents a journal, a record of a life as it is lived. Yet almost all the drafts also have titles that point to a unifying principle, often, as I have already suggested, grammatical or typographical. The flavor of DuPlessis's writing comes from the way it infuses the dailiness of life with unifying motifs of this sort. To see how DuPlessis's writing interweaves the various threads that here come together, "ply over ply," as Pound would say, it is necessary to follow the poet's path through one of the drafts. For this purpose I have chosen, more or less arbitrarily, "Draft 17: Unnamed" (DuPlessis 1997: 9–13). And in the hope of giving the reader some sense of how DuPlessis uses the full page as a field of play in her poems, I have allowed myself the spatial luxury of quoting this poem as verse, with the white space that sets off the lines. The subtitle of this poem at once denies the presence of a unifying theme for the poem and makes that absence itself the theme, for this draft is in significant measure "about" the evanescence or illegibility of the name and the condition of being nameless, lost to history. We begin in what seems to be a classroom with a chalkboard on which poems are being/have been written. The class period is over, the board is erased or is about to be, or at any rate the words are beginning to dissolve into some indeterminate space:

> It's true that every ending only erases the board
> rather than filling it.
> The poems are written in strange chalk
> strange, a chalk
> in some lights dark, plump with serifs
> on a scumbled, agitated whiteness,
> but mainly a white chalk on a whiter page.
>
> Which can hardly be read
> and that, only under angled light.

The physical immediacy of the words on the board (black or white?) is inescapable. But what do they say? The poet who chooses to write in white letters on a white page takes a certain risk.

At this point two metaphors offer themselves. First, we are invited to see the poem as a roll of paper towels, unfurling behind a toddler running up and down the hills. Here we're seeing a blaze of white against the dark. Or perhaps the poem is

> . . . dark as a mist
> hanging over the fill-built airport
> smoke brown, the sky looks daubed
> and of no depth.

We're in the territory of metaphor here, but the vehicle seems to swallow up the tenor, as the graphic image takes over. The world of things, objects emerges to establish a point or reference against which we can measure the translucence/opacity of words. And now the chalked words return, momentarily luminous:

> But the chalk (with luck, another turn) turns
> translucent, light on light
> which is, in certain lights, like dark on dark

but more
blinding.

Words,
scattered falling
arcs of shame,
glaze the flicker-ridden labyrinth—

Light and dark are, it seems, at some level indistinguishable. But if we scatter our words about, perhaps they will make a little light within the labyrinth. Why "arcs of *shame*"? We don't know yet, but perhaps we'll find out. In any case, the poet now wonders if the evanescence of those half-legible words may itself be the point:

Perhaps translucence is a quality of erasure.
The thing anyway looks like a Cy Twombly
strokes trailing each other and dibs, nibs,
flicks of the wrist and a dreamy evisceration of pencil.

But isn't art timeless, a monument to the ages? A nameless "he" now enters to tell the poet that while her "little valise is filled with souvenirs," the dribs and drabs of daily life, "none of them is 'art.'" Maybe not, but she wants to be ready for those moments when "the hole, the sufferance" falls open. At those moments we can hear "the shaped scream of a duration," the voice of "the same, the same, the same again." For she wants—and she want us to want, "'nothing but these facts and all these facts.'"

The focus shifts now from the problematics of language to the world that language claims to be "about." If the word has proved an unstable reference point, the world proves no more stable but no less inescapable:

Low song clouds in unbelonging places
emphasize the activities of light,
which is unspeakable.

While the sound, not just the light,
plays along certain vectors
pools in the force field

large, square, rent, timeless
void. Know?
Can barely know what labyrinth.

The grass clods push up
        between the lines and cracks
                of pavement. In the depth

of night, a street lamp
        looming behind them
                they rise and lurk,

turf tufts made near twice
        their "real" size
                by shadow.

In borrowing Williams's triadic line, DuPlessis also pays homage to his poetics of "no ideas but in things." "Song clouds" suggest some sort of transition from words to things, but things themselves turn out to be, as always, unspeakable. Indeed, perhaps they are merely vectors in the force field, and the field itself is perhaps a void—but the four incompatible adjectives that DuPlessis lines up to describe the void underscore how unspeakable the facts always turn out to be. We have a hard time knowing even what labyrinth we're in, much less where we are in it. But those clumps of grass that squeeze up through the cracks in the pavement are indubitably *there*, fracturing this imposed order. The Other cannot, it seems, be entirely excluded, even though the uncertain light makes it hard for us to determine what these objects are, or how large they are, or whether or not they mean us harm ("they rise and lurk").

As the phenomenal world forces its way into the poem, the historical world is not far behind, as the poem moves on to describe a woman who revisits a mass grave that she had come upon, fifty years previously, just after 155 Jews had been shot and buried there.

There, near a field of rye,
        she'd found dozens of notes and addresses

tossed away
        moments before their deaths.
                To this day,

she regrets
        that out of fear,
                she did not pick them up.

This image, DuPlessis tells us, implies a poetics. Many people are wandering about, trying to find those notes, "But they are not there." And yet, if we had found ourselves beside this grave on the day after the massacre, wouldn't we too "have left / all of them where they lay"? And to imagine that *we* are destined to find those notes and addresses left behind by the unnamed dead and thereby to redeem history—this is, DuPlessis acknowledges, a form of hubris.[22] Thus what she finds it possible for her to write

> . . . is not elegy
>   though elegy seems the nearest category of genre
>   raising stars, strewing flowers. . . .
>
> It's not that I have not
>   done this, in life or wherever I
>   needed to
>
> or throwing out the curled tough leather
>   of the dead
>   the cracked insteps of unwalkable shoes,
>
> but it is not the name or term
>   for what is meant
>   by this inexorable bending.
>
> And it is not "the Jews"
>   (though of course it's the Jews),
>   but Jews as an iterated sign of this site.

The "it's" here squirms painfully about, pointing us toward the unnamed and the unspeakable: the what-I'm-trying-to-say, the poem-I'm-trying-to-write. Rilke helps a little, but the elegiac mode won't do. We cannot walk in the shoes of the dead, so we throw them out, but as we do so we cannot not know that we are throwing out the "sign of this site," for the feet of the dead have shaped these shoes to their need. The "inexorable bending"—of the shoes, of time, of the words on the page—has no name or term, no limit point.

But turning back now to words, we discover that we can at least say what they are and are not:

> Words with (to all intents and purposes)
> no before and after

>   hanging in a void of loss
>   the slow and normal whirlwind
>   from which it roars
>   they had not ever meant to be so lost,
>   so little wordth.

The "it" now becomes the voice of JHWH from the whirlwind of time, the voice of all those words that, simply because they are timeless, also become the emblems of all we have lost: the sad words that didn't want this to happen and that in the end stumble into a lisp that telescopes "word" and "worth." We now do find at last some Rilkean angels, but they present themselves "without / choices or pleasure, stand [-ing] empty." And for a moment DuPlessis's text devolves into a jumble of miscellaneous stuff, a shift perhaps signaled by the shift to a right margin:

>   Late busses, glass smash, styrofoam containers.
>   Low sun plain wing
>   grey toyota
>   ormolu
>   soccer freshener
>   kith, soot,
>   food,
>   rainbows of oil.
>   But even this clutter of random objects conceals some
>   important directions: if you turn at "the intersection by
>   Dunkin' Donuts" and the Gulf station, you'll find that
>   all along you've been "coming / here."

And so the draft rises to something approaching a triumphal resolution:

>   So speak, stutterer, and stain the light with figments.
>   Rush, and brush, this evanescent shimmer
>   that does not even track
>
>   that does not
>   even fill and replicate
>   the historical air clotted here.

And Here
>   where all this is and are,
>>   this back and forth through time,

Alight.
>   It's never
>>   what you think.

And so the stuttering poet is freed to stain the purity of the light with her (necessarily impure) figments/fragments. The evanescent shimmer of the poem cannot reproduce or make itself coextensive with history. But it can allow us to alight (with the obvious pun on a struck match) for a moment Here (capitalized now), where the unnamed and the unspeakable are happening at this very moment, although "it" is "never / what you think." On the contrary, "it" is always *more*: more than you could possibly anticipate but more also than any mental categories can encompass. For whatever "it" may be, we did not create it; rather, we find ourselves always already in it.

It is a pleasure to quote writing like "Draft 17: Unnamed." In sheer propulsive force, in its capacity to engage the world while simultaneously keeping a close eye on those (always treacherous) words through which we define our place among the things of this world, in its polyphonic exploration of a full range of experience from the personal through the historical to the religious, in its sheer pleasure in the physicality of language, the poetry of Rachel Blau DuPlessis seems to me as satisfying as the work of any poet writing today. DuPlessis herself has described *Drafts* as "post-lyric, creolized writing: epiphanic moments are flattened and undercut; narratives are multiple and dissolved; heteroglossia is maximized; the symphonic space is the site of anarchic, wayward collages of language and investigations of textual markers" (1993: 108). I will let the reader determine the specific ways in which "Draft 17: Unnamed" may or may not show the influence of H.D. Certainly at first glance, "Draft 17" looks and sounds very different from, for example, *Trilogy*, H.D.'s best-known long poems, and DuPlessis has chosen to end her essay in this volume by emphasizing the differences between her poetics and those of H.D.

> I wanted exodus, the ex-odic, watchfulness into departures. H.D.
> wanted to return to plenitude, postulated as origins. I quarrel with

the nonpresence. "El" and the loss of L means oss, a bony site. She builds a space in which presence can reemerge. I want (and this from J.-F. Lyotard, painfully) "the forgotten never part of memory": "a demand for a form of thinking and writing that do not 'forget the fact' of the forgotten and the unrepresentable."

We could conceptualize these differences in many different ways: the postmodernist DuPlessis versus the modernist H.D., DuPlessis the radical New Yorker versus H.D. the (always intuitively conservative) child of suburban Philadelphia, even DuPlessis the skeptical, nomadic Jew versus H.D. the Moravian Christian, still longing to return to that magical manger in Bethlehem—and I would not question the validity of any of these oppositions.[23] But I prefer to end this essay by emphasizing not the differences but the continuities between these two poets, simply because DuPlessis has indeed "influenced" H.D., and my H.D. is in major ways the H.D. that DuPlessis has given me. And reading H.D. "through" DuPlessis, I see a poet who is not paralyzed by a nostalgia for a lost Presence but one who is strikingly open to new possibilities, both psychologically and poetically. *Helen in Egypt* and the long sequences collected in *Hermetic Definition* are, if not as disjunctive and polyvocal as *Drafts*, nevertheless almost as exploratory, recursive, and "nomadic" as the works of the younger poet. Nor can I see H.D. as (like, for instance, Eliot) a nostalgic Christian trapped in a hunger for transcendental Presence.[24] Not the H.D. who displaced the Logos of Greece with the Mythos of Egypt; who wanted both Christos the Lamb and "Amen, Aries, the Ram" (1973: 30); who rejected the claims of the theologians to explain the meaning of the Word and instead gave it back to the poets; who, in the face of the Judeo-Christian proclamation "Thou shalt have no other gods before me," asked,

> not on the sea
>
> shall we entreat Triton or Dolphin,
> not on the land
>
> shall we lift rapt face and clasp hands
> before laurel or oak-tree,
>
> not in the sky
> shall we invoke separately

Orion or Sirius
or the followers of the Bear,

not in the higher air
of Algorab, Regulus or Deneb

shall we cry
for help—or shall we?   (H.D. 1973: 50)

H.D. had no answer to this interminable question, but she did know that when we dismiss as demons the gods worshiped by those without the law, we have sinned against the light.

NOTES

1. I might also note, marginally, that DuPlessis is here interested in the "Oppen/open" rhyme, as well as the "Oppen/oddly" assonance.

2. In "f-Words: An Essay on the Essay," DuPlessis describes at length the distinctive generic qualities of the essay, offers a comprehensive bibliography of contemporary essay writing, and argues eloquently that the essay is uniquely suited to the needs of our cultural moment. And what am I myself writing here? An "essay"? An "article"? The latter label has an academic ring missing from "essay." But already I have committed myself to the endnote as an ancillary mode of discourse, and by my standards that makes this piece of writing an article—although DuPlessis's own essays usually have notes. Besides, if I were writing an essay, I would want to refer to my subject as "Rachel," which is how I think of her—I have known her for nearly twenty years. But in an article the first name takes on patronizing overtones, so here, dear Rachel, you will be, for better or worse, "DuPlessis."

3. DuPlessis herself, not unnaturally, tends to see her work in these three modes as all of a piece—all this writing is, after all, "hers": "My Poetry propelled my criticism, criticism propelled poetry, and essays were originally born in a growth spurt between them. Essays then further incited my main critical book, and even my next one, on H.D. The three genres I use offer (at least) three different and related subject positions, answerable to different social expectations and writing forums. But they were not separate tracks. Discoveries made in one mode led the way to work in another" (1993: 106). But looking at her work from the outside, I am more aware of the differences among the three modes.

4. In "Reader, I Married Me," DuPlessis reports that in 1980 she was turned down for tenure at Temple (1993: 107). It is my understanding that in the appeal process she was granted tenure at the rank of assistant professor, with the stipulation that promotion to associate professor would come only after she completed a major scholarly book then in progress; it is also my understanding that *Writing beyond the Ending* is the book in question. "I chose," says DuPlessis, "to write this book in

standard tones and modes of argument; it would have been professionally unstrategic (to say the least) to make another kind of work" (1993: 110). I detect in this terse statement some signs that DuPlessis is not entirely happy with "the standard tones and mode of argument," but the assertive "I chose" also bespeaks a certain pride in her ability to master these "tones and modes."

5. In "Reader, I Married Me," DuPlessis quotes a statement of purpose that she co-authored for *Feminist Studies*, on whose editorial board she served for fourteen years: "The feminist movement has demonstrated that the study of women is more than a compensatory project. Instead, feminism has the potential fundamentally to reshape the way we view the world. We wish not just to interpret women's experiences but to change women's condition. For us, feminist thought represents a transformation of consciousness, social forms, and modes of action" (1993: 104).

6. DuPlessis is not the only contemporary woman poet to write poems that stand, more or less, within this tradition: some other notable examples are Susan Howe, Beverly Dahlen, and Lyn Hejinian. Lynn Keller's recent *Forms of Expansion: Recent Long Poems by Women* (1997) discusses several contemporary long poems by women.

7. And William Carlos Williams, for while his work offers no specific precedent for the "drafts" form, some of the most eloquent passages in the sequence are written in his triadic line. Williams is also in obvious ways a less problematic model than Pound or Rilke.

8. In "Reader, I Married Me," DuPlessis says, "For some of the poetics and some of the intransigence, I was indebted to the work of the 'Objectivist' poet George Oppen, many of whose writings in poetics occurred in his self-chosen form: personal letters" (1993: 107). Oppen sent a good many of those letters to DuPlessis herself. I might add that I first met Rachel (I'm talking about the person here, not the authorial persona) through the Oppens. In 1979 I began to prepare a collection of critical and scholarly essays on Oppen, published in 1981 as *George Oppen: Man and Poet*. At my request, Mary Oppen gave me a list of potential contributors to this volume, and the name of Rachel Blau DuPlessis stood at the top of the list.

9. In "On Drafts," DuPlessis says, "At first, it seemed as if my plan was going to be the investigation of some 'little words'—pronouns and pronominals ('it,' 'she')— the shifters." But as she proceeded, this "conception eviscerated itself. . . . What was learned from the first ones was that there was a lot of 'it.' And one way or another, 'she' was going to have to deal with 'it.'" But even the later drafts, DuPlessis acknowledges, circle around issues of language. "For instance, a group of titles from 1988–1990 seem to intimate the materials of writing: 'The,' 'Page,' 'Letters,' 'Schwa'—'Letters' with the qwerty keyboard foregrounded as alphabet. . . . The examination of textuality is ongoing ('Title,' 'Traduction,' 'Incipit,' 'Segno') but this focus is not exclusive, for I am also interested in work, and mapping, and their results" (1996c: 147–48).

10. It is amusing to watch the amount of space allocated to H.D. in successive editions of the *Norton Anthology of American Literature* steadily expand from the 1970s to the present in direct consequence of the work of these feminist critics.

11. But I should add that over the years DuPlessis has become increasingly in-

terested in Moore. In "No Moore of the Same" (1988) she claims Moore as a feminist poet. In "Corpses of Poesy" she presents Moore's poetry as an alternative to a lyricism whose generic conventions inevitably re-encode women in the object position (1994: 85–91). And in "Manifests" she traces the poetic tradition in which she herself is writing back to Moore's poetry of the 1920s (1996b: 45).

12. For DuPlessis, "the career of that struggle" is precisely "the struggle not to be reduced, to be neither muse nor poetess" (1990a: 29).

13. In *Drafts*, says DuPlessis, "Definite motifs and thematic materials are at stake. A representative, although incomplete, list would include home and exile; writing and the scenes of writing; the minutiae of dailiness; death, and the dead linked with the living; silence and speaking. And as well the question what positions and discourses are adequate to speaking as a gendered 'I' while at the same time, there is a distinct downplaying of any 'I' (a word, incidentally, that rarely appears), and no more overt discussion of gender than anything else" (1996c: 150–51). So as perhaps befits a poet/scholar/essayist, DuPlessis has been far more willing than most poets to explain what she is up to in her poetry. See, in particular, the essay "Otherhow" in *The Pink Guitar* (DuPlessis 1990a: 140–56) as well as DuPlessis (1993, 1996b, 1996c).

14. For a full and lucid exposition of this latter reading of H.D., see Dembo (1966: 24–47).

15. See, for example, DuPlessis (1993: 107). See also DuPlessis (1990a: esp. 149–52). Or see "On Drafts": "I cannot believe in the perfection of lyric, the separation of lyric, the selectivity of lyric, the purity of lyric, the solitary language of lyric & cannot imagine what to 'do' next" (DuPlessis 1996c: 145).

16. It was, DuPlessis suggests, psychoanalysis, not as ideology but as process, that legitimated for H.D. this processual mode of discourse: "Freud's analytic procedure—the talking cure, the metonymic combinations playing across the axis of selection to construct a swelling, interminable reading of any sign, this associative, ruminative, atemporal and palimpsested style, the voice of 'chora,' was the definitive rupture from 'vanishing points of sterility and finesse'" (1986: 85).

17. At one point DuPlessis sums up this image of H.D. in a single, terse (if grammatically somewhat dubious) sentence: "H.D. is an anti-patriarchal symbolist; her yearning for centre and presence still rupture the unspoken attachment, in most symbolist poetic practice, to a phallocentric focus" (1986: 89).

18. A few sections later in this same sequence H.D. plays the trick again: meditating on the name of "Venus," she pulls away (in section 11) the external layers of association with impurity ("venery," "venereous") to un/recover (in section 12) the holy ("venerate," "venerator"), and then, in section 13, a voice speaks to H.D., telling her to "invent" a new name for the color of the mystery—and if we are not quite sure whether she is still thinking about that "ven" root, nevertheless the connection rises up to us from the page (1973: 75).

19. See the essay "Psyche or Wholeness," which DuPlessis decided not to include in *The Pink Guitar*. This essay is an extended meditation on/deconstruction of the writing of Neumann (DuPlessis 1979a).

20. And if we can do *that*, maybe we can also put Eliot and Moore and Stevens

and Stein into this same picture and undo all the cruel divorces among our great modernist masters.

21. "Especially when one is in the midst of a work—who can say the 'I' is exemplary, historical? One just writes as best one can" (DuPlessis 1996c: 154).

22. In an earlier draft (number 14, "Conjunctions"), DuPlessis had proposed that every poet must

> vow to write *so that*
> *if*, in some aftermath, a few shard words,
> chancily rendered, the potchkered scrap of the human
> speck
> washed up out of the torn debris, to write
> *so that*
> *if* your shard emerged from the shard pile
>
> people would cry *and* cry aloud "look! look!"

and then would proceed to rebuild the whole "infinite extended structure" out of your shard (1991: 84). But to imagine that *our* scrap is destined to survive is also obviously a form of hubris.

23. In "On Drafts," DuPlessis tells us that her poetic sequence is marked by "a number of allusions to elements of the Jewish tradition. It's a creolized mix: certain holidays and customs; certain compelling Hebrew scriptural stories such as Jacob and the angel; some words in Yiddish; a pervasive and incurable nomadism and sense of the exilic; a number of humble shadows of the Holocaust. Can this be summarized? The poem is inflected with a peculiar (and of course resistant) 'Jewishness' because it is about text and textuality? about debris? about 'anguage'—a cross between language and anguish, and maybe anger?" (1996c: 152–53).

24. I am perhaps unduly sensitive on this point because the last time I taught H.D. a student in class attacked her work on precisely these grounds.

The Blank Page: H.D.'s Invitation to Trust and Mistrust Language

KATHLEEN FRASER

---

we know no rule
of procedure,

we are voyagers, discoverers,
of the notknown

the unrecorded;
we have no map   H.D., *Trilogy*

With an authentic sense of beginning at zero, a poetically mature H.D. could write in the war years of the early 1940s: "we know no rule / of procedure." Yet her contemporary readers know that rules of procedure did exist at almost every level of her early life. Even in that nontraditional world of literature toward which she leaned, achieved forms stood in place. Nevertheless, she refused the finality of the already filled page. For while others' writings often thrilled her, they did not speak for the unsaid that burned in her.

Born from doubt and extreme privacy, her own tentative language slowly invented itself out of silence. Her gift was an ability to see the empty page waiting to be inscribed and to imagine—beyond the parchment metaphor of "palimpsest"—a contemporary model for the poem that would recover a complex overlay of erotic and spiritual valuings variously imprinted, then worn away, then finally rediscovered and engraved inside her own lines. Her vision lay in the conviction of plurality—that the blank page would never be a full text until women writers (and their reader-scholars) scrawled their own scripts across its emptiness.

Even within Pound's mentoring embrace, H.D. felt a certain cautionary guardedness around the unfolding, if uneasy, project of her own work. "Ezra would have destroyed me and the center they call 'Air and Crystal,'" she admits in 1958 in her journal entry from *End to Torment*. A month later, she writes: "To recall Ezra is to recall my father. . . . To recall my father is to recall the cold blazing intelligence of my 'last attachment' of the war years in London. This is not easy" (H.D. 1979: 35, 48).

She had survived two major wars and the tyranny of gender stereotype. But fifty years later she was still trying to sort out the impact of this strange, impassioned outsider, Ezra Pound, who identified and constellated her early poetic identity while at the same time limiting its very stretch by his defining, instructive approval.

That a strong push-pull dynamic progressively marks her writer-relation to Pound and her position "on the fringes of the modernist mainstream" seems evident from passages in her fictional works and in bits of letters and journals (Friedman and DuPlessis 1990: 24). Her artistic progress is marked by self-initiated shifts in attitude and ambition—notably, her decision to try to shed the once-useful but finally limiting description of "Imagiste" given her by Pound as her poet designator. It is instructive to mark her ambivalence toward—and discomfort with—male value judgments vis-à-vis her own work and to see how she climbed, repeatedly, out of these silencing effects to again recover her own voice and to trust its foraging instincts.

We read the following words written to Pound, anticipating his criticism, in a note H.D. sent along to him in 1959 with a copy of her complete *Helen in Egypt*: "Don't worry or hurry with the Helen—don't read it at all—don't read it yet—don't bother to write of it" (quoted in Friedman and DuPlessis 1990: 12). One hears the echo and ricochet of her wariness traveling all the way back to Pound's first decisive claim on her poetic gifts, the swift and confident slash of his editor's pencil and his literal initialing—or labeling—of her for purposes of identification and value in the poetry marketplace.

In H.D.'s life, this style of "help" manifested itself in various powerful guises, notably in encounters with big-affect literary friends such as D. H. Lawrence, whose charismatic male authority was often as much a source of anxiety as support. The delicate yet powerful mythic terrain wisely appropriated by H.D. afforded protection from a merely personal accounting of her highly volatile emotional life—the more personal lyric, so liable to deliver her into the hands of male "correction." Myth finally provided a route of independent travel, a large enough page on which to incise and thus emplace her own vision of the future, spiritually enlivened by values retrieved from female life.

When she directs our attention in *Trilogy* to "the blank pages / of the unwritten volume of the new," H.D. is issuing a literal invitation of breathtaking immensity and independence to contemporary women poets. Once perceived, the page is there and yours to remake. No more alibis. The challenge is at once freeing and awesome.

As a contemporary writer, I have been called back to this blank page again and again. Let me attempt to describe a largely intuitive gathering-up of poem materials for a serial work of mine, "Etruscan Pages" *(When New Time Folds Up)*, in which the layerings of old and new inscription were built from accretions of literal archaeological remnant bound together into current pages of language, visual figure and event (present-time dreams and letters).

I believe that it was H.D.'s profound connection to the contemporary relevance of ancient cultures—as well as her Egyptian experience with hieroglyph as a kind of telegram from the atemporal—that opened me and prepared me for my journey (May 1991) to the sites of three Etruscan necropolises—Tarquinia, Vulci, and Norchia—scattered north of Rome along the Maremma coast, each site marked on the map with an almost illegible triangle of black dots. Having deferred a long-held intellectual curiosity, early prompted by reading D. H. Lawrence in the sixties and an early draft of Rachel Blau DuPlessis's ground-breaking essay "For the Etruscans" in 1979 (and thinly veneered with bookish obligation), I finally took the occasion of a friend's visit to propose a journey to these three sites, and we set off early one morning with map and guidebook.

There was nothing that could have prepared me for the impact these places had on me—their absence informed by presence. The cliff tombs of Norchia might well have been entirely nonexistent if one were dependent only upon visual clues or signs along nearby roads. By guesswork we found ourselves climbing down through rough rock passages overgrown with foliage that seemed to have been there forever. The lack of any other car or human allowed the presence of birds, local wildflowers, and the more apparent ruins of Roman conquerors—planted just across the ravine from the Etruscan cliff tombs—to resonate powerfully. I felt as if dropped through time, less and less able to talk casually of our surrounds.

Days later, the poem slowly began to rise to the surface of my listening mind. And during that time a startling convergence of dreams and events worked to push the limits of the poem into something much more layered and much less personal than any account of my own private experience could have provided. A week after the Maremma trip, I returned to the Villa Giulia, the major Etruscan museum in Rome, to see again the dancers lavishly flung across urns and the sculpted bodies of husband and wife entwined sensuously on the limestone lid covering an elongated sarcophagus. It was then I could finally begin to piece together their celebratory moment on earth with utterly changed eyes. H.D.'s invitation had allowed me to step out of the skin of verbal overlay and late-twentieth-century gloss, rendering me available to the palpable presence of these women and men.

Here are several passages from a letter, early embedded in my "page," that narrate a dream and then an archaeological episode, both given to me during the weeks of the poem's writing, as if invented for the layered record I was attempting to rewrite:

> The night you left for Paros, I dreamt I was lying on a stone slab at the base of the cliff tombs at Norchia, preparing to make my transition from "this world" to "the other." I was thinking about how to negotiate the passage, when it came to me—the reason for all the layers of fine white cloth arranged and spread around me. I said to you (because you were with me), "You just keep wrapping yourself with white cloth and eventually you are in the other place."   (Fraser 1993: 26)

This from an unexpected conversation—days later—with an archaeologist:

> The other source [referring to etymological studies] is the "mummy wrapping," linen originally from Egypt (probably hauled on trading ships) covered with formulaic and repetitious Etruscan religious precepts written "retro" (right to left). Even though there are over 1,200 words covering it, the total lexicon is barely 500. The mummy text is preserved in the museum in Zagreb, thus "The Zagreb Mummy."

Her body had been wrapped in this shroud made of pieces of linen, written on through centuries [with Phoenician, Greek, and, finally, Etruscan characters], used as "pages" for new writing whenever the old text had faded. Her family had wrapped her in this cloth, this writing, because it was available.   (Fraser 1993: 27)

With these interventions, the actual making of the poem became immensely absorbing. H.D.'s exhortation to heed "the blank pages of the unwritten volume of the new" was pulling me away from her "air and crystal" language. My page wanted to be inscribed as if it were a canvas, my own linguistic motion and visual notation appropriating the Etruscan lexicon and alphabet as subject and object—inventions suggested directly from contact with tomb inscriptions and the beaten gold tablets at Villa Giulia, covered with the elusive remainders of their language.

For example, a passage on the imagined origins of the letter *A* is juxtaposed with a miniature lexicon composed of words that already existed throughout the larger poem's text, a word hand-scrawled in Etruscan letters (meant to resemble those scratched into burial stones), and a bit of quoted speculation by D. H. Lawrence. I wanted to place a close-up lens over particular words as well as to foreground the hand and mind at work making language through history.

Without H.D.'s precedent, it is very unlikely that I would have trusted my own particular rendering of the historic clues and layers of the Etruscan culture or understood the urgency of articulating another reading of it in the face of all the officially recognized studies preceding me, including Lawrence's narrative. While my poem "Etruscan Pages" intentionally acknowledges Lawrence's 1932 travel memoir, *Etruscan Places*, it writes the new word PAGE over the old word PLACE to tip the reader's attention in the direction of an alternative reading introduced through a formal shift of perception. Mine is a document meant to record an alternative vision of the predominantly male archaeological point of view already well installed.

Having given Lawrence's account a rather perfunctory skim in the sixties, I was curious to go back to it—once I had a fairly realized draft of my own—just to see what had occupied him. I was pleased but not that surprised to find that there were a number of physical details and baffling absences we'd noted in common (although sixty years apart), even to particulars of asphodel (he must have been there in May) and the "nothing" that seemed to be so present in the barren fields and shut tombs around Vulci, where a sensuousness of daily life had once been so radiantly apparent.

I decided to incorporate several fragment phrases from Lawrence's text as a way of marking our meeting in parallel time—a kind of palimpsest dialogue. But I was deeply relieved to find that he'd not been to Norchia, the site that most profoundly spoke to me. I didn't want his brilliant voice-print preceding me everywhere. Its definite authority and well-installed literary history might have in some way inhibited me from capturing my own barely visible version.

I'd like to return now to the issue of asserted literary dominion versus self-confirmation as it impinges on the working life of the woman poet. For in spite of her strategies for empowerment, we recognize in H.D.'s 1959 note to Pound a residual mistrust based on the tension between her deep desire for his approval and the necessary self-affirmation of her own unmediated—and thus uninhibited—vision and writing method. Even after fifty years, a lurking fear of not meeting his standards still seems to hover in her. It isn't a simple fear of critique, for she was obviously strong-willed and utterly conscious of her aesthetic choices by then; rather, it is more like the dread of having to tangle with the absolute ego of the beloved but intrusive father/judge, forever looming in the shadow just over her shoulder, and to risk the loss of his admiration.

Reviewing H.D.'s progress toward the trust of her own "page," a contemporary woman poet might well identify with this struggle to circumvent the tremendous pressure of prevailing male ideology that has so conveniently persisted, historically viewing women contemporaries as "receptacle-like muses rather than active agents," thus reinforcing long-dominant "notions of what was properly and naturally feminine" (Friedman and DuPlessis 1990: 16).

Recently reading through a selection of letters between Pound and the young Louis Zukofsky, exchanged between 1928 and 1930, I was generally amused until I came across such bits of Pound-heavy advice as his urging Zukofsky to form a new literary group of serious, high-energy writers but exhorting him: "NOT too many women, and if possible no wives at assembly. If some insist on accompanying their *mariti* [husbands], make sure they are bored and don't repeat offense." Later, advising Zukofsky about the selection of work for a new magazine, he says: "AND the verse used MUST be good . . . preferably by men [*sic*] under 30" (Pound 1987).

In these tossed-off bits of pecking-order jocularity are found the not very subtle codes of selection and disenfranchisement that were practiced to various degrees in the literary world I entered as a young poet in the early sixties. A primary difference between my world and H.D.'s was that nine-tenths of the once-published writing by modernist women was out of print, leaving very few female texts as models for the nontraditional poetics one felt compelled to explore.

Fortunately, change was in the air. By the early seventies, women scholars had begun to talk to each other about this problem and to investigate it in print.

This brings us again to the shaping hand of influence and the prevailing authority of installed standards of judgment—and how the effects of gender-specific valuing, editing, and explication can make a radical difference in the continuing life of the working poet.

Thinking about particular writers who shaped my early writing sensibility, I cannot find any direct H.D. imprint upon my poetics or practice, yet I know that somewhere along the line my mature writing has been significantly touched by her traces even though in the first decade of my exposure to modernist American poetry there was the now-documented, measurable obstacle blocking access to her writing.

I would guess that I first saw the initials "H.D." at the end of an anthologized poem sometime at the end of the sixties. No doubt that poem was one of the few safe and untouchable Imagist poems that editors began recirculating around that time to represent her work. We would later discover a much more complex, fecund, and demanding literary production. But for the moment, lacking any particular professor's or admired poet's passion for this mythic and (what seemed to me) very austere and impersonal voice, and swarmed as I was by every possible kind of innovative or jazzy poetic example, I was not available to H.D.'s spiritual and generative gift. I suspect that even if *Trilogy* or *Helen in Egypt* had been waved in my face at this time, I lacked sufficient conscious appetite for her alchemical and mythical vocabularies of transformation.

Eventually, in the mideighties, I had the opportunity to read *Trilogy* aloud with a small group of women poets and could finally hear H.D.'s voice, as if there were no longer any barrier. By then my inevitable share of human loss had prepared me.

In the sixties I was in love with everything that promised a fresh start and quite ready to shed a dominating mainstream "poetics of Self" that imposed its confessional hypnotic trance upon readers and young American writers. I was chafing at the confines of the typical "I"-centered, mainstream American poem that so theatrically and narcissistically positioned the writer at the hub of all pain and glory; it seemed reminiscent of pre-Renaissance science, before Galileo announced the radical news of his telescopic discovery:

Man is no longer at the center of the universe.

(H.D., of course, understood this afresh. The hierarchies forever asserting themselves were again toppled.)

Physics, action painting, field poetics, and new music—as well as fuller readings of Woolf and new encounters with Richardson, Moore, and Stein, the New York School, the Black Mountain poets, and the Objectivists—had all been registering a different dynamic involving energy fields, shifting contexts, and a self no longer credibly unitary but divided and subdivided until uncertainty called into question any writing too satisfied with its own personal suffering or too narrowly focused on cleverness and polish.

My devotion and intellectual curiosity had been claimed instead by a dozen highly inventive, nontraditional sorts of poets. I imagined, then, that I was equally open to all poetry, but, in fact, I was a young reader and writer, prone to the excitement of what I thought of as a high-modern tone and syntax, one whose surface diction and visual field promised to carry me away from what had begun to feel like the dangerous trap of lyric habit and ever closer to my own increasingly idiosyncratic compositions. I did not want to write within a language tradition too easily understood, too clearly part of an agenda rubber-stamped by most mainstream journals, but I had not yet articulated for myself the reasons for my resistance or the power relations dictating the limits of what I felt antagonistic toward.

The contemplative, as a desired place of knowledge, was beyond me; the contemporary implications and uses of myth hadn't yet hit— I mean, the understanding that myth is ahistoric, breathing in us and not merely confined to a narrative of the ancient past.

The seventies and eighties revealed a different grid, a detour meant to flaw the convenient, intact, uniform story of influence. As it turned out, H.D.'s linking of "hermetic" assignations with "secret language" and her conscious rejection of single-version narratives would become central in helping to define my own poetic process. It was not that I wanted to write *like* her but, rather, that I began hearing her urgency and experiencing in her work a kind of female enspiriting guide that I'd been lacking.

Constructing and *re*constructing this episodic moment across the space of my own blank pages, I finally understood that H.D. had used the scaffolding of locked-up myth to regenerate lopsided human stories with a new infusion of contemporary perspective. This meant the possibility—for herself and her readers—of being more fully included in the ongoing pursuit of knowledge and thus less personally stuck in the isolation of private anguish. There was, as it turned out, a place in language—even in its zero beginnings—to put one's trust.

"I am not of that feather": Kathleen Fraser's Postmodernist Poetics

CYNTHIA HOGUE

Breaking rules, breaking boundaries, crossing over, going where you've been told not to go has increasingly figured in the writing of the contemporary woman poet as a natural consequence of the restraints placed upon her as a child being socialized to the female role her class and culture prefer. The poem becomes her place to break rank.
                              Kathleen Fraser, "Line. On the Line"

we know no rule
of procedure,

we are voyagers, discoverers
of the not-known,

the unrecorded;
we have no map;   H.D., *Trilogy*

Influence is a mysterious process of invitation, trust, and intuitive intertextual engagement, as Kathleen Fraser's essay in this volume details. Fraser gives us a fascinating insight into a postmodern woman poet's bringing-to-consciousness of a "lost" modernist foremother. As such, it provides the basis for what will be my point of departure: H.D. did not "influence" Fraser in the conventional sense of reading an older writer as model in a young poet's formative years and absorbing (and denying) that predecessor's style. Rather, devoted to "intellectual curiosity," productive of an oeuvre that tracks and investigates process, that thoughtfully challenges and linguistically reforms itself, Fraser encountered H.D. as "enspiriting guide" at a crucial transitional period in her career.

The changes that feminist consciousness-raising had brought about by the 1970s enabled Fraser to trust her own artistic intuition and to explore possibilities of creative process that H.D. helped her to hear (Fraser repeatedly casts her response to hearing H.D. in terms of trust). As she remarks about her long sequence, "Etruscan Pages" (1993), for example, "Without H.D.'s precedent, it is very unlikely that I would have trusted my own particular rendering of the historic clues and layers of the Etruscan culture or understood the urgency of articulating another reading of it in the face of all the officially recognized studies preceding me, including [D. H.] Lawrence's narrative." Hearing a literary mother after a generation of silence encourages Fraser not to mute her own "rendering" because of a powerful paternal precedent.

Absent from the college reading lists of the 1950s and 1960s (like most of the other great female-authored modernist texts), H.D.'s work was represented in anthologies, if included at all, by a few of the early, Imagist poems by which she often remained anthologized until quite recently.[1] In the New York of the 1960s, "swarmed as I was by every possible kind of innovative or jazzy poetic example," Fraser simply couldn't "hear H.D.'s voice." Moving to San Francisco by the end of the decade, however, Fraser began to encounter H.D.'s voice indirectly, filtered through prominent Black Mountain poets like Robert Duncan and Robert Creeley.[2] By the 1970s and 1980s, feminist critics revealed for Fraser "a different grid, a detour meant to *flaw* the convenient, intact, uniform story of influence"; their critical work helped Fraser to understand H.D. in a way that opened up poetic possibilities:

> H.D.'s linking of "hermetic" assignations with "secret language" and her conscious rejection of single-version narratives would become central in helping to define my own poetic process. . . . I began hearing her urgency and experiencing in her work a kind of female enspiriting guide that I'd been lacking. . . . I finally understood that H.D. had used the scaffolding of locked-up myth to regenerate lopsided human stories with a new infusion of the contemporary perspective. . . . There was . . . a place . . . to put one's trust.

It is clear that Fraser never aspired consciously to imitate H.D.'s honed, signatory style. Quite the contrary: Fraser's essay celebrates H.D. rather for her invitation *not* to imitate, for her *blanking out* of inherited structures and her multiplying of "single-version" fictions. H.D. gives Fraser the poetic means to possess herself ("enspirits" her), to generate her own poetic structures, in turn helping her to define and orient herself. H.D. does not place *her* (as in locking her into place, fixing her in relation to Eliotic Tradition) but gives her a place *for* her "trust." This placement enables Fraser to gain confidence in her own "particular rendering." She headily celebrates H.D. for helping her to leap, as it were, into an emptiness she also sees because of H.D.'s work (H.D.'s "blank page" emptied of previous presence).

In 1983 Kathleen Fraser founded *HOW(ever)*, a journal established to bridge the gap between feminist scholars and experimental women poets, providing a place for "commentary on neglected [modernist/postmodernist] women poets who were/are making textures and structures of poetry in the tentative region of the untried."[3] H.D. is discussed often in the journal's pages over its nine years of publication, with entries by such major H.D. critic-poets as Rachel Blau DuPlessis, Adalaide Morris, Barbara Guest, and Alicia Ostriker (among others). Volume 3 (October 1986) celebrates H.D.'s centennial year with an issue "of writings in which the sign, the mark, the utterance of the unconscious comes through into present voice, with ancient echoes hovering."[4] The issue includes a substantial list of publications honoring H.D. (there were special issues, for example, of *AGENDA* and the *Iowa Review*) as well as an announcement for an Emily Dickinson/H.D. Dual Centennial Conference to be held at San Jose State University. In *HOW(ever)*'s final issue in 1992, Fraser quotes the lines alluded to above from *Trilogy* (which were fast becoming feminism's mots justes); H.D. then gets the last word in the issue, reiterating Fraser's quotation of those lines:

> she carries a book but it is not
> the tome of the ancient wisdom,
>
> the pages, I imagine, are the blank pages
> of the unwritten volume of the new;   (1973: 103)

They also conclude the publication as a whole. Out of context, the quotation functions not simply to reproduce but to reinterpret H.D.'s original reference to a transformed, and transformative, feminine spirituality, becoming an ongoing and ever-renewing "invitation" to pursue a new ("untried") feminist poetics beyond the frame of both *Trilogy* and *HOW(ever)*.

The second quotation used as epigraph above, another famous passage from *Trilogy*, is also employed as epigraph in "The Blank Page," in which Fraser spells out her sense that "H.D. is issuing a *literal* invitation" (my emphasis). In her opening paragraph, Fraser recontextualizes H.D.'s mystical "not-known" (i.e., of esoteric wisdom), rendering it very specifically the "unsaid" of one woman's historical experience. Fraser thereby leaps from the epigraph about "no rule" to an opening discussion that contemplates H.D.'s particular refusal of the pervasive, inherited "rules of procedure" that surrounded her in her youth. But the epigraph that refers us to *Trilogy* also, we discover by perusing *HOW(ever)*, refers us to an excerpt of Alicia Ostriker's essay on H.D., "No Rule of Procedure: H.D. and Open Poetics."[5] Asking how the poem's music contributes to its meaning, Ostriker suggests that "we are being *invited to trust* not a still point outside of ourselves, transcending this world, but our own interiority" (my emphasis). Astutely characterizing *Trilogy*'s paradoxical formalism as "neither rhymed nor not-rhymed," Ostriker goes on to enumerate some of the many "interior sound-echoes":

> *(here) there / (your) square / colour / hare . . . (there as here), enter /*
> *doors, (here) there, endures, (everywhere) air; fissure / endure fire / floor /*
> *terror / ember / what for?*   (Friedman and DuPlessis 1990: 21)

"By intensifying the overlap of sound," observes Meredith Stricker about H.D.'s signatory, Imagist poem "Oread," "H.D. creates expectations that the reader rushes to fill. . . . Every rhyme invokes the reader's consideration of semantic as well as sound similarities." Stricker aptly calls the reverberations of semantic, aural, and visual associations *"ghost rhymes"*: "the aural equivalent to palimpsest" (1989: 19). Thus, readers experience this "sound-play," as Ostriker terms it, not only as rhyme but also as formal and thematic premise: "that order, beauty and meaning remain permanently present in our shattered world, but not permanently obvious, and that the way to recover them is through the receptive psychic states of dream and vision" (Friedman and DuPlessis 1990: 21). Having accepted H.D.'s invitation to trust our "interiority" (our dreams and visions), we open to hearing the meaningful "sound-echoes" of the poem, which, Ostriker implies, reverberate beyond the poetic frame.

Invitation, hearing, trust. These recurring words indicate a process of attention that catalyzes poetic invention. Coincident with her learning about H.D., Fraser speaks in her 1989 essay, "The Tradition of Marginality," of encountering a "different kind of attentive [in the works of postmodern women poets]: . . . a listening attitude, an attending to unconscious connections, a backing-off of the performing ego to allow the mysteries of language to come forward and resonate more fully" (1989: 25). Stricker writes that the "more I read H.D., the more I feel loosened from categories." She suggests that H.D. created a "new species" of "literary form" (Stricker 1989: 1). Being receptive to "the other world" of "what wants to be said," as Fraser describes it ("Line on Line"), involves "a new structure of trust in one's discovered (not received) relationship with language and all that language encloses," Linda Kinnahan asserts (1994: 26). Hearing H.D. coincided with, and enspirited, Fraser's own process of discovery as she began to write poems that "make us see the world through a lens that would subvert, at their linguistic-perceptual root, habits of consciousness comfortable with the predominant cultural givens," as Marianne DeKoven puts it (quoted in Kinnahan 1994: 227). Fraser readily acknowledges that in her work she tries to "do something syntactically that will disturb or shift [a] person's way of reading," as she remarked during a 1997 MLA roundtable discussion on the long poem, in order to maintain what Peter Quartermain has described as "a vital perturbability" (Crown 1998).

I have been exploring a few of the Brief Commentaries, Alerts, and Postcards from *HOW(ever)*'s pages in some detail to give a sense of how much H.D.'s work and aesthetics permeated Fraser's intellectual and artistic milieu from the mid-1970s to early 1990s. As I leafed through the issues of *HOW(ever)*, I was struck by how often H.D. was discussed; every few issues there was an entry or two throughout the years of publication, as well as announcements about scholarly and critical publications, some excerpted briefly in *HOW(ever)*, like Ostriker's essay. In addition to some of the very specific reconsiderations and astute formal analyses of H.D.'s work, there are myriad kinds of other references: fascinating, informal scholarship (one entry by Virginia Smyers, for example, the librarian cataloging Bryher's books, detailing Smyers's discovery of H.D.'s annotations of a book on Christian mysticism [October 1986]); an extension of H.D.'s primary methodology to her poet-biographer in a lovely "Palimpsest for Barbara Guest" by Dale Going (summer 1991); even H.D.'s response to a 1929 questionnaire "What would you most like to do . . . ?" (H.D. was making films at the time: "I should like more than anything to . . . wander in and about Italian and Swiss hills making light do what I want" [April 1988]). I suggest that the layers of such references, in the context of the flowering of Second Wave and poststructuralist feminist scholarship on H.D. and other women writers, as well as feminist experimental writing in the 1980s, comprise a sort of cultural palimpsest, in H.D.'s sense of the term.

In her important essay on the line in postmodern poetry, Fraser in fact invokes the term in order to build on H.D.'s work as model for postmodernist women's writing:

> H.D. introduced the concept of the *palimpsest*: writing "on top of" other writing which . . . has been imperfectly erased . . . ; *this* moment in history is *re*-inscribed over the faded . . . messages of a female collective consciousness, a spiritual and erotic set of valuings essentially ignored by the dominant culture.   (1988: 155)

Fraser's revisionary "female collective consciousness" engenders linguistic traces ("messages") that coincide within the palimpsest, not only creating imaginary intersections where there could be none in history but also reinventing in the present what has been lost (Hogue 1999). Such a reinvention can never be whole or precise, however, and is achieved not through reproduction (the erasure of significant differences) but by having established affinities: a shared "spiritual and erotic set of valuings." Noting that a Fraser poem works like "a linear poem [but] in a deconstructed space," Kinnahan suggests that the structures of Fraser's work require "a reading and thinking in layers" (1994: 215)—that is to say, a palimpsestic, critical reading strategy.

To understand how Fraser's work responds to H.D.'s poetic project, it is useful to think of the "layers" in Fraser's work—the "bits and pieces of language, single words, alphabet fragments," to borrow Fraser's own description of "the palimpsest notion" (1988: 155)—as "potent" fragments full of insights discovered through or during, despite or even because of, the accidents of interruption. As she puts it in her afterword: "that in fragment lay potency" (Fraser 1997: 195). "The fragmented, broken up, interrupted time" out of which women writers have always tried to write—the traces of which Fraser conceptualizes and integrates into her work, rather than attempts to erase—works for her as an important creative principle (Crown 1998). We can approach these layers archaeo/logically, as excavations of levels of sociocultural experience embedded in and juxtaposed among personal and literary intersections. The creative/formal interactions produce—and are produced by—discovery: flashes of insight often catalyzed by the "merely" accidental. "The accidents / interest me," Fraser writes. A prose poem, "this. notes. new year.," for example, records the process of a woman's realizing, through the accident of a typo, that she has a very different relationship to "flaws" than the one she has inherited: "She wanted a 'flow' she thought, but in the translation it was corrected, displacing the *o* and substituting *a*. She could give herself to an accident" (Fraser 1997: 39).[6] In Fraser's ironic corrective of tradition, "flaw" (as in, traditionally, of feminine character) displaces "flow" (as in aesthetically pleasing), and conscious desire is "corrected" not by punishment but by "translation" (a typo leading to metaphor and insight [the self-as-gift]): an "accident" to which the woman can "give herself."

I want to consider specifically how Fraser's postmodernist work extends H.D.'s modernist poetics by turning to the last poem included in Fraser's selected poems, *Il Cuore: The Heart* (1997), a serial poem in ten parts, entitled "WING." As Fraser details in a recent interview, the series emerged from "seemingly disconnected levels" of social and historical context (several of which remind us of H.D.'s traumatic residence in London during the Blitz): the illness and death of a close friend from AIDS; two exhibits by artist Mel Bochner in Rome (one at the Museo Storico della Liberazione) that caused Fraser to ruminate about Italian fascist and Nazi imprisonment of Jews, Gypsies, and Resistance fighters during World War II; the archaeo/logical remnants of imperial Roman history evident in the architectural layers of Roman walls (becoming Fraser's palimpsestic *arche/text*); and (perhaps the most unconscious coincidence of Fraser with H.D.'s *Trilogy*) Fraser's fascination from childhood with the spiritual iconography of angels and wings.[7] Produced with visionary intensity during the London Blitz, *Trilogy* poignantly enspirits "WING," I would like to suggest, with its "haunting" by the history of Rome and World War II, by angels, by death, and, not least, by its invitation to inscribe "the blank pages / of the unwritten volume of the new."

"WING" opens with this direct allusion to *Trilogy*:

> The New comes forward in its edges in order to be
>   itself;

> its volume by necessity becomes violent and
>   three-dimensional
> and ordinary, all similar models shaken off and smudged
>
> .   .   .   .
>
> as if each dream or occasion of pain had tried to lift
>   itself
> entirely away, contributing to other corners, planes and
> accumulated depth.   (Fraser 1997: 184)

Because of "the new" at which H.D. arrived, Fraser is able to open with "The New." Most obviously, of course, Fraser's "New" isn't "unwritten" but writerly—"in order to be itself," it has "shaken off and smudged" all other "similar models." Where H.D.'s work pauses conceptually ("the unwritten volume"), Fraser continues with a graphic description of the palimpsest as material object on which new writing smudges and partially erases the earlier scripts. Fraser's text inscribes "The New" by describing what has for her become its concrete "volume" (through concretized wordplay)—imaginatively materialized, an entity both with real edges and edged with rhetoricized play between the abstract and concrete ("as if memory were an expensive thick creamy paper and every / corner turned now in partial erasure").

In Fraser's "New," the palimpsestic fragments of thought, observation, "nested" quotations, phrases, sentences, words separate from each other coincide, sometimes combine. The four verbal cubes of part 2, "First Black Quartet: Via Tasso," for example, depict what Fraser describes as "the breaking up of matter and its reformation"[8]:

> A cube's clean volume   shatters and reassembles
> its daily burnt mark   the New is used and goes
> backwards . . .
>
> .   .   .   .
>
> to unfold in expand   ing brilliant traces or
> stars: "that which   is known to us" or just
> improvised . . .
> picking, pecking at   our skins ghost or angel
> sent to tell us what   we didn't want to know
>   (Fraser 1997: 185)

The four spatially related cubes of part 2 illustrate a number of Fraser's formal innovations that echo H.D. (with all the aspects of distortion that accompany the phenomenon of echo). In Fraser's serious wordplay, "the New is used." Patterns of thinking, the mindset of line and power that H.D.'s *Trilogy* contemplates urgently as well, are shattered and reassembled ("that which is known to us"). Formal improvisation and visual/aural association ("picking, pecking") expand upon the semantic possibilities explored in H.D.'s aurally excessive but visually "contained" poetics.[9] H.D.'s revisionary "Tribute to the Angels" becomes, in Fraser's postmodern layering of loss, much less certain or reassuring: "ghost or angel" comes to tell us what "we didn't want to know"; a body-of-words (also a body-in-pieces) intersecting spatially so as to interact visually and semantically. Part 6, "Crossroads," for example, ends: "messenger: : wing"   (Fraser 1997: 189).

As a creative principle, fragmentation occupies an acknowledged, even exalted place in modernism, thanks to its best-known articulation by T. S. Eliot ("These fragments I have shored against my ruin"). Kinnahan persuasively argues, however, that in their paratactic collage and layers of "overlapping differences" (the term is Fraser's), Fraser's experimental compositions trace their roots to the work of William Carlos Williams, whose poetry in turn "carries the imprint of the women modernists"—Gertrude Stein, Marianne Moore, Mina Loy, and H.D. (1994: 218–36). Fraser's process of linguistic reassociation and the forms that "overlapping differences" create work to resist enculturated patterns of thought and to dislodge us from the received assumptions and perceptions to which we are attached. As she explores in "WING," we are very attached to words' attachments to each other (that is, to syntax and sense). Part 5, "Color: Via Della Penitenza," for instance, tracks the synthesizing, unifying leaps from partial, "retinal" glimpse to full-blown angelic vision:

> Even the New is attached or marked by attachment
>
> the shimmer of wing, which claim may tell us
>   everything
> in a white blink
>
> .   .   .   .   .   .
>
>   [an angel stands in technicolor as cosmonauts
>   look out
>   on   Jet-liner wingspan   attaching itself
>   collectively]

> these retinal bodies larger, remarkable for their
> iridescence   (Fraser 1997: 188)

In this passage, the signifying ability of a phrase like "marked by attachment" is enhanced by the very process of detachment, the materiality of which it both records and illustrates. The section refers to both narrative fragments embedded inside it (the cosmonauts glimpse a jet's wings and see an angel) and readers' extratextual, interactive process of (re)attaching syntactically what Fraser's text has detached (as I have here, to discuss the passage, as well). Imaginatively, we thereby *hear* with enhanced consciousness the levels that Fraser's poem activates, "loosening" ourselves from static "identity," from the "familiar," from the "known," as section 4, "Line," suggests (Fraser 1997: 187).

Finally, the poem opens to what Fraser herself has discussed as "covert error leading to unimpeded risk" and unfettered insight (quoted in Quartermain 1997: xi). Through an "accident" produced by the formal experimentation that she was conducting, section 10, "Vanishing Point: Third Black Quartet," concretely materializes "WING":

forward edge itself to be volume by necessity as if partial	erase
edge itself to be volume by necessity as if partial erase	other
itself to be volume by necessity as if partial erase	corners
to be volume by necessity as if partial erase	planes
be volume by necessity as if partial erase	accumulate
volume by necessity as if partial erase	depth
by necessity as if partial erase	condensed
necessity as if partial erase	in
as if partial erase	preparation
if partial erase	stagework
partial erase	historic
	tendons

(Fraser 1997: 193)

Fraser describes the process of writing this last section as the unplanned, formal contextualization of an "out-of-context" experience. An experiment with mechanical/formal repetition leads to a visual discovery (the shape of a wing) and an insight that "being taken outside of my normal frames of reference" catalyzes (Hogue 1998).[10] As she elaborates in her afterword, "Isn't the typo, after all, a word trying to escape its single-version identity? It wants deciphering. Just as the alphabet is 'at large,' so is the fugitive identity of the poem . . . on the prowl, looking for its next escape from the already known" (Fraser 1997: 197; Fraser's ellipsis). Hearing the reverberations and resonances of (among others) H.D.'s etymological wordplay, loosening her own approach to language and form from the poetically familiar as well as social and cultural hierarchies of dominance, Fraser "break[s] boundaries, cross[es] over," as she puts it in the passage from "Line. On the Line." quoted as my first epigraph. As such, she defamiliarizes world and word through a particular, gendered, and historical consciousness, because, she writes in the essay's closing, a "woman wants to fly" (Fraser 1988: 174). In winging it, "WING" opens its wings to the poetically possible or, put another way, to the ecstatically "New"—"itself the wing not static but frayed, layered, fettered, furling" (Fraser 1997: 193).

NOTES

1. By analogy, of course, it's as if Pound were represented solely by "In a Station of the Metro" and "The River Merchant's Wife."

2. Duncan began publishing portions of his *H.D. Book* by the late 1960s. Although teaching in the East, Creeley spent half of every year around San Francisco throughout the 1970s. My own initial exposure to H.D. occurred, as a matter of fact, in the spring of 1974, when at SUNY/Buffalo I took an independent study with Creeley, who gave me his 1973 New Directions edition of *Trilogy*, mentioning that I might be interested in H.D.'s work. I have cherished the gift for many years now, although we never talked about H.D.'s poetry, and it was never taught in his American modernism class (which focused on Pound, Williams, and Olson). Entranced by her jewel-like images and wordplay, I didn't really begin to understand H.D. until Susan Stanford Friedman published her groundbreaking *Psyche Reborn* in the following decade.

3. Fraser, "WHY HOW(ever)?" *HOW(ever)* 1, no. 1 (May 1983): 1. *HOW(ever)* was published for nine years, founded and edited by Fraser along with Frances Jaffer, Beverly Dahlen, Rachel Blau DuPlessis, and Carolyn Burke (among others over the years). I am grateful to Linda Kinnahan's groundbreaking critical work on *HOW(ever)*, first presented as a panel paper, "'A Peculiar Hybrid': The Feminist Project of *HOW(ever)*, Then and Now." A longer critical work is in progress.

4. See *HOW(ever)* 3, no. 3 (October 1986): 15.

5. Ostriker, "No Rule of Procedure," *HOW(ever)* 5, no. 4 (October 1989): 20–21, excerpted from a talk by Ostriker at the E.D./H.D. Conference, San Jose State University, 1987. The essay's full text was published in *Signets*, ed. Susan Stanford Friedman and Rachel Blau DuPlessis.

6. Quartermain also discusses this formal principle in Fraser's work (1997: xi). Fraser has discussed "accidents" and "errors" as principles of invention both in a recent interview (see Hogue 1998) and in Crown (1998).

7. As she remarks in her interview with the author, "I had been thinking for years about angels in Italian art, going back to my childhood connection to certain biblical passages, and the presence of angels in Rilke's elegies. What were they? Why is it that we have such an extensive iconography of wings, passed down in different religious traditions? What actually has happened to people who experience angels? I'd been collecting pictures of wings." On the pervasive iconography of angels in London during World War II, in the context of which H.D. composed *Trilogy*, see Schweik (1991).

8. In her recent interview, Fraser describes at length her emotional response to Mel Bochner's drawings of "cube forms hurtling through space" and his 1993 installation, *Via Tasso*, mounted at the Museo Storico della Liberazione di Roma, originally an apartment where the Italian fascists and Nazis had imprisoned Jews. This installation consisted of three six-pointed stars formed entirely of burnt match sticks. To Fraser, who has dedicated "WING" to the memory of a friend who died of AIDS, Bochner's work catalyzed the memories of personal and historical loss. See Hogue (1998).

9. One need only think of a passage illustrating H.D.'s linguistic, alchemical transformations formalized in couplets as an example:

> Now polish the crucible
> and in the bowl distill
>
> a word most bitter, *marah*,
> a word bitterer still, *mar*,
>
> .   .   .   .
>
> and change and alter,
> mer, mere, mère, mater, Maia, Mary,
>
> Star of the Sea,
> Mother. (1973: 71)

10. See also Stewart (1995) for an analysis of the attempt to convey within the space of the poem the quality of inspiration and transport that reputedly catalyzed it.

Three Thoughts on *Trilogy*

BRENDA HILLMAN

I have been asked to consider whether H.D. has influenced my work. Am I qualified to speak to the question? Do I have any temptation to lie? No to the first question; of course to the second. Poets lie about their influences because they believe that their originality lies in their singularities rather than in their unique power to speak past those singularities into the collective bounty of their age. If we admit to influences, we might lose the small credit we have accrued and can redeem for the image by which we can remake ourselves "at the end." But everyone is interested in the constructs inventors make about their sources, in how often they are coy when asked about whom they envy, will not name the inspiration for their verbal gestures and torques of phrase and syntax or anything else; frankly, this can be seen as any other form of play that writers engage in, even *sincere* ones, and shouldn't be worried about too much. Of course we don't name them. We don't even know them. I love thinking about these matters, especially in writers of genius like Dickinson who probably had her whole world turned twice on its axis by some tiny, wild, dangly turn of phrase gleaned from one of the Brontës. And so what if she did? Good for everyone. Influences come less from specific ancestors than they come from verbal climates or trends or tendencies set up by excellent poems, from what is popular, whether it is excellent or not (it well may be), and from waves of suggestiveness that writers, in their thin-skinned sensitivities, catch from the environment, the way single-celled pond animals know what nutrients to use from the watery goop that floats past them.

Like any writer, I've thought a lot about the influences I have been aware of having and have not thought about the influences I've not been aware of having. I don't think I can speak with any objectivity about whether H.D.'s influence is observable in *Death Tractates*, and what the reader might conclude from the disclaimer offered above is that I wish to hide some influence I am aware of. I prefer to address how her poems—or, perhaps, more fairly, how her poetic system—might be useful to contemporary writers, to how she was helpful to me, in the broadest sense as a poet who gave permission, and to voice some doubts I've had. In this task I've had three appreciative thoughts and three complaints that are also thoughts.

I read *Trilogy* in the mideighties in a reading group that consisted of women—mostly poets who work in what are now clumsily called "experimental" or "innovative" forms. I had not studied H.D.'s work before but had read it casually in anthologies. Reading the book at that time—Reagan was still in office making the three-trillion-dollar national debt, the stuffed Garfield dolls with suction cups were starting to appear, people were getting comfortable with their PCs—was enlightening, but enlightening like that moment in spring when you see daffodils around telephone poles—the odd news has always been there underground, next to something that resembles it. H.D. reminded me of some luminous news, although the something that resembled her— Robert Duncan, Kathleen Fraser, and others—had been in my life long before.

What struck me first in *Trilogy* was the largeness of her use of various orthodoxies. Instructed by the sweep of the three meditations in that book, I saw her as the first woman poet to make a triangular relationship between religious and mythological knowledge, historical material, and heterodox artistic practice. It is the blending of mythmaking and art-making that seems most striking and ambitious in her work as she invokes and announces, approximates to epic, makes grand encampments, stalwartly but vaguely conjuring deities in the face of the terrors of war. At the opening of "The Walls Do Not Fall," describing the bombing of London in spare, unornamented tercets, she also reports on the opening of the tomb at Luxor, setting up the connection between an act of revelation and many acts of destruction. This opening—bold and magical—suggests a triumph of the inside over the outside. Like the other modernists, she calls upon us to look even at complete devastation in light of the works of human imagination, and because, from the outset, the task seems futile, she immediately implores Spirit and asks what is salvageable about civilization.

When twentieth-century artists try to invent or reinvent the gods they rarely seem to believe that there is a retrievable innocence in this task or even in the inverted figures themselves. In appealing to the old Egyptian gods at the outset, H.D. wants to bring into alignment the ancient functions of the tripartite deities—poetry, magic, and healing. She calls for the spells, the caduceus, the power of the craftsmen. The old god/artist/helper is invoked and remade personally and impersonally. Especially instructive is the way she remakes the Magus/Magician/Hermes figure—or recovers him—at the start of the poem: "He is Mage / bringing myrrh." This powerful erotic figure comes from a time when poets were not useless trinkets in a utilitarian bellicose culture but dynamic makers of live dreams.

So I suppose the first thing to think about is the fact that she spoke of the real hope for the redeeming vision. Unafraid to confront the cultural values that would destroy books and the word, she makes an argument for the function of poetry and poets as a corrective for these horrors, though she doesn't offer a false utopianism in their stead. If the first poem of *Trilogy* has a kind of Coleridgean sorrow and darkness, the poet rallies by the end of that part to assume a role as a priestess, employing the ancient arts of magic, numerology, and alchemy for her purposes. So that's the first thing—her vision gives permission to think in the most inclusive sense about this task, this big druidic thing we are supposed to do, to connect the life of the soul and the making of art in a material world that doesn't recognize the divine or the human mysteries.

My complaint about this: it's not that the grandeur or even the grandiosity bothers me, it's that H.D.'s consciousness is singularly disconnected from the minute noticings that make for the most engaging forms of spiritual insight. In Dickinson there is vastness in those agonies of the spirit made possible by the tiny links of the need to get it right. H.D.'s concern is far less about this than it is about the great sweep of culture. The study of consciousness as it precedes (or makes) (or is at one with) (we still don't know) that culture—which is to me the most beautiful reason to read poetry—is less a concern for her. The compensatory system of angels and linkages, lovely as they are, often leaves me hungry for the study of a perception of that irremediable agony of being alive, of some specific but deeply general human pain that has qualities, various attributes that a great poet makes something new from. I went on reading despite this complaint.

The second thing I found was that H.D. attempts to reveal, rather than to conjure, an absolute metaphysical weirdness. Here I look to the second of *Trilogy*'s meditations, "Tribute to the Angels." The poem doesn't reject its own pluralism while assembling the apparatus for an essentially feminist vision. I love her weirdness. In a stiff—you could almost say nude-*with-clothes-on*,-descending-the-staircase—image she brings the Lady into the poem after covering a lot of spiritual mileage, from Hermes, to John, to angels and Mary, going from figure to figure as if visiting relatives in small midwestern towns, plain-ness, no antics, but also no sentimentality. If in her descriptions of buildings she gets to use exotic solids like jasper and lapis, she seems to go for the stripped-down deity, and thus the Lady comes almost as plain vanilla, the multipurpose goddess figure with many artists' hands laying a touch here and there. This figure has without a doubt had a huge impact on my work—and not just mine, the work of many other writers, including Duncan and Barbara Guest. In admiring H.D.'s stew of gods and spiritual presences, I learned that the human imagination, when it confronts what it might think of as god-ness, metaphysical abstraction, or even traditional religious iconography, doesn't have to be the agent of an impossible narrowness that we usually associate with belief. Another way of saying this is that she allowed me to go deeper and be strange, even inconsistent, in a worldview I felt I had inherited from inward traditions of American Protestantism and all the Western occult and esoteric traditions that had laced it like swirls of chocolate in marble fudge. H.D., quite simply, gave a sense about what needed to be remade.

What was most instructive about this figure of the Lady as I encountered her for the first time, marching slowly down, was that H.D. was enacting a revision of the visionary method. The figure of the Lady, appearing in her joyous, teasing, sort of sexy-mommy mood as Psyche, the anima, imagination, Venus, Aphrodite, you name it, carries the Book of Possibility, and this development of the goddess snatched simultaneously from tradition and personal sources is legible as a figure for the artist in our time. The dream comes in the middle. We want Gabriel but we get the Lady who steps down canyons, the one whom we cannot hold, ever, but who gives us everything. I was enchanted by the state of delirium H.D. described; it coincided with some experiences of reverie I had had in which an unnamed figure comes simultaneously as a helper and as a muse but who maybe turned into a pet image, the way a painted

Mexican mask that has been carved by a single hand to reinvent a single soul may also appeal to the generalized need.

The problem I encountered with this figure—this is my complaint—is the humorlessness and the occasional sanctimoniousness of the sacred one and of the speaker's relationship to her—not so much the polemical earnestness of the whole routine since, as I say, I had bought the nine-island cruise package early on, recognizing that H.D. works in circles of symbolic possibility. But writing like

> We see her visible and actual,
> beauty incarnate,
>
> as no high-priest of Astoroth
> could compel her
>
> with incense
> and potent spell;
>
> we asked for no sign
> but she gave a sign unto us;   (1973: 82)

makes me just want to jab my finger in H.D.'s swooning middle and say, "Stop fakin' it, girl, let's go outside and smoke." The weightiness in general—and in specific—of all the arcane presentation, however forceful and amazing it can be, of one figure after another makes me laugh, almost in the same way that watching certain rock videos in hotel rooms makes me laugh, not exactly with a snort but just with an "uh, yeah, right," though when rock videos are humorless it's exactly because they can reflect an awareness of how absurd the initial propositions are, and this is not a bit true of H.D.; she makes a reader wish the decor of the fairly tacky sublime were not so unironically gaudy and that there were a lot more displays of antic shame, or at least that the invisible that is promised had a few more tattoos of lizards and snakes.

Probably responding to the humorlessness and grandiosity was part of my purpose in *Death Tractates*. In many metaphors of religious rescue, the soteriological figures leave the rescued one with the nausea of intense longing even while arriving thoroughly; responding to *Trilogy*'s weightiness, though I admired its oracular dualism, I devised a speaker who makes asides and hesitates and makes a few jokes while she gives up having a "satisfying" relationship to the spirit world she so craves. The saviors function in a daily way rather than existing in a heaven the speaker believes exists and can't reach; this quotidian, with all its DMV papers and camellias and library slots and mockingbirds, keeps the lost body in the world as a paratactic accomplice of yearning. I don't suppose my vision is any more or less dualistic than H.D.'s, for all that, but I'm interested in the erotic besideness of the other in a different way, perhaps because it's cozier and sillier and more remote. Possibly writing about the spirit world can never be funny enough if the job for the first half of life is to grieve the passing of everything. I don't know what the main job for the second half is, quite yet. I suspect it's more fun.

And finally, along with the big historical vision and the specific metaphysical weirdness, hers is a craft that is simultaneously restless and obsessive. In her formal decisions, H.D. was trying to enact the only thing possible for an ecstatic introvert: she was trying to have it both ways. Therefore, her forms—though they are not entirely successful—are ambitious. Her relentless attempt to achieve such an epic range—not only in *Trilogy* but in *Helen in Egypt*—in a minimalist manner is heartbreakingly earnest. The vision of an evolving self has to do with resurrected beauty—the magical Christ in "Flowering of the Rod," the Lady in "Tribute to the Angels," and Hermes in "The Walls Do Not Fall"—and juxtaposes the linearity of existence to cyclical time, as do all epics. By trying to be simultaneously big and skinny, like the girl who is the first one to grow very tall in seventh grade, her spare, long strips of telling inspire respect. The writing is best when the account turns to story because experience is so long and invisible and ungainly. At the same time, she so yearns to achieve the Imagist's ideal for relaxed directness and lyrical naming.

It is at the level of the units that most matter to me in writing—the unit of the word, the phrase, and the sentence—that H.D. fails me. I know this is heretical to say, but though I find the idea of her ideas astounding, I do *not* feel the desire to memorize her poems line by line, to remember her great tricks, to say them to myself like Demosthenes with pebbles in my mouth until I can recite them, to sleep with her books under my pillow the way I have with the intense poetry loves. Finally, it's this in the notion of influence that matters most: that the music of the language is most changed by a new being inside of it,

simply because some new awareness—let's call it an author—has inhabited it in a different way, made love to it, made it her helper and
sister. In lines like

> Invisible, indivisible Spirit,
> how is it you come so near,

> how is it that we dare
> approach the high-altar?

> we crossed the charred portico,
> passed through a frame—doorless—

> entered a shrine; like a ghost,
> we entered a house through a wall;   (1973: 83)

there is great deal of wasted language and one really bad image—a
ghost through a wall. What would have been more interesting is an
accurate perception of the experience that could take us past the ghost
going through a wall. It is because she never quite enchanted me ver-
bally that she is probably a bigger influence on me than I know, and I
have wanted to talk back to her, to hover in uncertainty and to ask her
to keep me company in the next making.

"The Blank Pages of the Unwritten Volume of the New": Gnosticism in H.D.'s *Trilogy* and Brenda Hillman's *Death Tractates*

ALIKI BARNSTONE

H.D. wrote *Trilogy* out of the crisis of World War II; she writes, "that outer threat and constant reminder of death drove me inward." In *Trilogy* H.D. synthesizes Gnosticism, the Judeo-Christian theological tradition, and the Egyptian and Greek pagan traditions and comes up with a healing spiritual answer to war: "though there was whirr and roar in the high air, / there was a Voice louder" (1973: 12). That voice, which H.D. calls "Dream, / Vision" (1973: 11), seeks to bring together opposing forces: Word and Sword, spirit and matter, male and female, monotheism and polytheism, the old and the new. For H.D., hope rises out of utter destruction in the figure of "Our Lady," a synthesis of pagan goddesses and Mary who carries a book whose pages "are the blank pages of the unwritten volume of the new" (1973: 38).

Like H.D., Brenda Hillman is driven inward by crisis, uses Gnosticism as a major source, is inspired by a feminine spiritual force, and emphasizes the regenerative power of the word and her own creativity. For both poets, crisis collapses established epistemologies and leads to a revision of Gnosticism and of male-centered theology. Hillman's work can be seen as part of a resurgence of women's spiritual poetry, for which H.D. is a precursor. In this essay I'm most interested in the cue Hillman took from H.D. about how to revise theology and how to have the courage to be large-minded, to have "real hope for the redeeming vision," and, as a maker of art, to take on the enormous philosophical and spiritual questions. Hillman writes in her essay in this volume: "So that's the first thing—[H.D.'s] vision gives permission to think in the most inclusive sense about this task, this big druidic thing we are supposed to do, to connect the life of the soul and the making of art in a material world that doesn't recognize the divine or the human mysteries."

Hillman is honest about the ways in which poets are reluctant to reveal their influences, for such admissions about influence threaten their originality. Emily Dickinson, too, demurred when faced with the question of influence: "I never touch a paint mixed by another." Hillman points out that influence is not monolithic or traceable or linear: "Influences come less from specific ancestors than they come from verbal climates . . . set up by excellent poems, from what is popular, . . . and from waves of suggestiveness that writers . . . catch from the environment, the way single-celled pond animals know what nutrients to use from the watery goop that floats past them." Hillman also reveals in her ambivalence about H.D. that influence does not come like fundamentalist belief, without questions, vexation, or friction. She is refreshingly salty in refusing to be sanctimonious about H.D., regardless of her precursor's status as a great spiritual poet, philosopher, and revisionary theologian. I believe that H.D. would appreciate this kind of confrontational honesty—after all, in her *Tribute to Freud*, she asserts, "The Professor was not always right" (1974: 18). Hillman's "complaints" about H.D. are as instructive about influence and the process of being influenced as are her "appreciative thoughts" about her "as a poet who gave permission."

Hillman complains that "H.D.'s consciousness is singularly disconnected from the minute noticings that make for the most engaging forms of spiritual insight," that her portrayal and relationship to the Lady is humorless and sanctimonious, and that her language is not musically enchanting. (I disagree with Hillman's complaint that H.D.'s music lacks the power to get the voodoo going. *Trilogy* is full of modernist music; H.D. does not write in form but she uses formal devices. Her echoes of biblical language and her ecstatic breath *are* enchanting to my ear, especially in "The Flowering of the Rod.") It is precisely Hillman's refusal to accept anything or anyone wholesale that empowers her to sing her own song while stealing some melodic lines from H.D., just as before her H.D. took from Freud. The precursor gives permission, but the artist who does not feel friction with her influence, who will not reject, will seem merely derivative. So Hillman in *Death Tractates* appropriates H.D.'s large-mindedness, her Lady, her female-centered theology and fuses these appropriations with her poetics, which include "minute noticings" and humor and her own musicality.

Hillman's willingness to be critical allows her to find within herself "what needs to be remade." She establishes the borders (a word repeated throughout *Death Tractates*) between her poetics and those of her precursors. Even her essay here is full of her own idiosyncratic humor and diction, as in the contrasts she creates between philosophically abstract Latinate or Greek and the thingy foundation of the English language: the "verbal climate" that influences poets becomes "watery goop that floats past them." When the Lady calls on Hillman to re-create her, H.D.'s creation invites her to set herself apart from the cosmology of *Trilogy*. This distancing is ironic and appropriate, Hillman acknowledges, even as she says that sometimes H.D.'s lines about the Lady make her want to "jab my finger in H.D.'s swooning middle and say, 'Stop fakin' it, girl, let's go outside and smoke.'"

Trilogy promotes heterodoxy, even as it resurrects aspects of Christian orthodoxy. "What struck me first in *Trilogy*," Hillman writes, "was the largeness of her use of various orthodoxies." H.D. uses her inheritance of American Protestantism "to go deeper and be strange" and invites other writers to do the same. Hillman remakes orthodoxies as well and uses Gnosticism as a generative force for her re-creation. (Her essay here is Gnostic in its defiant spirit, since in it she eschews blind faith and obedience to H.D.'s theology in favor of individual knowledge and vision.) In *Death Tractates* Hillman makes H.D.'s implicit debt to Gnosticism explicit: in her "Note about the Book," Hillman explains that many themes and sources of *Tractates* (and *Bright Existence*) are Gnostic (1992: vii). She lets her readers know that her books perform "the big druidic thing we are supposed to do," to connect the light of the soul with the material world, which is the central Gnostic duality and which she acknowledges H.D. allowed her to do. Hillman also uses her reading of Gnosticism to transform H.D.'s Gnostic lady, "the new Eve" (1973: 36), who is a myth, into a personal and intimate dead loved one to whom the speaker is calling.

Gnosticism is a potent spiritual alternative for women poets, since it emphasizes that the feminine principle is appropriately powerful, that the path to God is a knowledge of the self, not faith through the clergy's word, and that the human and divine are the same. In contrast to the traditional Judeo-Christian Eve, whose sin of disobedience is responsible for death and expulsion from Eden, in Gnosticism Eve is a heroine who, because she gave humanity the gift of knowledge, has the ultimate virtue. She challenged the biblical Creator God who by creating humanity made the error of trapping our light spirits in matter.

Hillman writes that "the poem is the story of the writing of itself"

(1992: 25). In *Death Tractates* that story evolves out of crisis, for as Hillman notes, "my closest female mentor died suddenly at a young age" (1992: vii). Her death interrupted the writing of the companion volume to *Death Tractates, Bright Existence*. Although *Death Tractates*, like *Bright Existence*, uses Gnosticism as its source, *Tractates* differs from what Hillman calls its "fat sister" by creating a new cosmology in which to perceive death and mourning. She connects the death of the beloved with the light of the soul that has returned to light, to the original larger source-light of the soul of which it was always a part. In "First Tractate" the soul

> . . . was very clever, stepping
> from Lightworld to lightworld
> as an egret fishes through its smeared reflections—
>
> through its deaths—
> for it believed in the one life,
> that it would last forever.   (Hillman 1992: 3)

The poem is the description of the living speaker questing toward the light of the dead beloved. The speaker calls to her who

> . . . had become invisible,
> . . . had become subtle
> among the shapes—
>
> and at first she didn't answer; everything
> answered.   (Hillman 1992: 3)

In the course of her voyage, she doubts whether she can connect with the light of the dead one or find a language for her poem, for the knowledge of the beloved's light is embodied in the poem by virtue of the medium itself, which consists of the borders and forms of words; the poem, in other words, is neither "invisible" nor "subtle / among the shapes." She calls out and, when "everything answers," records the answer of the world of matter. The speaker observes that "all of this compared to her seemed bulky" (Hillman 1992: 5).

The light of knowledge is attained through the writing of the poem. But writing is an imperfect means of coming into that light because it is also a way of materializing what, through the traumatic experience of death, has become dematerialized. H.D. describes this process in

Trilogy. In "Tribute to the Angels," she writes:

> I do not want to name it,
> I want to watch its faint
>
> heart-beat, pulse-beat
> as it quivers, I do not want
>
> to talk about it,
> I want to minimize thought,
>
> concentrate on it
> till I shrink,
>
> dematerialize
> and am drawn in to it.   (H.D. 1973: 77)

H.D.'s speaker quests toward the ineffable, sees traditional nomenclature collapse, wants to commune with the spirit, and to "dematerialize."

Likewise, Hillman's speaker wishes to commune with the spirit, "to go back 'from whence' I came" (1992: 4), to the original light her loved one has joined by dying. She observes that "without her / everything seemed strange to me in this world; / just the taste of oranges: imagine!" (1992: 5). This strangeness, this imagining, is the world deconstructed by the dead one, who is for the poet the agent of light, as if

> Only being dead were fragile enough
> for what the earth had to say.
>   . . . For a while
> it was too much to go on living.
> Roadside acacias—
> I could not bear them. All unzipped,
> like meaning.
> The ostinatos of the birds.
> Magnolias—dog's-tongues—curved
> to spoon up rain. Too much shape.   (1992: 5)

Everything the speaker perceives—acacias, ostinatos, magnolias, dog's-tongue, meaning itself—is unbearably infused with the loved one's death; all things are "unzipped," their borders challenged by immaterial light.

"Who shall be safe from the anguish of borders?" asks the speaker in Hillman's "Yellow Tractate" (1992: 18). "Borders" are the containers of light needing to become the word. And as I face the blankness of the page on which these words take shape, as I face you now, I face a central conflict in Hillman, in H.D., in Gnosticism. Gnosticism holds that the error of creation was to trap the endless light of the soul in matter. Yet unless the light of the soul is trapped in matter and in the shapes of words, there can be no human existence and no language to communicate that light's vastness. So the anguish of borders is the anguish of shape, it is the Gnostic anguish of the light of the soul trapped in the living human shape, and it is the anguish of the writer trapping the light of her knowledge in the shapes on the page.

> But anything that had a shape
> was cheating her.
>
> A minuet. The dresser
> for example. An afternoon
>
> at the DMV—such shape! The living
> have such shape in them!
> The official taking the multifoliate forms
> and pressing down with his ballpoint
> hard, harder, and the pen
> maintaining smooth shapes for him.
> Patient people in line with their hats and scabs and skin
> holding them in as they watch
> each letter being made—   (1992: 17–18)

In these lines Hillman connects quotidian and bureaucratic events with the anguished duality of spirit and matter: the body acts to form words, the official's pen presses "hard, harder," creating the shapes of letters, just as the "hats and scabs and skin" of the people hold them in, contain them in the borders of their bodies. Though "anything that had a shape / was cheating" the dead one, the only way for her light to shine into this world, paradoxically, is for the poet to shape her into words: "And the poems: / things kept getting into them" (Hillman 1992: 18). These things are both the concrete images of the DMV and the official's ballpoint pen and abstract spiritual ideas held inside them. In Greece trucks are painted with the word *metaphora*, which means, literally, transportation, so, too, the shape of metaphor transports the reader to the light of the poem's idea.

> Where is my dead one?
> Shape makes life too small.
>
> But I needed borders to do the remembering.
>
> .   .   .   .
>
> . . . I needed them
> in order to be anything at all—   (Hillman 1992: 19)

The speaker realizes that she cannot search for the lost one without borders, for without borders neither the speaker nor the dead one exists at all.

Hillman's speaker must *speak* "to remember" the dead one, and to remember is to create language, a language that combines the voice of the poet with the voice of the beloved. In both H.D.'s *Trilogy* and in Hillman's *Tractates* the question of voice is a central, agonizing concern. In *Trilogy* H.D. sets the voice of "Dream, / Vision" against utilitarian matter, the sword of war:

> Without thought, invention
> you would not have been, O Sword,
>
> without idea and the Word's mediation
> you would have remained
>
> unmanifest in the dim dimension
> where thought dwells   (1973: 11)

H.D., like Hillman, deals with the anxiety of shaping the light into speech, the ineffable into visible things, yet understands that without borders there can be no affirmation of the psyche's light, which is represented by the butterfly. H.D. writes:

> I know, I feel
> the meaning that words hide;
>
> they are anagrams, cryptograms,
> like boxes, conditioned
>
> to hatch butterflies.   (1973: 39)

Similarly, Hillman sets the voice of spirit against what she calls "all the awkwardness of living":

> I called her more quickly,
> told her how much I missed her,
> pausing at the edge of the screen
>
> that kept me from her
> in all the awkwardness of living,
>
> and she said it was not up to me
> to live without her
> or make the voice be single,
>
> she said every voice is needed.
> Every voice cries out in its own way—   (1992: 8)

Hillman, like H.D., hopes that the borders of words will hatch the butterfly of spiritual voice. She writes: "Pretty soon the borders won't bother you either. / Pretty soon your loved one / will speak forward: into this world" (Hillman 1992: 11).

Hillman allows the loved one to "speak forward" by seeing a "panel" or "screen" between the dead and the living, light and dark, spirit and matter. This heaven where the dead one—whom Hillman calls her "bride"—resides is parallel or sideways. "What lived / lived on both sides," the poet writes. "What lived / went back and forth across the panel" (Hillman 1992: 12). So the panel mediates between the two worlds, and the dead one, the bride, marries both the spiritual light and the poet. Hillman's vision of heaven is specifically feminine and anti-hierarchical; she looks "sideways" across a neighborly, horizontal panel to reach the loved one:

> I simply looked across the row of days
> to what she had become—
>
> a little wild around the edges,
> shining, unavailable,
> across the serious spaces.
> Across! Such an odd direction. Not like the men,
> who travel "up" or "down"—
> across.

So instead of the descent into hell
it seemed I had learned death
by looking sideways. (1992: 40)

This panel is spiritually and materially the blank page, for Hillman in-
serts in the center of the book a blank page that is very much like H.D.'s
"blank pages of unwritten volume of the new." H.D.'s and Hillman's
blank pages resemble each other as well because, as Susan Gubar writes
in "The Blank Page and Female Creativity," for them the blank page is
"a female space, represents a readiness for inspiration and creation, the
self conceived and dedicated to its own potential divinity" (1982: 91).
Because both poets commune with a female muse, the blank page does
not represent the female object but the female subject. H.D.'s Lady "is
not imprisoned . . . / She is Psyche, the butterfly, / out of the cocoon"
(1973: 38). Hillman's loved one "will speak forward into this world,"
her voice mediated by the blank page. Just as in H.D.'s *Trilogy*, Hillman's blank page serves to mediate between the living and the dead, the
old and the new, the unwritten and the written.

The blank page or panel, then, mediates between dualities. At the
same time the panel represents the blankness of loss and the blankness
of letting go. In the poem before the blank page, the speaker asks,
"What do you fear in a poem?" and the answer is "the moment of excess" (Hillman 1992: 22). Asked again, the answer is:

(I fear that moment of withholding—
especially inside what I thought was free;
and I feared the poem was just like her,
that it would abandon me—)   (Hillman 1992: 22)

At this moment the reader faces the blank page, the moment of withholding, loss, and abandonment. The reader also faces the light of spirit,
the excess and immensity of whiteness, which as Melville tells us "ap-
peals" and "appalls" since it is "the visible absence of color, and at the
same time the concrete of all colors" (*Moby Dick*). And as Gubar observes, "the blank pages contains all stories in no story" (1982: 89).
When you turn the blank page the next poem starts in medias res:
"—So the poem is the story of the writing of itself" (Hillman 1992: 25).
The poem needs the intervention of borders and shape in order to
emerge out of immensity:

> So, put yourself in the way
> of the poem. It needed your willing
> impediment to be written. Remember the lily,
> growing through the heart of the corpse?
> You had to be willing to let it through the sunshine
> error of your life,
> be willing not finish it—   (Hillman 1992: 25)

So the voice of the dead one speaks through the "impediment" of the self and through "the sunshine error" of life, which is the error of light trapped in matter. Not to finish is to finish it, to give the poem—and the light of the dead one—a life beyond its ending; poetry, like life itself, must have within it a continuation.

In "Split Tractate" the speaker struggles to let go, to allow the impediment of the self and the world to come between herself and the dead one. She fears "her soul didn't / miss me":

> I looked for her in anger,
> behind sunsets,
> along the iron tracks of the personal:
> I looked for her in planes of agony
> and she was quite close by.   ·
>
> They said I had to let go of her.
> She said so too. Let go she said from the
> What.
> The screen between me and her.   (Hillman 1992: 29)

Even though everything says, "Let go," the speaker says, "Holding on is my specialty," and she looks for her, hears her in the mockingbird, whose verse sounds like "teacher-teacher-teacher / police! police!" (Hillman 1992: 30). In her search to find her lost one, in describing her journey, her doubt, her special failure to let go, she ends up letting go, letting the world and herself be "willing impediments":

> Sweet afternoons of exhaustion. Trips to the library
> with the other moms. Taking the books
> to the chrome mouth of the book deposit
> and hesitating
> before letting the slender paperback slide down

on its very own bardo journey;
Maybe I should have warned it
not to attach itself to its travels,

not to identify with the suffering,
that is the main thing.
. . . .
What is this so-called
death what is it

Let go said the so-called
What.
Let go said everything.

Even the poem said it.
Said it would come in its own good time
as I leaned forward to see death's face
though there was always this gap
between my hand and the page,

I had only to trace the pen
over the words;
the poem was already written—
    (Hillman 1992: 30–31)

The speaker lets go by not letting go, by describing her journey of attachment. She wants to warn the book not to "attach itself to its travels," but, of course, books are the record of travels. She wants it not "to identify with the suffering," but a book's identity is its identification with suffering. The speaker lets go as well by questioning the boundaries of perception: "Let go said the so-called / What." The poem is the journey of one who, through death, has lost established categories. Every meaning is "unzipped," and the voyage of the speaker perceiving that unzipped meaning is the new poem in which she "so-calls"— or names—death an unzipped "what," leaving it open and borderless. Once she has described her journey of doubt, disorientation, and grief, she sees that the poem "was already written."

Hillman fills "the blank pages of the unwritten volume of the new" with concrete images, with shapes and borders, with mockingbirds and libraries, the DMV and bureaucrats. The abstract notions of ecstasy and union with the light need the particularity of the living world in order to be understood. In the last poem in the volume, "Quartz Tractate," Hillman reveals "the idea of reverse seeing": "My friend saw backward into this world. / In the tent, where wisdom is eaten / by the snake, the poem sees into us" (1992: 48). In a Gnostic-like move, Hillman reverses the Eden story. Rather than the snake tempting Eve to eat the fruit of knowledge, the material snake eats the light of wisdom. Likewise, the light of the dead one sees backward into the world of the living, and the poem, in all its materiality, snakes from line to line and consumes the light of the page, seeing into—and describing—the light of our souls. Death returns the soul-light of her friend to the living so that it can be captured in the radiant forms of the poem. The "story of the writing" is the story of the poet's continuing relationship with her "female mentor," of living matter infused with the light of the soul. H.D.'s poetry is the poetry of regeneration, for the "Lady" carries "The Book of Life." Hillman writes a book of death, but for her, too, the poem is regenerative, for out of the blankness of death and crisis comes "the splendor" of a new, relational vision between the lost soul of light and the thingy awkwardness of the living: "I go to the hill where 'she' lies and see / it's true. Things borrow splendor" (1992: 48).

Interior Scrutiny: Example of H.D.

LESLIE SCALAPINO

In my writing I've worked on occurrence of simultaneous times in relation to the writing's structure, how time and events unfold or appear simultaneously as if existing vertically/horizontally in a "visual" field.

I've always written series or sequences, never short individual poems, because the perspective in beginning to write a piece would always need to change; perspective itself would alter as it went along. That is, perspective in the writing would, as it were, alter how something's seen as well as what is chosen to be viewed.

Thus I've been drawn to texts or visual, spatial demonstrations (of perspective or relations in space) such as Japanese scrolls vertical and horizontal; Japanese panels or screens, *The Tale of Genji*, and illustrated books in which the text being vertical has small pictures showing a part of the action embedded in (beside) it or pictures on the opposite page; Indian miniature paintings in which the text and borders are inside the picture and have a relation to it (similar Japanese prints in which the language is within); Classic Comic Books or Romance Comic Books in which the text is in bubbles on stacked frames both vertical and horizontal; paintings where diverse events, in expanded historical scheme as multiple, are occurring at the same time as if at once minute and expanded.

I first began to read H.D. in 1983; I started with *Helen in Egypt* and *Notes on Thought and Vision*. I was interested in the sequential structure of *Helen in Egypt*, a 304-page poem in units of books within which are numbered poems, creating the sense of a vast spatial expanse (the subject "historical," vision as seeing/reading: the transmigration of Helen to Egypt after the Trojan War) in which the past, future, and present occur at once and are the same.

Yet these (time schemes) are also differentiated, and that differentiation (as the presentation or repetition solely of the relations between other relations, implying continual change) is motion and also stillness at once. There is a sense of this simultaneous motion and stillness reverberating through the entire structure as well as in each "location" or single poem. That is, the "same" motion and stillness are simultaneously on the minute and on the expanded scale.

Her extended poem is a schema of points of relation only (Achilles is Dis/Proteus/Osiris, for example—the past is the future). That is, the points of relation have no relation except her designation of that. This relativity itself is the sole ground of observation, being at once a spatial location, movement, and interpretation of same.

Thus designation is the mind; occurrence is people. In *Helen in Egypt*, the characters, such as Helen and Paris, are only their symbolic or fixed meaning (implying, I think, the mass of people through time); one character or figure is many figures who are other symbols (which are visual site/sight as hieroglyphs). So a person is qualities that are static (or generic?) yet multiple.

Therefore, interpretation is not psychological in the sense of personal entity; rather, it is relational—qualities or components don't change, but the group relation or configuration of these to each other changes. It's almost a molecular structure: history transcending as "one" (as if all the events and motions are in the mind of one).

While admiring the structure of *Helen in Egypt*, I still found its circularity (vision as visual reading/seeing, H.D.'s circular time scheme in which everything refers to everything else) to be too static to account either for history or event in the present—my regarding action as undetermined even after it has occurred.

I think that the latter thought is H.D.'s intention also (as well as mine) and in her work is probably best realized in *Trilogy*. For her, physical seeing ("vision," which she associates with seeing history as if reading hieroglyphs) is transcending of history.

Robert Duncan once spoke (in informal talk) of *Trilogy* as coming out of H.D.'s greatest crisis; it was written in the midst of World War II during the bombing of London, where H.D. was living. For her, that "present" *had* to transcend history.

The sense that action is undetermined even after it has occurred—
the syntax or language-shape that is that action—constitutes continual
change throughout a serial or sequential writing.

My sense of sequential or extended writing is that the present is in
continual movement. It is not that the writing is fragmented; rather,
events are "seen" again—first, before they occur.

For me, reading is "seeing" texts as if one sees on the surface of
one's retina, where the action of reading is out ahead of one—*is* actions
outside. Actions or events are "read," and—perhaps similar to H.D.'s
physical seeing of hieroglyphs as "reading the past"—this action of
reading is itself the present-time.

This sense of "reading" is interior scrutiny, which is at once observation of the outside.

The following, for example, is my note on a sequence *(Friendship)*
that itself is in (and it is also a commentary on that sequence) a series of
sequences titled *The Public World/Syntactically Impermanence* (written
from 1995 to 1998). The time scheme of this work is past/present/
future occurring at once. (I was taking into account as much as I could
the Japanese philosopher Dogen's view of being as time.)

Note (on *Friendship*, a sequence in *The Public World/Syntactically
Impermanence*):

Friendship is a spatial syntax, as if rendering interior that is oneself
which is (also) being rendered as space of actual geographical location. It's space-based, written in China while on the Yangtze River
and here.

Though geographical space was determining the space that is
one's (present) apprehension as the syntax: a different space occurs
that is outside mind—also—by being within it.

In the whole text that is *The Public World*, the intention is to propose observation of one's own culture by superimposing "outside"
on it. *Friendship* is an "outside" geography (in Asia, in this case)
rendered as one's interior spatial sense. Land as thought.

"One" is not obliterated by land.

Geography cultural analysis as rendered/filtered only interiorly—
is here scrutiny. Using geographical location (as only configuration,
i.e., spatial conceptualization/syntax) *Friendship* is the converse of
definition *by* place. Time as being—syntactically impermanence.

Another example from my own writing: one has to write "on" "sub-jectivity"—as that being without entity: as such, contentless—*by* being subjectivity (by having only that ground; and by that being seen to be "subjectivity" as socially devalued characteristic per se). By being "not" is—(contentless):

For example: eroticism per se as writing (said to be that as genre) may be contentless as being outside the "social" (in the sense of outside by not being what is given high value because seen to articulate "impor-tant" social relations—i.e., this implies erotic as *defined* as unimportant [in convention]: so there it "can be" contentless only negatively as lust without relation to other, i.e., as sexism). So eroticism would have to be there as "that" (eroticism) only, a double that is "doing nothing."

Therefore, one could "return" to a ground of eroticism "only"—not as "obsession" or reaction but a gesture observing itself, therefore "contentless."

My *Instead of an Animal* is a "serial" that is substitution: only as sexual behavior being there (of children for adults or adults for "animals" or any for unknowns). Interpretation of it "in terms of its content" belies it. It's "the opposite" of obsession. As serial, it is and it isn't what it claims to be—so it's outside of definition (starting with being outside and its own "definition" as its shape/in simple repetition but which is change). That is, is outside of being "on" sexual gestures only *or* "being contentless," either.

H.D.'s bitter jewel/worm-cycle ("the real actions of/in the world" what we experience as real, with oneself, together) is seen as merely the self, which when the *world* allows only itself, isn't of the "real." Con-versely, H.D.'s saying self is only being the "real."

I'm comparing gestures of mine as possibly being akin to H.D., rather than saying these come from her. Poets write in relation to oc-currence, and they're informed from the outside. H.D.'s writing em-barks on, implies, the confluence of boundaries of "commentary," "au-tobiography," "poetry," conflating one's interior (mind/psyche) and what she called one's "over-mind" in order to "read" the outside.

"Over-mind" as far as I can understand is akin to one's state of con-centration or meditation, which is aware of, takes in, the details and nature of the individual and is at once expanded seeing that is compre-hending the entire space—outside one's mind, by being in it.

Her writing is revolutionary in investigating one's own mind *being* present action, as *being* history, and being also future "outside."

Thus she opened a terrain for other poets that is investigation as sound and shape-as-syntax, rather than prior categories ("givens") that would be the form of the thought ("autobiography" "poetry").

This influence has been instrumental to poets (starting in the 1970s and 1980s) beginning to develop forms that are conscious transgressions of boundaries in "essays that are poems," "poems that are essays"—in which thought/apprehension is allowed to take the varied quirks it demonstrates in one's mind, which is what thought is.

An essay I wrote on *Helen in Egypt* in 1983 (titled "Re-living") was the first time I wrote a "poem that's an essay"; I attempted to render the "relations" laid out in the original work by delineation or duplication that by imitating the work's gesture would "see" and apprehend it.

To learn the pattern by "seeing" it spatially.

RE-LIVING

Egypt is the act of love, in *Helen in Egypt*. It is being dead, so time values are altered. Present is past, past is future: "The whole heroic sequence is over, forgotten, re-lived, forgotten." Achilles, in life, is immortal; after death he's left with only the Achilles-heel. The soul was in life, in the past—which is now the future. The body exists in death:

> it was God's plan
> to melt the icy fortress of the soul,
> and free the man

Achilles is Osiris, Proteus, Dis. He's the ice-star. Paris, who's Helen's lover prior to Achilles, is Eros, Dionysius, the child of Helen and Achilles. The first lover having been created by the last lover. Spring is always in the past. Achilles, keeping Helen in the past, obliterates time—so it's the present:

> can spring defeat winter? never,
> spring may come after
>
> but the crystal, the center, the ice-star
> dissembles, reflects the past

but waits faithful

*   *   *

Paris will never find me;
I reflect, I re-act, I re-live . . .

The question is asked, "Is the disguise of death, love . . . are we homesick for what has been?" Love is in the past, just as spring is. The scattered dead Greek heroes are the Egyptian flower, also the limbs of Osiris. The thousand-petalled lily is a hieroglyph repeated endlessly so time stops in it. Postulates or pictures are projected from a single reality. The writing is expressed in things: "The secret of the stone-writing is repeated in natural or human symbols. She herself is the writing." People are more than one symbol.

So the pattern can't be "read" or deciphered completely but only expressed in statements that are declarations of relationships between things. The most abstruse hieroglyphs are the most simple memories, so seeing is in terms of surfaces. Certain sights or pictures through their lines are direct entrances to vision, which occurs in over-mind consciousness. In *Thought and Vision*, H.D. says that Leonardo da Vinci, for example, "saw the faces of many of his youths and babies and young women definitely with his over-mind. The Madonna of the Rocks is not a picture. It is a window. We look through a window into the world of pure over-mind."

The over-mind is a lens, really two. The center of consciousness is either the intellect, which is in Greece, or the love-region of the body, in Egypt. The two lenses work separately, "perceive separately, yet make one picture." The dream as delirium/trance/ecstasy, Helen in Egypt and Helen in Leuké, is the subconscious world: "The subconscious world is the world of sleeping dreams and the world great lovers enter, physical lovers, but very great ones." The state of being awake and seeing clearly, remembering and not remembering, is the waking dream: "The over-conscious world is the world of waking dreams and the world great lovers enter, spiritual lovers, but only the greatest." Helen's soul is snatched from its body—with its body—by the gyrfalcon Achilles.

Theseus is Freud, who's to "teach me to remember . . . teach me not to remember," which is the state of the waking dream. Intellect being the bridge between subconscious and overconscious mind, which looks back on thoughts: "Into that over-mind, thoughts pass and are visible like fish swimming under clear water."

Helen's the hollow shell, death/Leuké/mind. Having found or being found by Dis. She's inside the eggshell, in Hades. The dead Greek heroes are "as one soul, one pearl" asleep in the shell. Re-living, being in time, in thought, reduces time to a finite moment in which there's "all song forever." "There is only a song now and rhetorical questions that have been already answered. The song is the frieze." The song's in herself (in the shell/the mind/the writing) and the sea enchantment.

So only being in the waking state will free her from enchantment. Paris before and after Egypt is Eros so there's only the present:

> there is no before and no after,
> there is one finite moment
> that no infinite joy can disperse
>
> or thought of past happiness
> tempt from or dissipate;
> now I know the best and the worst; (1961: 303)

The world of death is the highest life. Only Dis/Achilles (he's in the past and therefore future time) can break his heart and the world for a token, "a memory forgotten." Which means remembering and forgetting at the same time, the waking daydream or window. In terms of the song, it's "a rhythm as yet unheard."

Things and people being translations, they are lacquered, frozen. In *Hermetic Definition*, she gives birth to Dis at the end of her life, though he's said to be Osiris/Paris/Perseus. He'd died, was much younger than she, so it's seasonal. The rose unfolds through her, unfolding to an impossible degree:

> no, no, this is too much,
> we cannot escape to a new continent;
> the middle door is judgment,
>
> I am judged—prisoner?
> the reddest rose unfolds,
> can I endure this?   (1972: 11)

There are other roses. The rose that's reddest is therefore formal and external. So it's frenzied, finding in itself "the exact intellectual com-

ponent / or the exact emotional opposite." The lover/opposite is perfect. Permitting her to be nothing, to be dead. The writing, therefore,
far away, outside oneself. Re-living is out-living:

> and you draw me out
> to compete with your frenzy;
> there are other roses,   (1972: 33)

"Time-less or Hieroglyph": Self and Simulacrum in H.D. and Leslie Scalapino

ELISABETH A. FROST

Leslie Scalapino opens her volume *The Front Matter, Dead Souls* with an assertion that recurs implicitly in over ten books of poetry, prose, and criticism: "A dialogue about love is utterly crucial to the re-making of the modern world in writing" (1996: 1). It is a comment that echoes elements of H.D.'s *Notes on Thought and Vision*, for H.D. locates "over-mind consciousness," the greatest level of human insight and creative thinking, in the "love region of the body" (1982: 19). Scalapino's own "dialogues" on love, gender, and language have taken similarly provocative, elliptical forms in the recasting of what she calls "the erotica genre" as well as in a reimagining of sexual reproduction and the body itself. Yet in Scalapino's serial poems we find not just a "dialogue about love" but also a radical revision of the very notion of identity—a rejection of the conception of the fixed self that Scalapino traces, in part, to H.D.

While there is a world of stylistic difference between Scalapino's highly fractured serial compositions and H.D.'s mythic epic poems, Scalapino nevertheless shares with H.D. strategies fundamental to an alternative vision of the self. And, in a more pointed fashion than many readers of *Trilogy* and *Helen in Egypt*, Scalapino casts H.D. in the role of precursor—a deconstructive poet whose daring uses of the structures of "illusion" challenge the nature of identity. While H.D. is frequently seen as unearthing a repressed feminine principle in Western culture,[1] Scalapino emphasizes the ways in which H.D. reveals the instability of the self, thus providing a means to theorize the construction of gender difference as illusory. Scalapino's statements about H.D. focus more on form than on either writer's views about gender. Yet parallels between Scalapino's depictions of erotic experience and H.D.'s earlier experiments with the shifting nature of sexual identity offer a way to reveal the kinship between the two poets and to place their linguistic explorations of identity as simulacrum—as a projection, representation, an often indecipherable hieroglyph—in the context of feminist poetics.

Scalapino is attracted to what she sees as H.D.'s rendering of simultaneous events and perspectives in her long poems, particularly *Helen in Egypt*, H.D.'s epic unraveling of the story of Helen of Troy. Scalapino's writing of serial poetry emerged, she says in her essay in this volume, from a need for a similarly expansive form, in which "perspective itself would alter as it went along." [2] Such shifts in perspective draw Scalapino to visual representations—from Japanese screens to comic books—and to H.D. as well. In *Helen in Egypt*, Scalapino finds "a vast spatial expanse . . . in which the past, future, and present occur at once and are the same." Scalapino acknowledges that a central role is reserved for "the professor" in *Helen in Egypt* (as Theseus, Helen's "analyst"), but, unlike many readers, she does not see an integration of personality or a psychoanalytic interpretation consonant with Helen's reconciliation of past and present.[3] Instead, in *Helen in Egypt*

> the characters . . . are only their symbolic or fixed meaning; . . . one character or figure is many figures who are other symbols (which are visual site/sight as hieroglyphs). So a person is qualities that are static (or generic?) yet multiple.
>
> Therefore, interpretation is not psychological in the sense of personal entity; rather, it is relational—qualities or components don't change, but the group relation or configuration of these to each other changes.

Characters perceived as their own "symbolic or fixed meaning," their visual occurrence as "hieroglyphs," are thus not iconic figures in Freud's family romance but, rather, the elements of a complex structure ("It's almost a molecular structure") based on "vision as visual reading/ seeing." Thus Scalapino links the "relational" poetics of *Helen in Egypt* to the poem's intricate and often challenging modular structure, one that can be compared with Scalapino's even more fragmented seriality. This characterization of H.D.'s "relational" poetics as comprising simultaneous events and multiple perspectives and as requiring a fracturing of narrative linearity underwrites a fundamental aspect of both poets' work: their shared view of the contingent, shifting nature of gender and the self.

Scalapino's reading of *Helen in Egypt* doesn't focus on gender, despite that poem's exploration of Helen's sexuality and the blame she endures as feminine "cause" of the war. Yet Scalapino's texts consist of a similarly "molecular structure" that breaks down gender identity as well as delineations of self. In this respect Scalapino's strategies can be likened to H.D.'s dismantling of gender difference and identity more broadly. In *Trilogy*, for example, H.D. challenges sexual difference, exploring spiritual, linguistic, and sexual fluidity. As Susan Stanford Friedman has shown, the basis for H.D.'s gender ambiguity in the poem lies in Gnostic and alchemical texts that rely on a mixture of feminine and masculine traits in androgynous deities (1981: 205, 275). H.D. uses these ancient sources to recover the gender indeterminacy at the root of Western thinking. H.D. renders the caduceus, for example, with combined male and female qualities—it is the "scepter" or rod of power, but it is also feminized, "crowned with the lily-head / or the lily-bud" (1983: 512). Regendered as both masculine and feminine, it represents the cultural renewal that H.D.'s epic, written during the devastation of World War II, envisions. A second motif that suggests indeterminacy is the mollusc that "gives birth" to the pearl, a central figure in *Notes on Thought and Vision*, a motif in H.D.'s novel *Paint It Today*, and a frequent image in Gnostic texts. The mollusc begets through self-fertilization. This "oyster, clam, mollusc" is an "amorphous hermit" that lives according to nonhuman laws: most molluscs are hermaphroditic, and it is this differently gendered being that consistently intrigues H.D. as a counter to sexual divisions.

The pearl reappears in a series of unusual nativity scenes. The inverse of reproduction—ingestion—is followed by a yielding forth that is an alternative to conventional birth. In one such passage, the speaker observes, "I in my own way know / that the whale // can not digest me" and advises,

> be indigestible, hard, ungiving,

> so that, living within,
> you beget, self-out-of-self,

> selfless,
> that pearl-of-great-price.   (H.D. 1983: 513–14)

Adapted from the Gospel of Matthew, the "pearl of great price" takes the inanimate as a symbol of "begetting," and the creation issued is not exactly a fellow creature but something that remains, like its source, "indigestible, hard"—and genderless. In *Notes on Thought and Vision*, H.D. observes: "The oyster makes the pearl . . . So the body, with all its emotions and pain in time casts off the spirit, a concentrated essence, not itself, but made, in a sense, created by itself. . . . Because the spirit, we realise, is a seed" (1982: 51–52). Rejecting Cartesian dualism, H.D. proposes a procreation in which the spirit, seed or pearl, is a *product* of the body and is "created by itself."

H.D. also offers moments of linguistic indeterminacy to demonstrate the destabilizing of language, gender, and the self.

> Splintered the crystal of identity
> shattered the vessel of integrity,
>
> till the Lord *Amen*,
> paw-er of the ground,
>
> bearer of the curled horns,
> bellows from the horizon:
>
> here am I, Amen-Ra,
> *Amen*, Aries, the Ram;
>
> time, time for you to begin a new spiral,
> see—I toss you into the star-whirlpool;
>
> till pitying, pitying,
> snuffing the ground,
>
> here am I, Amen-Ra whispers,
> *Amen*, Aries, the Ram,
>
> be cocoon, smothered in wool,
> be Lamb, mothered again.   (1983: 526–27)

First, the "crystal of identity," its "integrity," is "shattered." Following this "splintering" of the self, the "Lord *Amen*" appears, in whom the Egyptian god Amon and the Christian prayer "Amen" are conflated, just as, in Egyptian mythology, Amon and Ra were fused to create a combined deity who represents the sun-god, who controls reproduction, life, and death. Such syncretism re-creates gender and the self: "here am I, Amen-Ra whispers, / *Amen*, Aries, the Ram, / be cocoon, smothered in wool, / be Lamb, mothered again." The passage invokes a Lamb (of indeterminate gender) as product of a birth that occurs not from a "womb" but from a different sort of generative space: the "cocoon" with its "wool." Like the pearl "born" from the mollusc, the Lamb emerges from encasement without sexual reproduction in anticipation of a novel "mothering." In a recasting of the Virgin birth, H.D. replaces sexual difference with ambiguity. But another kind of new relation is also at play: sonic repetitions, puns, and echoes (as in "cocoon" and "wool," "smothered" and "mothered") emphasize relationship rather than difference. Emblematic of H.D.'s transformations, the play of signification helps create the "birth" of a new being.[4]

A similar dismantling of difference appears in Scalapino's play with gender and the sign. Like the H.D. of *Notes on Thought and Vision*, Scalapino suggests that if language helps enforce the rules of identity, a different *kind* of language might help obliterate them, opening up new avenues for individual action. Scalapino outlines an anti-essentialist politics:

> My articulation of feminism is in the gesture of trying to unravel
> how something is packaged or mirrored back to me—as part of the
> whole web of what's around us. . . . One's decisions about what one is
> as a formed being, as a woman for instance, are like placing the con-
> clusion or the hypothesis on something before one has done it. It's
> a process of unraveling the hypothesis and the conclusion—there
> should *be* no hypothesis.   (Frost 1996: 20)

Passages from the serial poem *way* (1988) show how Scalapino "unravels the hypothesis" of difference.[5] Through a sexual iconography similar to H.D.'s ambiguous alchemical figures, Scalapino depicts the sexual act in serial fragments and in a highly stylized manner; the strangely *un*anatomical representation of what is in fact an intricate depiction of sexual intercourse leads one to disassociate the "act" from the (human) body, even as the sexuality of the passages is inescapable. The central motifs are the "lily pad" and "bud"—both nonhuman (though naturalistic) symbols. These terms clearly recall both H.D.'s "thousand-petalled lily" and "lotus bud" motif from *Helen in Egypt*, as well as the "lily-head / or the lily-bud" from *Trilogy* (1983: 512). At first, the "lily pad" and "bud" are synonymous in Scalapino's syntax:

the

women—not in

> the immediate
> setting
> —putting the
> lily pads or
> bud of it
> in
> themselves
>
> a man entering
> after
> having
> come on her—that
> and
> the memory of putting
> in
> the lily pad or the
> bud of it first,
> made her come.   (1988: 65, 66)

There is a disruption of location ("not in / the immediate / setting")
and sequence ("after," "first," "memory"). The plural ("women") in-
explicably shifts to the singular ("her"). Further, what is "put in" contributes to the erotic moment: it is, in part, "memory" that "made her
come." As I have argued elsewhere, the figures of the bud and lily pad
are reminiscent of Taoist icons of sexual organs through which one offers praise to the deity.[6] This section might well be conceived not as
challenging difference but, to the contrary, as placing value on the
"female," for Scalapino provides the woman's point of view and, in
her description of this section as the "floating" series, alludes to the
amniotic.

Yet in the floating series, the lily bud, which is initially inserted into
the female body, eventually is an object "ingested" (not unlike H.D.'s
"pearl" in "The whale can not digest me") by the male:

> having
> swallowed the
> water
> lily bud—so having
> it in

him—when he'd
come on some
time with her
a man'd swallowed
the bud
of the water lily—and
had
it in
him that way.   (Scalapino 1988: 85)

The "translation" of the hieroglyphic sign of sexual exchange—
whether "entering" man or woman—is rendered impossible to finalize
or to fix. Thus the most crucial aspect of Scalapino's text is the "relational." Various fragmented sections of *way* underline the importance
of the reader's awareness of how the subject's positionality, like sexual
difference itself, is unstable. Sexuality is, at best, a construction or
"custom" that places one in (arbitrary) relation to an other: "—the /
sexual / being that / relation to / that / custom" (Scalapino 1988: 46).
"Position" is everything: "our / being / that //—as in / the middle"
(Scalapino 1988: 83); identity ("our / being / that"), location, sequence,
and even class ("in / the middle") shift, unfixed. Each is a hieroglyph
that, however indecipherable, forms the text on which we base the
"reading" of ourselves. The "relation to / who oneself is" (Scalapino
1988: 120) is posed as the poem's preoccupation, and yet that "relation"
is continually being undone:

told
others are
not like
the nature of
themselves
by
a man or
someone
being that.   (Scalapino 1988: 27)

Sexuality, then, is one element of the "self" that surfaces as simulacrum. The epigraph to *way*, from David Bohm's *Causality and Chance in*

Modern Physics, concerns the paradox of the "identity" of matter over time; ultimately, Bohm concludes, "*no . . . thing can even remain identical with itself as time passes. . . .* we admit also that nevertheless there still exists an absolute, unique, and objective reality" (Scalapino 1988: n.p.). This contradictory state of affairs, as it concerns men and women as social subjects, is the "subject" of Scalapino's text.

Yet even more fundamentally than the dismantling of sexual difference, Scalapino questions any fixed notion of identity on which delineations of self depend, and her preoccupations are anticipated by H.D. Scalapino discusses *Trilogy* in terms of what she calls "the tiny self": the poem, Scalapino argues, effects a dialectic between self or interiority and "actions in the world," so that "the 'world' is part of and 'within' the defenseless self. H.D. allows the imbalance: a sense of an infinite structure of possible actions that is the world overwhelming the tiny self"; this, in effect, "is the *form* of the writing" (1994: 3). Thus, in H.D.'s poetics, the ego is repositioned as an appropriately "tiny" part of a larger scheme: "One's small, static, limited," and, rather than the self's isolation, "The world/oneself/nature are enmeshed" (Scalapino 1994: 4). What Scalapino calls H.D.'s "tiny" self, the personal ego put in proper perspective, is the progenitor of the figures who populate *way*: the "characters" of Scalapino's poem are part of a spectrum we perceive in isolated textual fragments. These parts, including the scenes that depict the sexual act, can be understood only in relation to one another as linked elements of a more elusive whole.

This awareness of "relation" also informs Scalapino's reading of *Helen in Egypt*. In H.D.'s epic, "The text/dream is a 'timeless dimension' in which 'Time values have altered, present is past, past is future.'" This simultaneity is enacted in the projection of both self and "external" event: "At times all projections are one, the self, which are maintained separate; these are the form of the structure itself" (Scalapino 1994: 6–7). In *Helen in Egypt*, self and structure are enmeshed, but both are "illusion": "H.D.'s nerve was to openly base the structure on illusion made precarious by the apparent base of the self (thus *it* is illusory). Seeing the psyche as structure as myth/as illusion, the incremental structure is set free" (Scalapino 1994: 7).

The liberation of "incremental structure" is thus an *effect* of the "illusion" of selfhood. In "Pallinode," H.D. adapts Stesichorus's account that during the Trojan War Helen was spirited away to Egypt. (In

H.D.'s version even this much "plot" is in question, as the "location" of Egypt is at times presented as the afterlife and at times a trance state that defies both sequence and physical location.) In H.D.'s text, Helen is a simulacrum of female beauty; she represents the masquerade of femininity, the enforced performance of gender difference.[7] As counter to this pernicious "illusion," the eidolon, or image, of Thetis instructs Helen at the close of "Pallinode" and returns (in the past) as the wooden figure worshiped (in image only) by her son, Achilles. H.D. casts this series of "illusions" into a lyric structure whose short sequences shift continually, subverting narrative and defying logic and sequence—the very bases of epic construction.

At the opening of *Helen in Egypt*, Helen asserts that the "power" that drew the assembled hosts to the image of herself on the ramparts was

> but the phantom and the shadow thrown
> of a reflection;
>
> .   .   .   .   .   .
>
> a hieroglyph, repeated endlessly,
>
> upon the walls, the pillars,
> the thousand-petalled lily;   (H.D. 1961: 5, 20–21)

This "illusion" is the icon that fuels the war: just as the "lily" is trans-mogrified into the "flower" of the "chosen" (Achilles' assembled "host" [H.D. 1961: 17, 25]), so the "hieroglyph" that appears upon the walls is the image of femininity in the text of masculine conquest, a signifier of "woman" that takes shape in the minds of a host of readers. Yet Helen's own version of a hieroglyph appears outside the Egyptian temple when "a night-bird hooted past." She tells Achilles,

> "I am instructed, I know the script,
> the shape of this bird is a letter,
>
> they call it the hieroglyph."   (H.D. 1961: 13–14)

It is a visual sign whose meaning she projects ("dedicates" to Isis), even as "this great temple's / indecipherable hieroglyph" (H.D. 1961: 21) eludes her; it posits, like herself, a challenge to both meaning and identity. At their initial meeting, Achilles at first fails to recognize her. Even later, she must wonder of herself, "Helena? who is she?" (H.D. 1961:

37). As a prose introduction to one of the cantos answers, *"She herself is the writing"* (H.D. 1961: 22).

Through the figure of the hieroglyph, H.D. links identity to the structures of language and explores the possibility of transcending fixed selfhood through the trance state of "time-less time." The hieroglyph "upon the walls" of Troy is a simulacrum, yet the hieroglyphs upon the temple are also Helen's means of defying linear time through an extraordinary act of reading. The prose commentary asserts that "Helen achieves the difficult task of translating a symbol in time, into time-less time or hieroglyph" (H.D. 1961: 13); thus a "symbol" is translated into yet another representation, a hieroglyph that defies sequence and location, suggesting not the "integration" of self but its dissolution.[8]

Scalapino writes of *Helen in Egypt*, "Present is past, past is future: 'The whole heroic sequence is over, forgotten, re-lived, forgotten'" (1989: 55). For Scalapino H.D.'s disruption of linear sequence is crucial: "The thousand-petalled lily is a hieroglyph repeated endlessly so time stops in it" (1989: 55). Both "things and people [are] translations . . . they are lacquered, frozen" (Scalapino 1989: 57). They "mean" most not as "selves" but as reflections of our inability to "translate" what is signified: "the pattern can't be 'read' or deciphered completely, but only expressed in statements which are declarations of relationships between things" (Scalapino 1989: 55–56).

It is Helen's "time-less time," the hermetic yet transformative power of hieroglyph, that supplies Scalapino with a recurring figure for one of her most elliptical serial poems. In *The Front Matter, Dead Souls* (1996), Scalapino's allusions to H.D., particularly to *Helen in Egypt*, reveal the extent to which her exploration of simulacrum is aligned with her "reading" of H.D.'s similar dismantling of the self. Scalapino explains that the book "is a serial novel for publication in the newspaper," also suitable for "billboards or outdoors as murals." It was composed "during the [1992] election campaign" (Scalapino 1996: 1). This serial poem/novel[9] is "scrutiny of our and 'one's' image-making," in which "the writing of events is not a representation of these events"; instead, actions are presented "artificially" (Scalapino 1996: 2, 1). H.D.'s structure of mythic revision (whose "circularity" Scalapino describes in her essay in this volume as "too static to account either for history or event in the present") is transmogrified in Scalapino's quintessentially postmodern text into a leveling of myth and "reality," self and simulacrum. Scenes are presented as elements of a simulacrum-culture whose billboards, TV screens, and abject public spectacles furnish the "reality" of individual consciousness. The "self" is no more than the internalization of contemporary culture: "I'm taking the outer now current culture *to be* the inner self drawing it in as one's core or manifestation—which it isn't. Then, it is externalized as oneself and is projected outward again as one's sense of real. That actually *is* one's inner self by acting upon its projection." Selfhood *is* illusion: "To be 'dislocated' never remaining as the same person by continual disruption is the creation of that 'one'"; "neither memory nor the present occurs" (Scalapino 1996: 5, 6, 11).

While fragments of a plot emerge, the real "event" in *The Front Matter* is the reading of a hieroglyphs of self/society. On the model of H.D.'s thousand-petalled lily, though with the crucial difference of a marked topicality, Scalapino constructs a series of contemporary hieroglyphs: the "action" takes place in a Los Angeles rife with police corruption, drug trafficking, and conspicuous consumption in streets lined with the poor and disenfranchised. In this abject setting (typified by the grotesque display of bodies and violence at a carnivalesque version of Venice's Muscle Beach), the text flattens historical occurrences and locations. While political references abound (the Iraq war, the Rodney King trial, the confirmation of Justice Clarence Thomas), interspersed with these references are recurring, surreal hieroglyphs: the disembodied head of a sumo wrestler; the figure of a greyhound on the track; a "fetid" corpse; a hyena that takes the form of news anchorman, businessman, and politician. In depictions of sexual and political violence, of crime and exploitation, *The Front Matter* assaults the reader with the dystopia of America run amok.

This panoply of contemporary violence is a postmodern descendent of H.D.'s account of a different period of war and sexual violence. As in *The Front Matter*, Scalapino argues that "actions" in *Helen in Egypt* have "no other occurrence except as their delineation" (1994: 6). The "artificial" nature of H.D.'s text interests Scalapino and provides language similar to her description of the "inner self" as "projection" in *The Front Matter*: "The delineations (reading hieroglyphs as pictures on the wall), which are the minute movements of the writing, don't mimic reality, but appear with reality: / Maintaining the imbalance and the separate delineation is the utter illusion and transience of one" (1994: 6). For Scalapino, in *Helen in Egypt* "being in history" is likewise "illusion" (1994: 5). But while H.D. employed Egyptian hieroglyphs for Helen's acts of "reading," Scalapino self-reflexively recycles H.D.'s hieroglyphs.[10] H.D.'s "lily-bud" is transformed into bombed-out Iraqi "burning lily fields" (Scalapino 1994: 37). Similarly, H.D.'s thousand-petalled lily (which Scalapino labels elsewhere "Helen . . . the thousand-petalled lily the self" [1994: 6]) becomes a hieroglyph for the character "Akira who's in the LAPD," who "is corrupt and is into drugs." We are first told that "Akira is stabbed" as he enters the sumo ring. A later passage asserts: "The burning fields billowing in another waft, open. Akira is H.D.'s thousand-petalled lily" (Scalapino 1994: 36, 33, 43). How is Akira H.D.'s thousand-petalled lily? And why is he connected to the other hieroglyph, of Iraqi fields burning under American bombs? In a strange twist, Akira serves as a contemporary version of Helen herself—the bodily emblem of a culture's inability to escape its own political and sexual violence. Thus Akira's sexual exploits (a recurring motif) are not disjunct from the devastation of the Iraqi war. Akira's very body—his "self"—becomes a hieroglyph we struggle to "read." The futility of the gesture is underlined in another H.D. hieroglyph—the hawk ("Eros, the Hawk Horus" in *Helen in Egypt*): "The thousand-petalled lily on that aquamarine, a hawk is flapping not sustained, and drops" (1961: 41, 43). Helen's "nightbird," a "living hieroglyph," is fused with "the Hawk with the thousand pinions" (H.D. 1961: 46), itself a play on the thousand-petalled lily. But here the "hawk" is not "sustained" and therefore "drops," as though to its own death.

Neither of these hieroglyphs is fully "readable" in Scalapino's difficult text.[11] Scalapino's infrequent "I" makes no effort to complete the "hermeneutical circle."[12] As Scalapino explains, "my writing is fabrication of self, of subjectivity (which itself is seen to be 'cultural abstraction'), yet in it the 'self' is not separable from its own illusion" (Frost 1996: 6). These motifs signal Scalapino's debt to H.D.: the linking of body and word, making space for a critique of self as illusion, marking the impossibility of any subjectivity's establishing itself independent of textual surfaces, of simulacra.

In her essay "Pattern—and the Simulacral," Scalapino writes, "Deciphering oneself entails what one is; the concept of that entails the action of what the text is. We mime the simulacra, 'syntax mimes space,' in order to get at the real" (1989: 30). Scalapino continues: "A manifestation of postmodernism: the proliferation of the particular—has to do with recognizing social definitions . . . as not intrinsic to reality or oneself" (1989: 35). Scalapino's writing focuses on the collapse of distinctions between masculine and feminine, "reality or oneself." H.D. and Scalapino are both fascinated by time-less time, by the hieroglyph of identity. H.D.'s legacy to Scalapino lies in her interrogation of language and difference, while Scalapino's readings of H.D.—a crucial forebear—bring to light both H.D.'s fascination with the simulacrum of identity and Scalapino's own politics of the dismantled self.

NOTES

1. Friedman's *Psyche Reborn* (1981) remains the most significant of such readings of H.D.'s poetics.

2. Conte defines serial form as discrete units potentially infinite in number, rather than structured by generic constraints or the linearity of a definable beginning, middle, and end.

3. Friedman's and Gelpi's readings emphasize Helen's integration of self through the recovery of repressed memories. See Edmunds (1994: 2–4) for an account of the generations of feminist critics of H.D.

4. The Lady's emergence in "Tribute to the Angels" represents a similar birth, through a cocoon—that of the "butterfly" or Psyche, the soul. H.D. employs the trope of the soul as bride of Christ ("we are her bridegroom and lamb" [1983: 571]), reversing genders by figuring the Lady as deity and the soul as bridegroom. In such passages H.D. both uses the Lady as a feminine symbol and attempts to rewrite the dualism on which such symbols depend.

5. In this respect Butler's metaphor of "gender trouble" applies to Scalapino's poetics as well as to a number of other feminist avant-garde poets, both modern and contemporary.

6. See my "Signifyin(g) on Stein" (1995) for a fuller statement of this argument, particularly concerning the intertwining of "private" experience (sexuality) with the public sphere in *way*.

7. Joan Rivière first described the notion of masquerade—an exaggerated femininity that helped a female patient compensate for her intellect, an effort to placate the "father" for her theft of phallic power. In Irigaray's later version of masquerade, women "recuperate some element of desire, to participate in man's desire, but at the price of renouncing their own" (1985: 133).

8. Chisholm argues, "It is not the woman, Helen . . . whom her palinode [*sic*] proposes to rehabilitate, but the palimpsest, the tracing and retracing of the Helen myths and legends." There is "no original Helen outside the poetry and history" that construct her (1992: 169). The poem decenters Greek thinking to recover "Egyptian hieroglyphs whose pictoideographic character is not reducible to phonological elements"; H.D. liberates "meaning from the stronghold of the logic of

binary opposition, the logic of difference" (Chisholm 1992: 169), including that of gender. See also Riddel's (1979) and Korg's (1995: 151) readings of hieroglyph in the poem.

9. Scalapino elides generic distinctions, challenging established literary categories. In an interview she described *The Front Matter* as "a novel, really a poem" (Frost 1996: 17).

10. Scalapino calls the time-less time that Helen enters the "light elation": "The place (the outside) is change *per se*. It is the light elation, a state of dreaming that is awake" (1994: 5). In *The Front Matter* the light elation motif is an alternative to self (ego), an awareness that, as in H.D.'s text, transcends time and place: "The elation is clear and real, that the physical state is endless"; "continual worry is barred by the elation in a light lucidity"; "no days are sustained in the light elation. No worrying comes up in it" (Scalapino 1996: 19, 21, 36). But as acts of sex and violence proliferate, "light lucidity" and "no worrying" seem elusive indeed.

11. The "thousand-petalled lily" is repeated three times in *The Front Matter*, twice referring to the character Akira (Scalapino 1996: 43, 87) and once related to emotional distance and response: "The response, there, has to be increased continually, like some still drug. H.D.'s thousand-petalled lily" (Scalapino 1996: 51).

12. See Hart (1995) for a reading of the circular movements of memory and forgetting—in his view a hermeneutical process—in *Helen in Egypt*.

Palimpsestic Stagger

NATHANIEL MACKEY

"I tend to pursue resonance rather than resolution, so I glimpsed a stubborn, albeit improbable world whose arrested glimmer elicited slippages of hieratic drift" (Mackey 1997: 17). This was in 1979 in a letter inscribed above a signatory initial, one of the letters attributed to composer/multi-instrumentalist N. that comprise *Bedouin Hornbook*. I didn't consciously have H.D. in mind, but the fact that her initials are there in the last two words, "hieratic drift," seems appropriate. Helen says in *Helen in Egypt*: "yes—I drifted here" (H.D. 1961: 174). I'd had H.D. consciously enough in mind in an earlier letter, writing of Ba cutting itself off from Legba to hide out in Egypt like Stesichorus's Helen, but here her presence was more faint, more at a remove, written over as in a palimpsest—which also seems appropriate. No one, after all, has done more to bring that term to our attention than H.D.

The work this particular letter was prompted by, a pastel from Irving Petlin's *Lake As a Furnace* series, is itself palimpsestic, posing geologic features as inscriptions upon earlier features, revisions and partial erasures of earlier features. Furnace precedes lake in a series of pastels presenting surfaces water will efface, parched, arid landscapes water will eventually cover or, if not entirely cover, differently articulate. It's as if the lake has been rubbed away to reveal a previous level of imprint, erased or partially erased as though geologic strata were a series of drafts. The revealed stratum itself partakes of a draftlike provisionality; differing kinds and degrees of definition and finish merge, coexist. The revealed stratum, in its unequal development, implies and partly reveals other coexistent strata. This is also true of the human or quasi-human figures populating these landscapes, just as in H.D.'s work human de-

velopment is crippled and complicated by the palimpsestic presence of
earlier steps along the way:

> and anyhow,
> we have not crawled so very far
>
> up our individual grass-blade
> toward our individual star.   (1973: 23)

So it was that, years after seeing a Petlin pastel for the first time, I chose
one of those in the *Lake As a Furnace* series for the cover of my compact
disc *Strick: Song of the Andoumboulou 16–25*. The Andoumboulou, as
I've explained elsewhere, are an earlier, failed form of human being in
the cosmology of the Dogon of West Africa, a flawed, earlier form I
think of as a rough draft of human being, the rough draft we continue
to be, compounded of starward reach and, as H.D. puts it, "the palimpsest / of past misadventure" (1973: 6).

It was Robert Duncan and his companion, Jess, who introduced me
to Petlin's work. I first saw one of his pieces at their house in San Francisco in 1979. The pastel that prompted the *Bedouin Hornbook* letter I
quoted from hung on the wall of a stairwell. It was also Duncan who
ushered me into H.D.'s work, albeit indirectly. It wasn't that I hadn't
read H.D. before meeting him or that I hadn't read her prior to reading
his readings of her in *The H.D. Book*. Though neither deeply nor especially well, I had read the Grove Press *Selected Poems* in my late teens.
The image of her that has had so much currency—classical, chaste, austere—probably got in the way of that reading. It wasn't until some years
later that I could recognize the discrepant strain running counter to that
image, the mixed-metaphorical promiscuity of such lines as:

> . . . inviting mountains
> of snow-clad foam-tipped
> green walls of sea-water
>
> to rise like ramparts about her.   (H.D. 1961: 278)

Reading more and more of Duncan's work led me to read H.D. more
deeply. Her importance to him had been made clear enough by three
pieces in *Roots and Branches*, the first book of his I bought: "A Sequence
of Poems for H.D.'s 73rd Birthday," "After Reading H.D.'s *Hermetic
Definitions*," and "Doves." Still, it was my reading, during the early seventies, of the sections of *The H.D. Book* that could be found in maga-

zines and journals that led me to return to H.D.'s work. I went this time
to the long poems *Trilogy* and *Hermetic Definition*, which had only recently, at last, been published, and *Helen in Egypt*, which had been in
print for a while.

There is, however, a sense in which I'd read H.D. more deeply even
before this, a sense in which I'd become a reader of her work upon
becoming a reader of Duncan's work. When, browsing in a bookstore
in 1965, I happened upon a copy of *Roots and Branches* and pulled it off
the shelf, I was drawn in by lines behind or beneath which lay, I found
upon my return to H.D.'s work in the early seventies, these lines from
Helen in Egypt:

> there is no before and no after,
> there is one finite moment
> that no infinite joy can disperse   (H.D. 1961: 303)

At the time I pulled *Roots and Branches* off the shelf I was in the habit of
turning first to the backs of new, unfamiliar books, so the first lines of
Duncan's I ever read were those at the end of the last poem in the book,
"The Continent," the eleven lines of its concluding section, section 6:

> There is only the one time.
> There is only the one god.
> There's only the one promise
>
> and from its flame
> the margins of the page flare forth.
> There's only the one page.
>
> the rest remains
> in ashes. There is only
> the one continent, the one sea—
> moving in rifts, churning, enjambing,
> drifting feature from feature.   (Duncan 1969: 176)

These lines drew me in, reeled me in, immediately made me one of
Duncan's readers, one of H.D.'s readers. They were lines in a sense I
would later hear Duncan himself speak of: lines *cast*, as in fishing. I was
caught.

Among the elements I was caught by, caught up in, was Duncan's
much-remarked-on music. It was also the straight-out metaphysical
wont of the first three lines that drew me in, an annunciative assurance
whose willingness to advance vatic risk shows that it sees itself to be

such once we get to "from its flame / the margins of the page flare forth." The order of statement loomed large among the elements that drew me in—that and the accumulative, incremental furtherance given to statement, the apparently confident assertions of singularity ("There is only the one time. / There is only the one god") whose apparency has to do with a subsequent mix of qualifications and contagion. That there could be "only the one page" and an ashen remainder as well, "only the one time" but a reminder as well, reveals annunciative assurance to have been other than the declaration or proclamation it appeared to be, reveals it to have instead been a proposition (that word Duncan liked so much), having to do with lure, of course, but implicitly confessing lack. That the final assertion of singularity and totality ("There is only / the one continent, the one sea") is followed and refigured by lines that give the last word to rift, drift, fragment, fracture, ushers rhetorical swell into a rhythmic retreat into fractal subsidence, subtended ends of a tidalectical swing between annunciative ebb and annunciative flow.

"Tidalectical" is a term I borrow from another poet whose work has been important to me, Kamau Brathwaite. Another of his coinages comes to mind as well: "driftword." The bookstore I first read those lines of Duncan's in was in a shopping mall in southern California in a town called Costa Mesa, not far from Newport Beach, but I felt I stood on an erosive, remoter coast. I've been drawn repeatedly to articulations of a coastal poetics, a coastal way of knowing, H.D.'s prominent among them. "An enclosure. Each wave is as to grasp / is an enclosure," I wrote in "Song of the Andoumboulou: 2." And later: "Wet sand and water / wet our feet, all / shore dissolves" (Mackey 1985: 38). The "desolate coast" on which Helen and Achilles meet in *Helen in Egypt* poses coastal knowledge as dissolute knowledge, repetitive, compulsive knowledge, undulatory, repeatedly undone and reconstituted—dissolute enough to call Paris's knowledge into question:

> But what could Paris know of the sea,
> its beat and long reverberation,
> its booming and delicate echo,
>
> its ripple that spells a charm
> on the sand, the rock-lichen,
> the sea-moss, the sand,
>
> and again and again, the sand,   (H.D. 1961: 304)

This reiterates its earlier assertion "I say there is only one image," an assertion echoed in Duncan's palimpsestic "only the one time . . . only the one god . . . only the one promise . . . only the one page."

Antonio Benitez-Rojo writes in *The Repeating Island*:

> The culture of the Peoples of the Sea is a flux interrupted by rhythms which attempt to silence the noises with which their own social formation interrupts the discourse of Nature. . . . [T]he cultural discourse of the Peoples of the Sea attempts . . . to neutralize violence and to refer society to the transhistorical codes of Nature. . . . [T]he culture of the Peoples of the Sea expresses the desire to sublimate social violence through referring itself to a space that can only be intuited through the poetic, since it always puts forth an area of chaos. In this paradoxical space, in which no one has the illusion of experiencing a totality, there appear to be no repressions or contradictions; there is no desire other than that of maintaining oneself within the limits of this zone for the longest possible time, in free orbit, beyond imprisonment or liberty.   (1992: 16–17)

This is what I felt or found in those lines on the last page of *Roots and Branches* and felt or found again a few years later in H.D.'s work. But the sublimation of social violence is only that, and the poetic knows it. Thus the need for a crosscut or cross-accentual tug between rapture and erosion, the tidalectical to-and-fro the poem gives the last word to. Hence the Soninke tale of Gassire's lute in which the violence the poetic would otherwise sublimate is not only acknowledged but exulted in, the tale of a lute being fed by the blood of war. It is a tale Duncan had recourse to, a tale H.D., following a suggestion by Homer, offered a Greek version of:

> was Troy lost for a subtle chord,
>
> a rhythm as yet un-heard,
> was it Apollo's snare?
> was Apollo passing there?
>
> was a funeral-pyre to be built,
> a holocaust of the Greeks,
> because of a fluttering veil,

> or because Apollo granted a lute-player,
> a rhythm as yet unheard,
> to challenge the trumpet-note?   (1961: 229)

In 1980 I appended two epigraphs to *Gassire's Lute*, my study of Duncan's Vietnam War poems: Rene Char's "Art knows nothing of History but helps itself to its terror" (1973: n.p.) and Charles Olson's "We drink / or break open / our veins solely / to know" (1983: 175). I meant them to suggest historical terror's ability to vex ostensible knowledge, ostensible witness, something the title of my book of poems *Eroding Witness* was also meant to suggest. I saw and see such vexation, a necessary vexation, answering or inoculative by turns, in H.D.'s as well as Duncan's work.

But noting such precedence as that of H.D.'s "Eros? Eris?" (1961: 115) to Duncan's "Eris in Eros" (1968: 6) wasn't all my return to her work entailed. A confusion or a conflation of coastal sand with desert sand, undulatory premises with ambulatory premises, emerged from my reading *Trilogy* in close proximity to *Helen in Egypt*. The latter's "new Mortal" Achilles, having "limped slowly across the sand" (H.D. 1961: 10), would eventuate in *Bedouin Hornbook*'s conjugation of Legba, the limping god of West Africa, or, more exactly, of Ba, an amputated, Egyptian rendering of Legba, with Stesichorus's Helen. Such ambiguation, early on, seeded itself in reflections on serial poetics nourished by H.D.'s use of the poetic sequence. Her insistence upon a singularity beyond or beneath seriality, the "one image" the sequencing of poems cannot capture but is included by, suggested that the gaps between poems in a sequence owned up to, if not advertised, a possibility of unitary consciousness beyond the sequence's reach:

> . . . I do not want
>
> to talk about it,
> I want to minimize thought,
>
> concentrate on it
> till I shrink,
>
> dematerialize
> and am drawn into it.   (H.D. 1973: 77)

Looking over my copy of *Trilogy*, I see that during one of my readings I wrote out a passage from *Frontiers of Consciousness*, edited by John

White. From an essay by Keith Floyd, "Of Time and Mind: From Paradox to Paradigm," which likens our normal perception of time and motion (lower-case consciousness) to the cinematographic illusion of motion created by a succession of still frames, I copied the following: "In Consciousness, the one frame is every frame, storing an infinitude of images in an infinitely creative pattern of pure and perfect ambiguity." This I followed with an etymological note on the word "ambiguity": "L. *ambigere*, to wander about." The advantage of the serial poem (or, more modestly, its honesty) appeared to lie in its not effacing the borders around the frame, the break between frames, its acceptance of an itinerary and a multiplicity it would get beyond but admits it can't.

H.D.'s recursive, desultory way of moving through the long poems furthered the sense of a desert ethic, a nomadic measure I'd begun to be taken by. Alain Robbe-Grillet's work, which I'd read during the late sixties, particularly *Jealousy*, *The Voyeur*, and *In the Labyrinth*, had already pointed me in this direction. The haunting, unpredictable way in which, in *Jealousy*, the squashing of a centipede comes up again and again, each time by an alternate route, a different chain of events, had especially stayed with me, charged with an air of obsession, ambiguations of possession and dispossession I recognized and took to in H.D.'s work as well. *Trilogy*, *Helen in Egypt*, and *Hermetic Definition* appeared driven, all their affirmations notwithstanding, by apprehensions of desertion or destitution. A sense of unremitting disquiet, unremitting extremity, susceptible to endless revisitation and variation, meandering transit through mixed emotional states, seemed as much of moment as those affirmations. (It wasn't until the early eighties that I read H.D.'s prose. I found this quality even more evident there.) Her suggestion in *Helen in Egypt* that "Crete would seduce Greece, / Crete inherited the Labyrinth from Egypt" (H.D. 1961: 169) recalled Robbe-Grillet's use of the labyrinth as a figure for the predicament recursive movement seeks to be done with or to undo. She goes on to write, self-reflexively:

> my meanderings back and forth,
> till I learned by rote
> the intimate labyrinth
>
> that I kept in my brain,
> going over and over again
> the swiftest way to take

through this arched way or that,
patient to re-trace my steps
or swift to dart

past a careless guard at the gate;
O, I knew my way,
O, I knew my ways,   (H.D. 1961: 265)

That the labyrinth, in her case as in Robbe-Grillet's, is also a figure
for recursive movement itself shows nomadic measure to be desperate
measure.

Reading *Trilogy*, *Helen in Egypt*, and *Hermetic Definition*, I was also
particularly drawn to the prominence of Egypt in H.D.'s work. The
black studies revolts of the sixties had indicted racism on a variety of
fronts, canonical renderings of history and cultural inheritance among
them, particularly, in significant instances, as these had instituted and
perpetuated a disassociation of Egypt from Africa. Egypt was contested
ground, reclaimed for Africa in a range of texts I was then reading:
Cheikh Anta Diop's *The African Origin of Civilization*, John G. Jackson's
Introduction to African Civilizations, E. A. Wallis Budge's *Osiris and the
Egyptian Resurrection*, Ishmael Reed's *Conjure* and *Mumbo Jumbo*, Amiri
Baraka's *In Our Terribleness* and "From the Egyptian." In addition, va-
lorizations of Egypt were to be found in the music I was listening to.
Sun Ra had been invoking Egypt in various ways for years, but there
were also others: Cecil Taylor's *Nefertiti, the Beautiful One Has Come*,
Pharoah Sanders's "Upper Egypt and Lower Egypt," John Coltrane's
Sun Ship, Alice Coltrane's *Ptah, the El Daoud*, "Lovely Sky Boat," "The
Ankh of Amen-Ra," and "Isis and Osiris," Wayne Shorter's "Nefertiti."
And in Duncan's *Tribunals* I read:

> . . . Egypt, the image of
> Heaven, Africa
> Her land, Her plants, Her animals,
> Osiris, the ever flowing
> returning river out of Africa.   (1970: 7–8)

Egypt's Africanity isn't as explicitly acknowledged in H.D.'s work, but
she clearly, consistent with Herodotus and others, views Egypt as importantly antecedent to Greece. She insists on pushing her immersion
in Greek tradition back to Egypt, implicitly debunking the false begin-

ning made of Greece by what Martin Bernal in *Black Athena* calls the Aryan model of Western civilization.

H.D.'s Egypt is a measure of lack, the excised ancestor on whose excision Western civilization Westernized itself. It persists like a phantom limb, advancing a critique of the rationalist-materialist premises Western civilization arrogates to itself, a critique of the arrogation if not the premises themselves. In *Trilogy*, these premises exact a toll during World War II, returning a repressed Egyptian disposition in the form of a pun:

> yet give us, they still cry,
> give us books,
>
> folio, manuscript, old parchment
> will do for cartridge cases;
>
> irony is bitter truth
> wrapped up in a little joke,
>
> and Hatshepsut's name is still circled
> with what they call the *cartouche*.   (H.D. 1973: 16)

In *Helen in Egypt* Egypt relativizes the reality and reach of such premises. It is more real, *"an ecstatic of semi-trance state,"* *"another dimension,"* *"a transcendental plane,"* a way of looking at the world aslant: "Did her eyes slant in the old way?" (H.D. 1961: 109, 112, 255, 245). The desire to *"bring Egypt and Greece together"* or to go *"back to Egypt but in a Greek mode"* gives way, as if in reference to the historical excision, to "Crete-Egypt must be slain" (H.D. 1961: 80, 178, 182).

But it cannot be slain. It is, along with everything else it is, the no-madic, recursive measure itself. It is returned to in "Winter Love":

> O unseen and unknown,
> wrap me round and round
>
> with Egypt's linen as the dead are wrapped,
> mystically cut, cauterise
> as with fire, the wound from which
>
> the heart and entrails were drawn out;
>   (H.D. 1972: 109)

It returns or is returned to not only as a carrier of cultural critique but as something personal, felt, a remnant, a reminder, some first, unfulfilled promise:

> there is something left over,
> the first unsatisfied desire—
> the first time, that first kiss,   (H.D. 1972: 91)

I shouldn't end without saying that the sting of unrelieved longing spoke to me as deeply as anything in H.D.'s work—so much so I wasn't thinking of these lines when I wrote in "Melin":

> Never another time
> like the first but
>   to be free of its
>
>   memory.
> This they'd pick their
>   hearts out aiming
>
>   for.   (Mackey 1993c: 23)

Angles of Incidence / Angels of Dust: Operatic Tilt in the Poetics of H.D. and Nathaniel Mackey

ADALAIDE MORRIS

This is an essay about alignments. Its intent is to make a tangent between two complicated poetics, both, as it happens, articulated through a mix of math and myth. H.D.'s "Tribute to the Angels," book 2 of her World War II *Trilogy*, and Nathaniel Mackey's *Djbot Baghostus's Run*, book 2 of his serial work "From a Broken Bottle Traces of Perfume Still Emanate," are tangential in a geometric sense; they touch, that is, without intersection or overlap. Mackey, the younger writer, does not cite H.D.; "From a Broken Bottle" is prose, not poetry; its angel is more Afro-Caribbean than Judeo-Christian; its angle, more Riemannian than Euclidean. The event this essay graphs is a reading— "[an] angle," as H.D. puts it, "of incidence"—that is also, inevitably, an "angle of reflection" (1973: 45). The extravagant, self-reflexive, mythopoetic word-work that aligns these poets helps to explain the ways in which their writing exceeds not only the gendered and racialized vocabularies so often deployed to analyze it but also the modernist and postmodernist paradigms most frequently used to position it. The metathetic wobble between *angle* and *angel* is, for both poets, much more than a trick: it is a habit of thought, a method of reasoning, an improvisatory, self-reflexive, over-the-top poetics: "operatic extremity," in Mackey's phrasing, "operatic tilt" (1993b: 186).

Like much of H.D.'s and Mackey's writing, "Tribute to the Angels" and *Djbot Baghostus's Run* are constructed stereoscopically. They work, that is, like the optical instrument that creates three-dimensional illusions by bringing into a single focus photographs of the same scene taken from slightly different angles. The flash of depth—the stereoscopic moment—occurs in the instant the viewer's eye makes one picture out of two or more angles. H.D.'s evocation of this phenomenon comes in her description of the book carried by the Lady in the vision at the heart of "Tribute to the Angels." The pages of this book, H.D. suggests, will reveal a tale told from two or more distinct angles:

> a tale of a Fisherman,
> a tale of a jar or jars,
>
> the same—different—the same attributes,
> different yet the same as before.   (1973: 105)

The wavering, perspectival energy of the writing in H.D.'s poem, like the narrative—"written / or unwritten" (1973: 105)—in the dream of the book within the poem, is a flicker, a shimmer of angles, a stereoscopic vision.

Mackey's evocation of the stereoscopic in *Djbot Baghostus's Run* is equally elaborate. As in "Tribute to the Angels," it emerges from the narrator's struggle to account for a series of dreams of a woman. In Mackey's book, the Lady is the drummer sought by the narrator's band, the Mystic Horn Society. In one night, all five band members dream of a genius, a genie, variously called Jeannie, Djeannine, Penny, or, when she finally appears in the flesh, Drennette. "I saw it all," the trumpet player Aunt Nancy says, giving her slant on the collective vision, "as though from a distance, as if thru an eye made of opera glass" (Mackey 1993b: 47). Aunt Nancy's odd phrase—one eye made out of a double-tubed opera glass—generates the first paragraph of the book's extravagant opera starring Djbot Baghostus, aka Jarred Bottle: "I sat down and began a new after-the-fact lecture/libretto," Mackey's narrator N. explains in a letter to his interlocutor, the mysterious Angel of Dust. "The first paragraph . . . came so effortlessly it seemed to be writing itself: 'Jarred Bottle's I made of opera glass dropped out'" (Mackey 1993b: 50).[1]

Like H.D.'s tale of "the same—different—the same," Mackey's lecture/libretto is multiple in plot and in construction. Layering sound as a stereopticon layers sight, its first sentence—"Jarred Bottle's I made of opera glass dropped out"—functions as an overture that the opera proceeds to develop in exuberant detail. "Jarred Bottle" is a bottle shocked, a bottle unbottled, a signifier warped to release multiple signifieds.[2] In the aural torque of N.'s phrasing, Aunt Nancy's "eye made of opera glass" twists into Jarred Bottle's "I made of opera glass"; the lingering

phrase "Bottle's I" reaches outward toward its wind-instrument muta-
tion, "Bottle's sigh"; and the drift of a final consonant across the di-
vide between segments turns the verb "dropped out" into the directive
"drop doubt." These sound effects—the lush transformations, the pho-
nemic overlaps Garrett Stewart terms "transegmental drifts"—register
for the ear the multiplicity stereoscopy registers for the eye. What the
ear hears in the sentence's operatic tilt is the convergence of two or
more angles of sound: "an aural," in Stewart's words, "rather than scrip-
tive palimpsest" (1990: 246).

To enter the both/and world of the pun, it is necessary, as Mackey's
transegmental waver suggests, both to drop out and to drop doubt. In
the momentum of polyphony, the "eye" that becomes an "I" also
evokes, in its unfolding, an operatic "aye": an assent, in this case, to the
pluralization and destabilization of signifiers crucial to serious wordplay. If the conventions of reasoning that govern law and logic depend
on discrimination, the poetics of operatic tilt places its bet on assimilation: the wager of the pun is that words that sound alike are also—
overtly or covertly—alike in meaning. Simplicity, earnestness, and sta-
bility are not foundational to the poetics of "Tribute to the Angels"
and *Djbot Baghostus's Run*.[3] The logic of these texts rides on surprise
and surmise: the surprise of aural overlap, the surmise of polyphonic
thinking.

In operatic tilt, sound leads thought. Puns, for H.D. and Mackey, are
"wit" in two mutually imbricated senses: not just ingenious engagements
between discrepancies but also, more importantly, a kind of intelligence,
perception, or understanding, a manner or method of thought. In his
essay "The Puncept in Grammatology," Gregory Ulmer devises the
term "puncept" to make this point: for him, as for Derrida, the pun is
"the philosopheme of a new cognition" (1988: 165), a way of knowing
that marks the postmodern. Like a "concept," Ulmer's "puncept" is a
thought or notion that joins elements that have specific common properties, but unlike concepts, which establish sets on the assumption of
similar signifieds, puncepts establish "sets formed on the basis of similar
signifiers." "If it seems intuitively possible (if not obvious) that puncepts
work as well for organizing thought as concepts . . . ," Ulmer writes,
"then you are likely to possess a post-modernist sensibility" (1988: 164).

Ulmer aligns the difference between concepts and puncepts with the
difference between the logic of mathematics and the logic of semiotics.

"Unlike physics, in which two bodies may not occupy the same space," he explains, "language is a material in which the same names are capable of supporting several mutually exclusive meanings simultaneously" (Ulmer 1988: 165). One example of punceptual cognition would be the set formed by "eye," "I," and "aye," the triplet that generates the extravagant initial sentence of Mackey's "antithetical opera" (1993b: 7); another would be the set formed by the metathetical waver of "angels" and "angles," a puncept Mackey and H.D. share with a much earlier Gregory (Pope Gregory the Great), who, inquiring as to the tribe of two pagan English boys in the Roman marketplace, rejoiced in the connection between their name and their beauty: "'They are called Angles,' he was told. 'That is appropriate,' he [replied], 'for they have angelic faces.'"[4]

In carrying us back toward the punceptual blend of mathematics and mythology in "Tribute to the Angels" and *Djbot Baghostus's Run*, Pope Gregory's wordplay points to a limitation in Ulmer's argument, for the puncept is not just a philosopheme of the postmodern but also a structural unit in premodern and/or non-Western modes of thought. For the classical philosophers H.D. admired and the Dogon philosophers Mackey invokes, puns are not so much quirks of language as its quick, its essence, its vital core.[5] Against the high modernist search for stable definitions and unified, monological meaning, Mackey poses the dynamic he calls in *Bedouin Hornbook* (the first volume of "From a Broken Bottle . . .") "slippages of hieratic drift" (1997: 23). N. invokes this phrase to describe forms of art that "pursue resonance rather than resolution" (Mackey 1997: 23): his examples are the eroding colors of a canvas in pastels and the smudged notes of a jazz improvisation, but his phrase also fits the verbal play that again and again in these texts moves from similarities in sound toward similarities in signification.

In contrast to wisecracks, which close in a flash, "hieratic drift" is open-ended, allowing meanings to slip one from another in a swift generative series. The locus classicus of this process in H.D.'s work is the semiotic alchemy of "Tribute to the Angels": "Now polish the crucible," H.D. begins, speaking to herself as well as to her readers,

> and in the bowl distill
>
> a word most bitter, *marah*,
> a word bitterer still, *mar*,

... till *marah-mar*
are melted, fuse and join

and change and alter,
mer, mere, mère, mater, Maia, Mary,

Star of the Sea,
Mother.   (1973: 71)

Gender-based readings of this passage tend to anchor its "hieratic drift" in one or another stable meaning—the re-vision of patriarchal tradition or restoration of female divinity in Susan Stanford Friedman's inaugural reading (1981: 228, 254), the claim of "gender authority" in Rachel Blau DuPlessis's summary of the struggle of H.D.'s career (1986: 86–100)—but Mackey's notion of "slippage" suggests a more radical reading practice, a practice that uses the generativity of language to undermine the way of knowing whose constraints it brings to light. Instead of progressing along H.D.'s series of charged words—*marah-mar*, mer, mere, mère, mater, Maia, Mary—as if they were steps toward the "right answer," "Mother," readings that start from the idea of slippage "get the drift" by privileging process over outcome. Instead of a "right answer" (a logic of mathematics, in Ulmer's terms), we enter instead into the generative logic of semiotics.[6]

The opus of operatic tilt is a practice of extravagant, open-ended meaning-making that is for H.D. and Mackey at once a poetics, an ethics, and a politics. For H.D., in "Tribute to the Angels," the vehicle of this insistence is alchemical; for Mackey, in *Djbot Baghostus's Run*, it is "operatic"; for both, more importantly and in the term's many meanings, it is an "operation." Improvisatory and transformative, operatic tilt distinguishes "radical modernism"—a way of reading such writers as Stein, Williams, Pound, H.D., Duncan, and Mackey—from its two better-known alternatives, "high modernism," on the one hand, post-structuralist postmodernism, on the other.[7]

Of necessity, in what follows, I use these terms—the binary pair "modernism" and "postmodernism" and their interrupter, "radical modernism"—in a shorthand fashion, for they are useful not as truth claims but as speculative formations, heuristics that distinguish the poetics of H.D. and Mackey from the practice of high modernists like

T. S. Eliot, on the one hand, and postmodernists like John Ashbery, on the other. All three terms are vexed, complex, and variously deployed. As a rough guide to their differences, it is helpful to recall Brian Mc-Hale's distinction between modernism as an epistemological practice whose logic is that of the detective story and postmodernism as an ontological practice whose logic is that of a science fiction tale. Like the questor in "The Waste Land," on the one hand, high modernism looks to locate an answer, solve a problem, or lay out a structure of truth; like a speculator in an Ashbery poem, on the other, postmodernism looks to project or construct a world (or a world-within-a-world), a zone of imaginative constructions that supports, for a moment, a play of suppositions. The term "radical modernism" provides a third alternative. Its roots lie in the operations—the "operatic extremity, operatic tilt"—of language. Radical modernism challenges "natural," "realistic," or scientistic epistemologies by situating language as an entity with properties of its own rather than as an instrument to be used neutrally or transparently to transmit a pregiven communication. At the same time, however, radical modernism challenges postmodern notions of epistemic randomness by insisting on a fit—albeit, in Mackey's words, a "rickety, imperfect fit," a "discrepant engagement" (1993a: 19)— between word and world.

To understand the semiotic logic of "Tribute to the Angels" and *Djbot Baghostus's Run*, it helps to turn for a moment to a seminal document of radical modernism: Ernest Fenollosa's *The Chinese Written Character as a Medium for Poetry*, written prior to Fenollosa's death in 1908, edited by Pound between 1913 and 1916, first published in 1919 in the *Little Review*, put out in book form by Stanley Nott in 1936, and reprinted as a pamphlet by City Lights Books. "The roots of poetry," Fenollosa declared, "are in language" (1936: 6). By "roots" Fenollosa meant not just poetry's origin, source, base, support, or core but also, in a linguistic sense, its radical: the element that carries its main freight of meaning. The basis from which words are derived by adding affixes or inflectional endings or through phonetic changes, a radical is flexible, generative, "alive and plastic" (Fenollosa 1936: 17). Because in Fenollosa's view Chinese written characters are a hieroglyphic language of radicals, they allow us to discern the join of word and world; they offer, that is, "a vivid shorthand picture of the *operations* of nature" (1936: 8, my emphasis).

The ideograph was crucial to Fenollosa and to Pound because they believed it to be capable of evading or exceeding the logic of scholasticism. Scholastic philosophy, for Fenollosa, is a language of nouns, "little hard units or concepts" (1936: 26); poetry, by contrast, is a language of radicals or roots. Like Ulmer's distinction between "concept" and "puncept," Fenollosa's argument pits monological and rigid signifieds against polyvalent and flexible signifiers, but the difference between Ulmer and Fenollosa is that for Fenollosa ideographs are "always vibrant with fold on fold of overtones *and* with natural affinities" (1936: 25, my emphasis). As an example of the Chinese written character in operation, Fenollosa points to the ideograph *ming* or *mei*, constructed from the sign of the sun together with the sign of the moon. The ideograph sun-and-moon is genetic code for the operation of light, verbal DNA for a core meaning *to shine, luminosity, bright*. Appearing with the ideograph for "cup," it can mean, all at once or by turns, "the cup sun-and-moons," "the sun-and-moon of the cup," "cup sun-and-moon," "sun-and-moon cup" (Fenollosa 1936: 17–18). In apprehending *ming*, Fenollosa concludes, returning us to H.D.'s alchemy and Mackey's opera, "we attain for a moment the inner heat of thought, a heat which melts down the parts of speech to recast them at will" (1936: 17).

When, for H.D., the words in the poem-bowl melt, fuse, change, and alter, the poet's alchemy at once distills them—separates or extracts their essential elements—and de-stills them—sets them into motion, restoring to them a vitality beyond parts of speech. The parallel operation in Mackey's series is the Mystic Horn Society's practice of jazz improvisation. In an enlightenment culture that privileges prediction, precision, and reproducibility, alchemy and improvisation become the abjected others of science and notated composition: expedients, in the popular view, tricks, even flat-out quackery. Just as *Trilogy* supposes that the alchemical operations of medieval Arabs involved sophisticated and advanced science, however, Mackey describes the improvisations of the musicians in *Djbot Baghostus's Run* as highly structured assertions, counterassertions, and argumentative advances characterized by intense preparation, design, and method.[8] As Mackey explains in an interview with Ed Foster, the jazz improvisations of avant-garde musicians like Cecil Taylor are not "free play" but "a language of reflection" (Mackey 1994: 77). Postbebop black music—the "new jazz"—makes "a significant break . . . with the tradition of the black musician as an embodiment of instantaneity, instinct, pure feeling, in some unmediated way uncomplicated by reflection and intellect" (Mackey 1994: 77). Its conversations require from players and audience alike a practice of sustained and rigorous listening.

The Mystic Horn Society's tribute to Monk, Marley, Mingus, and Lightnin' Hopkins performs what Mackey means in telling Foster that postbebop's "key ethic is improvisational" (Mackey 1994: 77). The tribute occurs at a specific time and place—"a three-night stint at a club called Earl's up north in Albany"—and is motivated by "the news that Monk had suffered a cerebral hemorrhage and was in a coma" (Mackey 1994: 172). "Three years ago Mingus, Marley last May, now Monk," one band member says, to which N. adds, "Lightnin' having died the week before" (Mackey 1994: 172). The band's response to the erosion of this generation is not to imitate their music but to regenerate it: like alchemists, that is, they break down and reconstitute—melt, fuse, change, and alter—the elements of compositions by Mingus, Marley, Monk, and Hopkins in a performance they call, formulaically, "Three M's and an H" (Mackey 1994: 173). To borrow Paul Zumthor's distinction between knowledge transmission in predominantly oral and predominantly literate cultures, their tribute is not a display of "memorization" but an act of "remembrance": characteristic of cultures that depend on writing, memorization abstracts knowledge from its context so it can be precisely replicated in any place, at any time, by any agent; characteristic of cultures that depend on oral—or, in this case, aural—transmission of knowledge, remembrance regenerates knowledge by integrating it into new contexts. "Three M's and an H" is, in this sense, the Mystic Horn Society's reflection on previous incidents, a riff on the trigonometry of "Tribute to the Angels" (Mackey 1994: 45).

The words "angularity" and "incidence" anchor N.'s description of the final segment of "Three M's and an H," the Mystic Horn Society's improvisation on Charles Mingus's "Free Cell Block F, 'tis Nazi USA."[9] As Mackey explains in his essay "The Changing Same: Black Music in the Poetry of Amiri Baraka," to call the music of composers like Monk, Andrew Hill, or Eric Dolphy "angular" or "oblique" is to stress its "spirit of interrogation and discontent." Less a mood than an argumentative tack, angularity undermines any knowledge that claims to be straightforward, complete, or sufficient. Because by definition it bends away from a previous assertion, improvisation underscores "the partial, provisional character of any proposition or predication . . . advancing a vigilant sense of any reign or regime of truth as susceptible to qualification. It thus calls into question the order by which it is otherwise conditioned on the basis of conditionality itself" (Mackey 1993a: 43). The sign of angularity in Mingus's piece is not the music itself, which has, N. tells the Angel of Dust, "uptown flair and good feeling" (Mackey 1993b: 177), but rather its title, which Mingus added after reading an *Ebony* article on southern prisons. The title is, therefore, Mackey summarizes, "a time-lapse equation linking before-the-fact tune with after-the-fact . . . intent" (1993b: 177). In testing and qualifying the tune, the title makes the music only the beginning of the story.

The band's performance of this part of "Three M's and an H" pays tribute to Mingus's improvisatory technique. They open by reading in unison the first paragraph of Ralph Ellison's *Invisible Man*, jamming Mingus's "Nazi" into Ellison's *not see*.[10] In a solo that takes off from this alignment, Penguin, the Mystic Horn Society's alto saxophonist, elaborates the phrase "not see" along the line of Mingus's indictment. "The Greensboro killings came up," N. tells the Angel. "The Atlanta child murders came up. The lynching last March in Alabama came up, as did a number of other such 'incidents' people choose not . . . to see for what they are" (Mackey 1993b: 178). Following Penguin on the tenor sax, N. torques *nazi* into the punceptual *note C*, which he plays over and over again, jumping octaves, varying placement and duration, insisting, until the audience gets the drift and yells, "Yeah, I hear you," "Yeah, break it down" (Mackey 1993b: 179). In the improvisational alchemy of this moment, the listeners—who themselves now enter the composition—remember, witness, and take a stand by pushing the hieratic slip, the drift, from *not see* to *see*.

In a pun that neatly superimposes the mathematics and mythology of *Djbot Baghostus's Run*, N. refers the Angel of Dust to "the doo-wop hyperbolics" of the Penguin's "Earth Angel," which he describes as an "exponential aria" that "offers a clue to the sort of opera I'm working toward" (Mackey 1993b: 186–87). Foregrounding the generativity of operatic tilt, the term "exponent" means both advocate or interpreter and the number or symbol placed to the right of and above another number, symbol, or expression to mark the power to which it is to be raised. In the Mystic Horn Society's improvisations, the interpretations of the five members of the band raise the power of the music of

Monk, Marley, Mingus, and Hopkins. The equation for their performance might be written $(3m + b)^5$, but the audience's response suggests
it could just as well be written $(3m + b)^n$. Just as *Trilogy* is a response to
the Nazi bombs falling on London—"an incident," as the newspapers
liked to put it, "here and there" (H.D. 1973: 3), "Free Cell Block F" is
an ongoing, open-ended speaking back to the totalitarianism of Nazis,
southern prisons, and the "incidents" in Greensboro, Atlanta, and Alabama, an angle of political, historical, and ethical reflection, an "anti-
thethical opera" (Mackey 1993b: 7).

There is, however, an important difference between the
mathematical formulations in H.D.'s "Tribute to the Angels" and those
in Mackey's "From a Broken Bottle Traces of Perfume Still Emanate,"
a difference that helps to clarify the variant deployments of radical modernism in these two writers. The formula H.D. embeds in *Trilogy* depends on a match or adequation between two angles, visible in figure 1.[11]

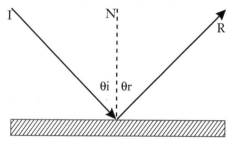

Although many elements fall and rise again in *Trilogy* (among others,
lightning, rain, flaming stones, bombs, cities, and angelic messengers),
it's easiest to imagine figure 1 as a depiction of a ray of light approaching and reflecting off a flat mirrored surface. The approaching ray of
light is the incident ray (labeled I in the figure); the ray of light leaving
is the reflected ray (R). At the point of incidence where the ray strikes
the mirror, a line can be drawn perpendicular to the surface of the mirror (the normal line, labeled N). This line divides the angle between the
incident ray and the reflected ray into two equal angles. The angle between the incident ray and the normal is known as the angle of incidence; the angle between the reflected ray and the normal is known as
the angle of reflection. The law, then, states that when light bounces off
a surface, the angle of incidence is equal to the angle of reflection.

In Mackey's "Broken Bottle" series, the operant rule is not equivalence but rather the principle Jarred Bottle calls in *Bedouin Hornbook* "*the fallacy of adequation. . . . The lack of any absolute fit*" (1997: 171), reiterated by N. in *Djbot Baghostus's Run* as "a principle of nonequivalence, an upfront absence of adequation" (1993b: 49). The figure N. invokes to demonstrate the lack of absolute fit is the asymptote, defined as "a line considered a limit to a curve in the sense that the perpendicular distance from a moving point on the curve to an axis approaches zero as the point moves an infinite distance from the origin."[12]

The limit of the curve, visible in figure 2, is measured by the evernarrowing gap between the line of the curve and the reference lines *x* and *y*. The term *asymptote* comes from the Greek, meaning nonintersecting, not converging, for the curve, by definition, approaches the axes or reference lines but never actually touches them.

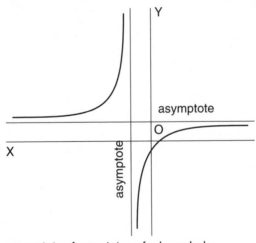

asymptote: Asymptotes of a hyperbola

In a text studded with geometrical curves (ellipses, hyperbolas, circles, and spirals, many set into motion and/or set to music),[13] the asymptote is *Bedouin Hornbook*'s most characteristic dynamic, the arc of its emotional, intellectual, physical, and musical operations. Members of the band suffer "asymptotic shivers," Jarred Bottle moves along an "asymptotic slope," a musician plays "an elliptic, asymptotic wisp of a theme," and all take care to respect the "asymptotic 'inch'" that generates their creativity (Mackey 1997: 46, 169, 202, 216). This "ontic, unbridgeable distance, a cosmogonic, uncrossable gap" (Mackey 1997:

170) in *Bedouin Hornbook* becomes in the next volume the "run" in *Djbot Baghostus's Run*: its pace, act, slope, distance, momentum, and freedom, "asymptotic sprint," "asymptotic pursuit," and "arch asymptotic aria" (Mackey 1993b: 191).

Mackey's asymptotic semiotics are anticipated in a second founda-tional document of radical modernism, Gertrude Stein's "A Carafe, That Is a Blind Glass," overture to *Tender Buttons*. Bouncing off a title that has the syntax of an equation (an *x*, that is a *y*), Stein's word portrait enacts the fallacy of adequation, the lack of any absolute fit. Her carafe is a variant of Williams's "bottle: unbottled," H.D.'s "tale of a jar or jars," Stevens's jar ajar in Tennessee. In "A Carafe, That Is a Blind Glass," Stein writes, "A kind in glass and a cousin, a spectacle and noth-ing strange a single hurt color and an arrangement in a system to point-ing. All this and not ordinary, not unordered in not resembling. The difference is spreading" (1990: 9). Like the rest of *Tender Buttons*, this paragraph is a "run" that swerves away from any act of equalizing or adequation. It emphasizes "not resembling" in the same instant it in-sists, like an asymptotic diagram, on the fact that it is "not unordered." Its waver of "the same—different—the same" is at the same time a waiver or deferral of "fit."[14] The litotes "not unordered," the oxymo-ronic "blind glass," the paradoxical phrase "a system to pointing" all gesture toward a gap language cannot quite cross. In case we miss this idea on a conceptual level, the paragraph performs it again for the ear in "the same—different—the same" of rhyme: a blind glass/a kind in glass, in/cousin, strange/arrange, not ordinary/not unordered. The meaning of "A Carafe, That Is a Blind Glass" is not—cannot be— equivalence. In its operatic tilt, the lack of adequation is not a failure but a release: a "difference [that] is spreading," the generative ongoing-ness and dispersal of punceptual thinking.[15]

The theories of language that underlie "Tribute to the Angels" and *Djbot Baghostus's Run* suggest a parallel way in which the poetics of these two writers differ in response to the politics and ethics of their times. For H.D., the working model is once again a match or adequation, here between word and thing or, less loosely, signifier and signified. "The Walls Do Not Fall," *Trilogy*'s first section, charts a straightforward and untroubled transit from concept to thing through the mediation of the word:

Without thought, invention,
you would not have been, O Sword,

without idea and the Word's mediation,
you would have remained

unmanifest in the dim dimension
where thought dwells,

and beyond thought and idea,
their begetter,

Dream,
Vision.   (H.D. 1973: 18)

In the fourfold passage from dream or vision to thought to word and
at last to thing, the Word is a go-between: messenger, mediator, rec-
onciler of difference. H.D.'s object of address in this passage—"O
Sword"—is symptomatic, for the difference between *Word's* and *Sword*
is not essence but position: *Sword* is *of the Word*, its anagram. As in the
biblical story of the Creation, the word makes manifest, brings forth,
generates, or realizes—makes real—that which has been "unmanifest
in the dim dimension / where thought dwells." This genealogy lays the
foundation for the linguistic alchemy of the next section, "Tribute to
the Angels," in which *marah*, *mar*, and *mater* are transformed to *Mary*
and *mother* by recombining the consonants *m*, *t*, *h*, and *r*. Although the
letters are rearranged, as in an anagram, they exist in equivalence: they
are made to balance, more or less, equally.

Mackey's principle of nonequivalence moves his thought in the opposite direction. Where H.D. tends to mute or suppress the discrepant,
Mackey amplifies and foregrounds it. For him, the relation of words to
things is oblique and angular—less an engagement of discrepancies
than a "discrepant engagement." *Discrepant Engagement* is, of course,
the title Mackey gives his collection of essays on Amiri Baraka, Robert
Duncan, Robert Creeley, Charles Olson, Kamau Brathwaite, Wilson
Harris, and other twentieth-century innovative and improvisatory writers. The title is asymptotic, "coined," Mackey explains, "in reference to
practices that, in the interest of opening presumably closed orders of
identity and signification, accent fissure, fracture, incongruity, the rickety, imperfect fit between word and world" (1993a: 19).

Unlike H.D.'s vision of the Word, which glances back at Genesis, Mackey's looks back to the creation myth of the Dogon of West Africa. In Dogon cosmology, as the sage Ogotommêli explains it to anthropologist Marcel Griaule, the making of cloth represents the cycle of life. The various components of the process—the warp, woof, footrest, shuttle, and heddles, the block on which the loom rests—stand for aspects of generativity: the opening and shutting of the womb; the phallic in-and-out of the serpent-shuttle; the stretched threads, which represent procreation; the woven cloth, which wraps the dead. "The craft of weaving . . . ," Ogotommêli concludes, "is the tomb of resurrection, the marriage bed and the fruitful womb" (Mackey 1993a: 73).

The loom rests on a solid piece of hard wood, to which the Dogon give the name "the creaking of the word." This creaking is, Mackey explains,

> the noise upon which the word is based, the discrepant foundation of all coherence and articulation, of the purchase upon the world fabrication affords. Discrepant engagement, rather than suppressing or seeking to silence that noise, acknowledges it. In its anti-foundational acknowledgment of founding noise, discrepant engagement . . . voic[es] reminders of the axiomatic exclusions upon which positings of identity and meaning depend. (1993a: 19)

The buzz, the resonance, the semiotic spread in Mackey's texts perform his version of "the creaking of the word" in a refusal of adequation as sustained and resolute as Stein's. Like the eponymous perfume, whose traces emanate from the shards of a broken bottle, like notes that fan out into chords or compositions reprised in multiple keys, words in Mackey's texts again and again split out into bracketed pairs or triplets, multiplying "ascent" into "accent" and "assent," for example, or breaking "compost" down to "compose" (1997: 25, 92).

Although H.D.'s story of the word's mediation moves in the direction of adequation rather than discrepancy, *Trilogy* also buzzes with not quite coincident aural doublets and triplets. In two often cited examples, "Venice" slides into "Venus," a word previously split out into "venereous," on the one hand, and "venerate," on the other (H.D. 1973: 74–78), as "Osiris" builds into "O, Sire, is" and breaks down into "zrr-hiss, / lightning in a not-known, // unregistered dimension" (H.D. 1973: 58). This thick and flickering ascent and breakdown in the work of H.D. and Mackey, this over-the-top extravagance, is the work of "operatic extremity, operatic tilt."

To an unsympathetic reader, "operatic extremity, operatic tilt" may seem merely "operatic": histrionic, that is, or, worse, hysterical. As if to blunt such a reading, both H.D. and Mackey embed it preemptively in their texts. The detractor in the first section of *Trilogy* sneers at the poet's

> . . . perilous ascent,
> ridiculous descent; rhyme, jingle,
>
> overworked assonance, nonsense,
> juxtaposition of words for words' sake,
>
> without meaning, undefined; . . .   (H.D. 1973: 44)

The detractor in *Bedouin Hornbook*—the first speaker at a press conference in a record store—is more succinct. His target is not convergence—"overworked assonance"—but dispersal: the Mystic Horn Society, he says, has a "tendency to . . . 'go off on tangents.'" "[A] piece of music should *gather*," he adds, to the applause of a knot of people in the classical section, "rather than *disperse* its component parts" (Mackey 1997: 16). Set like a trap at the beginning of each serial work, this critique acknowledges that operatic extremity is perilous, perhaps even, in a minimalist time, "ridiculous," but neither H.D. nor Mackey concedes that it is "without meaning, undefined," decorative, decadent, or irrelevant.

In the work of H.D. and Mackey, operatic tilt is an act, a habit, a praxis that moves outward, away from the "I," eroding the basis for any criticism that seeks, as Robin Blaser puts it in his essay on Jack Spicer, "to wrap itself around a personality" (Spicer 1989: 272). Operatic extremity cannot be recuperated to a pathology, for it does not point inward toward the psyche or soul. Blaser's name for this poetics is "the practice of outside." This practice is constitutive rather than descriptive, its truth lies in what it makes rather than what it describes, and it seeks, Blaser says, *"reopened language,"* one that "lets the unknown, the Other, the outside in again as a voice in the language" (Spicer 1989: 276).

The parallel to reopened language is reopened form, the run, the slip, the serial composition, which occurs, N. tells the Angel of Dust, in "submission to a processional muse" (Mackey 1997: 26).[16] H.D.'s definition—led by the triplet *have no, haven, heaven*—moves toward a similar conclusion. *"We are voyagers,"* H.D. writes,

> *. . . discoverers*
> *of the not-known,*
>
> *the unrecorded;*
> *we have no map;*
>
> *possibly we will reach haven,*
> *heaven.*   (1973: 59)

Exploring the dynamics of serial composition in a letter to Blaser, Spicer emphasized the necessity "not to search for the perfect poem but to let your way of writing of the moment go along its own paths, explore and retreat but never be fully realized (confined) within the boundaries of one poem" (1989: 61). This process, which Spicer attributes to Robert Duncan, Duncan absorbed at least partially from H.D. and passed on, in turn, to Mackey.[17] There is, however, an additional twist to the serial progressions of H.D. and Mackey: if with no set outcome—no heaven, no haven—the choice lies between the random and the experimental, H.D. and Mackey pick the latter over the former. Unlike aleatory postmodernists, their procedure is to move not just from event to event but also from event toward law.

The mystical mathematics or mathematical mystics of "Tribute to the Angels" and "From a Broken Bottle . . ." record a passage through destruction into generativity. What falls, H.D.'s law of angles implies, rises again, be it moisture, fire, a city, or a civilization, be it "angles of light" (1973: 150) or, in a deft slippage (a metathesis intensified by a transegmental drift), "angels of flight." "Tribute to the Angels" ends with the assurance that the war's *"zrr-hiss, / lightning in a not-known dimension,"* the incendiary "whirr and roar in the high air," is equal to the *this is* of another here and now: *"This is,"* "Tribute" concludes, *"the flowering of the rod, / this is the flowering of the burnt-out wood"* (H.D. 1973: 58, 19, 110).

The mathematics of angles in H.D. meets the mathematics of the asymptote in Mackey at just this point: the point of genesis or generativity. Here, N. tells the Angel of Dust, "the muse of inclusiveness awakens one to a giddy sense of spin, a pregnant, rotund integrity eternally and teasingly and whirlingly out of reach . . . a sense of asymptotic wobble" (Mackey 1993b: 71). At the end of *Djbot Baghostus's Run,* Jarred Bottle returns to amplify N.'s point by invoking "the tiny primeval seed"—the place of all-flowering—in two incidents, one musical and the other cosmogonical.

The incidents occur in two quotations in Djbot Baghostus's mind in the final scene of *Djbot Baghostus's Run.* After the drummer, Dannie Richmond, had been in Mingus's band for nine months, the first story goes, Mingus asked him, "Suppose you had to play a composition alone. How could you play it on the drums?" and then supplied an answer: "Okay, if you had a dot in the middle of your hand and you were going in a circle, it would have to expand and go round and round, and get larger and larger and larger. And at some point it would have to stop, and then this same circle would have to come back around, around, around to the little dot in the middle of your hand" (Mackey 1993b: 190). This spiral movement in two directions coincides with Ogotommêli's figure for creation in the second quotation: "The internal movement of germination was prefigured by this spiral movement in two directions, which is the movement of [the tiny primeval seed the Dogon call] the *po.* It is said: 'The seed grows by turning.' Inside, while germinating, it first spins in one direction, then, after bursting, that is, after the emergence of the germ, it spins in the other direction, in order to produce its root and stalk" (Mackey 1993a: 190). This radical wobble—improvisational, alchemical—is the creative force in action.

"It's exactly here," N. tells the Angel of Dust, "that revelation and recuperation lock horns, the latter almost inevitably the victor" (Mackey 1993b: 71). The binaries that stop the spin or abort the wobble are to interpreters of the last three decades of this century what scholasticism was to Pound and Fenollosa in the first two: a mark of the limits of Western logic that poetry bids to bypass. In the moment of recuperation, N. explains, "the potential breakthru, the asymmetrical fissure which begins to be glimpsed, is almost immediately closed off, almost immediately traded away for the consolations of a binary opposition" (Mackey 1993b: 71).

The operatic poetics of radical modernists like Pound, Stein, H.D., and Mackey is a struggle—not always, or even often, successful—to dodge these consolations. Although both "Tribute to the Angels" and

Djbot Baghostus's Run respond to gendered and racialized readings, neither text follows a binary logic of realism. This is a strength, not, as has sometimes been implied, an embarrassment or deficit. In their excess, their operatic tilt, H.D. and Mackey swerve away from the accessible and familiar politics of opposition. "My view," Mackey writes in the introduction to *Discrepant Engagement*, "is that there has been far too much emphasis on accessibility when it comes to writers from socially marginalized groups. This has resulted in shallow, simplistic readings that belabor the most obvious aspects of the writer's work and situation, readings that go something like this: 'So-and-so is a black writer. Black people are victims of racism. So-and-so's writing speaks out against racism'" (1993a: 17–18).

The inaugural readings of H.D.—the readings that made her accessible to my generation—speak out eloquently against oppression based on gender and on race, but it is time to complicate the oppositions of these readings by following her into more intricate, mystical, and chaotic territories. This is one benefit of reading H.D. next to Mackey or, to turn the spiral in this collection of essays, reading H.D. and Mackey next to Mackey reading H.D. "We find the traditions that nourish us," Mackey told Peter O'Leary in a recent interview. "We make them up in part, we invent the traditions and the sense of the past, the genealogies, that allow us to follow certain dispositions that we have, to be certain things we want to be, to do certain things we want to do" (O'Leary 1997: 37).

The benefits of reading Mackey in accord/in a chord with H.D. are not only an intensification of important complexities in his thought but also an appreciation of his radical modernist genealogy, a lineage he traces back though Duncan to H.D., Pound, and Williams as well as forward from Clarence Major and Amiri Baraka to Kamau Brathwaite and Wilson Harris. As Aldon Lynn Nielsen argues in *Black Chant*, his important study of the languages of African-American postmodernism, "If an intertextual history of African-American poetics is to succeed, it must also take as part of its assignment a study of the multitudinous ways in which black writings relate themselves to those writings by whites that seem to afford openings for transracial signifying practices. If American postmodernity is to be comprehended in its transracial plenitude, critical readings will have to follow black poets as they read and transform the texts of whites" (1997: 36). The resonance of transracial and transgender signifying practices in the work of H.D. and Mackey not only gives access to elements we cannot see if we concentrate only on the binaries of their antitotalitarian politics but also lets us hear the peril in the chime of "not see" with "Nazi" and perhaps also the promise of an off-tonic operatic tilt that is "not C" but, perhaps, in a couple of its variants, the signet H.D. or the indefinite number N.

NOTES

1. Like H.D.'s permutations on the initials that form her name, the name of Mackey's narrator, N., has many possible extensions, among them Nathaniel (his own first name), Narrator (his function), and N (the mathematical symbol for an indefinite number).

2. Mackey's name for his protagonist—Jarred Bottle—recalls the "bottle: unbottled" by the fire in book 3 of William Carlos Williams's *Paterson*:

> An old bottle, mauled by the fire
> gets a new glaze, the glass warped
> to a new distinction, reclaiming the
> undefined.   (1963: 142–43)

3. In a letter in *Djbot Baghostus's Run*, N. cautions the Angel of Dust "against confusing solemnity with truth" (Mackey 1993b: 144). Like Jonathan Culler and the essayists in his collection *On Puns*, H.D. and Mackey find echoic wordplay "not a marginal form of wit but an exemplary product of language or mind" (1988: 4).

4. For this famous anecdote, see Bede's *Ecclesiastical History*, book 2, chap. 1 (1968: 99–100).

5. For an excellent discussion of puncepts in classical writing, see Ahl (1985).

6. In *Bedouin Hornbook*, N. makes this point in reference to Coltrane: "It's like those people who used to say that Coltrane sounded like he was searching for some 'right' note on those long runs of his that at the time were called 'sheets of sound.' What he was up to was no such cover at all. He wanted each and every one of those notes to be heard, not to be erased by the eventual arrival at some presumably 'correct' (or at least sought-after) note" (Mackey 1997: 28–29).

7. "Radical modernism" is a term Charles Bernstein uses in his essay "In the Middle of Modernism in the Middle of Capitalism on the Outskirts of New York," presented at the Socialist Scholars Conference in 1987. Although like Bernstein I use this term to emphasize political and institutional ramifications of this writing, Bernstein's emphasis is on the term's Socialist valence, mine on its linguistic valence.

8. For an excellent discussion of the dynamics of improvisation and a convincing argument that "the composition/improvisation dichotomy doesn't exist," see Bailey (1993: 140).

9. This composition is recorded in Mingus's album *Changes Two*, originally issued as Atlantic #1678, October 1, 1975.

10. "I am invisible," Ellison's narrator emphasizes, " . . . simply because people refuse to see me" (1952: 7).

11. Figure 1 comes from a high school physics tutorial available on the web at http://www.glenbrook.k12.il.us/gbssci/phys/Class/refln/u13l1c.html.

12. See Microsoft Bookshelf 98 dictionary.

13. See, for example, N.'s "Deaf Diagrammatic Perspective on the Toupouri Wind Ensemble's Harvest Song" in *Bedouin Hornbook* (Mackey 1997: 134) or in *Djbot Baghostus's Run* his "Suspect-Symmetrical Structure of Misconceptual Seed's Parallactic Dispatch" (Mackey 1993b: 109).

14. For Stewart's play with the term "waiver," see his essay "Modernism's Sonic Waiver: Literary Writing and the Filmic Difference" (1997).

15. The erotic resonance of Stein's "spreading" resonates with Mackey's many allusions to the ultimately unquenchable desire that drives his writing, "a sexual 'cut'" that signifies "an exegetic refusal to be done with desire" (1997: 38, 52).

Another mathematical term that Mackey uses for the left over is the "aliquant factor": "Remainder and thus reminder of what's left over, what's left out," the difference that "[blows] the lid off totalizing assumptions" (1993b: 151).

16. N. goes on in this passage to invoke a geometry that rejects the grid for the asymptotic curve. Noting that submission to a processual muse is a kind of rowdiness that "openly takes to the streets," he adds, "I hope I can say this and still keep clear of a strictly euclidian sense of 'the streets.' . . . I should stress the word 'openly' perhaps" (Mackey 1993b: 26).

17. Mackey's Ph.D. dissertation (1974) took up the work of Robert Duncan, which would have led him to H.D. through Duncan's serial readings of her work in *The H.D. Book*. For Mackey's essays on Duncan, see *Discrepant Engagement* (1993a).

H.D. after H.D.

CAROLYN FORCHÉ

In a quiet seminar room lit by windows open to a coppery autumn, I encountered my first H.D.: hermetic poet of the chiseled lyric, truest Imagist, distiller of the mythic-imaginative psyche quest. I was eighteen years old and had been writing formal verse for nine years, in isolation and ignorance of the whole of *verse libre*, unaware that there were many living poets until, under the tutelage of Professor Linda Wagner, I heard their voices on reel-to-reel tapes for the first time and, startled into possibility, read in their strangely cadenced work the surviving presence of the poetic art. It was language and the other of language.

For H.D. it was a work built, as she wrote in *End to Torment*, "on or around the crater of an extinct volcano," around the wound perhaps of what must be abandoned for the work's sake, and that may have been, as Rachel Blau DuPlessis suggests, "the possibility of heterosexual love without phallocratic bondage . . . [or] sexual passion itself" (1990: 28). I read it as built on the rim of a mysterious, turbulent force that might at any moment erupt but that remained for the poet silent. I had not yet been enthralled, was not yet sexually active, and had not read deeper into the classical thought than my former teachers, of the Order of the Preachers of Saint Dominic, permitted as they wielded Roman Catholic doctrine against an abridged version of the pagan, Hellenic world. I had studied Latin but not Greek and, daunted by the prescriptions in Pound's *ABC of Reading*, found in H.D. a wand-bearing guide through the labyrinth of antiquity.

In my youth, of course, I mistook the task as one of acquainting myself with a cast of mythic characters, mortal and divine, and of reading Homer, Aeschylus, Euripides, the Greek lyric poets, and Ovid, toward

illuminating not only H.D.'s richly allusive work but the as yet impene-
trable darkness of Western thought. The mistake was of course to suppose that H.D.'s *Sea Garden* was "all about flowers and rocks and waves
and Greek myths, when it is really about the soul, or the primal intelligence, or the *Nous* or whatever we choose to call that link that binds us
to the unseen and uncreated" (John Gould Fletcher, quoted in Burnett
1990: 14). The Greek myths and the phenomena of nature were, for
H.D., an emanation of the sacred in the visible and invisible worlds
of the living present. For her the Greek poets and their myths were
"as vivid and fresh as they ever were, but vivid and fresh not as literature (though they were that too), but as portals, as windows, as port-
holes . . . that look out from our ship, our world, our restricted lives, on
to a sea that moves and changes and bears us up" (Burnett 1990: 61).
Decades passed before I would begin to apprehend the Herculean work
of this visionary poet, in her palimpsestic understanding of time and
history and her vertiginous explorations of the dichotomies of mind.

For a young poet, the principles of Imagism distilled the poetic task:
"direct treatment of the 'thing' whether subjective or objective," the
admonition "to use absolutely no word that does not contribute to
the presentation," and composition "in the sequence of the musical
phrase." While the articulation of these principles was Ezra Pound's,
credited with providing "H.D. with a discipline that enabled her to control the surges that arose from the depths of her violently responsive
nature" (H.D. 1983: xiii), it is also true that the principles originated
from her work to mark the early, radical break of her poetic thought.
She would not remain long confined to them.

My first H.D. was the "Imagiste," who freed me to abandon the iam-
bic pentameter of my poetic childhood, and while not yet understanding what was meant by "the musical phrase" (erroneously believing it
to be without form), I began writing in brief, breath-torn lines, measur-
ing by syllables and attempting a music of alliterative and assonantal
patterns. I took a paring-pen to my ornate descriptiveness, omitting
superfluous words until there was nothing left: from writing back to the
abyss of the blank page, which markedly improved upon what I had
written. Pound was the stern taskmaster: my poems, like the sunfish of
Agassiz, were in an advanced state of decomposition, but like his imaginary Post-Graduate student, I had begun to know something about
them. What enchanted me most was the challenge to "direct treatment

of the thing." Pound distinguished between "the poetry which seems to be music just forcing itself into articulate speech, and, secondly, that sort of poetry which seems as if sculpture or painting were just forced or forcing itself into words" (Pound 1968: 380). Despite my love of speech music, breath-rhythm, chant, and liturgy, I felt myself to be the latter, a poet of visual transcription. The writings of the young Imagists of 1912 distinguished the merely illustrative and descriptive from the image as thing in-itself. My early attempts produced a constellation of fusions: snow with flesh, bread, manna, a field lit by fireflies, night and a melon-opening dawn, which I imagined as the incision of sun in sky, the cantaloupe color, the cool wetness of daybreak. My images were attempts at phanopoeia, but they were static, stationary, immobile. I sent these poems to Robert Bly when I was nineteen and received a generous letter in response, in which he counseled me to attend to verbs and to understand the image as active. I would later recognize this in Pound's corrective, from image to vortex, but at the time the challenge to activate the image seemed insurmountable.

Returning to H.D., I read within the spare, chiseled, and "crystal-line" lyric of the earliest poetry a brave confrontation with the problem of evil, an embodiment of consciousness, and an interrogation of phenomena. This was not a language confined to thingness: the rose, leaf-mold and earth, wind and tide, seabirds and rubble were not rose, leaf-mold, and rubble but were rather freed of material stasis, the body was "more than raiment" (H.D., review of *The Farmer's Bride* by Charlotte Mew, quoted in Burnett 1990: 135). Poetry had begun to seem more than musical language "charged with meaning." It had begun to seem the very method and embodiment of a form of knowledge.

I encountered my second H.D. two decades later while attempting to formulate a mode of reading that might deepen and complicate our readings of poets marked by the impress of extremity: warfare, military occupation, imprisonment, and exile. In compiling exemplary works that might illuminate the legibility of this impress, I encountered H.D.'s *Trilogy*—"The Walls Do Not Fall," "Tribute to the Angels," and "The Flowering of the Rod"—and I began to reevaluate the sources of her poetic impetus. In an unpublished review of William Butler Yeats's *Responsibilities*, written during World War I, H.D. had voiced a polemic on "the relation between poetics and politics in a world defined by war" (quoted in Burnett 1990: 8). She writes, "The chief enemy . . . is the great overwhelming mechanical daemon, the devil of machinery, of which we can hardly repeat too often, the war is the hideous offspring" (quoted in Burnett 1990: 9–10). She lauded the generation of the nineties for having had "at least held one common law as sacred, at least [they] never condescended to the worship of material efficiency." The generation of the nineties was, she argued, at least "not efficient, neither did they fall down before some Juggernaut of planes and angles." Yeats was praised for his "worship of beauty other than the grace of the steel-girder." Some of the (male) poets of her own generation, however, had "merged into this struggle with its own much lauded guns and aeroplanes. . . . The guns they praised, the beauty of the machines they loved, are no more as a god set apart for worship but a devil over whom neither they nor we have any more control" (Burnett 1990: 9). H.D. set her work against this daemon in *Trilogy* by laying open the originary wound, the splitting of human consciousness, then cleansing and suturing that wound with a re-imagined mythos. At the same time, tragically, world war was continuing. Mankind was mechanizing genocide and splitting the atom, forever sundering the certainty of human futurity from its postnuclear contingency.

War, for H.D., threatens to destroy poesis. She had been deeply affected by the horrors of World War I: upon hearing of the sinking of the *Lusitania*, she suffered the stillbirth of her first child; her husband, Richard Aldington, enlisted to avoid conscription and was transformed into a hardened soldier whose breath smelled of gas and whose presence was suffused with death; her brother, Gilbert, was killed in France and her father died from shock. Public and private worlds collided, but H.D. refrained from explicitly addressing the war, although "Loss" and "Prisoners" from *Sea Garden* (1916) and "The Tribute" from *The Egoist* (1916) allude to its destructive force. In her 1916 review of John Gould Fletcher's *Goblins and Pagodas*, H.D. writes, "In grimmer moods, it is the swirl of guns, cannon, terror, destruction. And through it all, it is the soul or mind or inspiration of the poet, knowing within itself its problems, unanswerable; its vision, cramped and stifled; the bitterness of its own insufficiency" (quoted in Burnett 1990: 17).

H.D.'s suffering of that war was deeply personal but as yet removed, available to her in news reports and telegrams, in the war-hardened eyes of Aldington and the grave of her brother. I recognize now that this was

the manner in which I perceived the Vietnam War: in the gray flicker
of the cathode ray, in still shots of carnage, in the letters from soldier
friends scrawled on blue military paper. Insofar as that war had forever
transformed my life, it remained at once remote, and in its aftermath,
the resolve to put the war "behind us" obscured but did not obliterate
the impossibility of doing so. None of the poems in my first published
book rendered visible its mark.

In H.D.'s experience, the Blitz of the Luftwaffe bombers began on
September 7, 1940, destroying

> the Woolwich arsenal, the wharves and warehouses of the London
> docks . . . Victoria and Albert docks, the West India dock, and the
> Commercial docks. Ships were sunk, bridges collapsed. The bomb-
> ing of London's East End and other residential areas left hundreds
> dead and thousands injured and homeless. . . . Over the next seven
> days thousands of Londoners were killed, wounded or entombed in
> rubble. . . . During the night raids people sought shelter in basements
> or in subways. Soon pieces of railing began to disappear; they were
> needed to be melted down for munitions. . . . H.D. lived as a Lon-
> doner through this terror.   (Robinson 1982: 305)

"The Walls Do Not Fall" was written in the aftermath of her walk
through the ruins in a language indexically cratered by the aerial bombardment. The first H.D., she who had constituted herself as artist,
mother, lover, analysand, was gone; "the girl who had written the
poems in the library of the British Museum was dead; the library itself
was burned and gutted" (Robinson 1982: 307). The poet writing her
Trilogy is not that same poet, nor does her poem "record" that poet's
experience. It is not an account but the excavation of a consciousness
intact and in ruins. "Who is this lady?" she asked in June 1941.

> Yes, it is part of myself, I conclude, that had died . . . She was wise,
> she was not so much arrogant in her wisdom, as lost. She had only
> this peculiar garment of my own body to live in. It must have been
> a burden to her. There were very few occasions when she could ex-
> press herself, sometimes I wrote for her, stalactite-shape running
> verse . . . broken . . . frozen. . . . I am free of her, she is dead. She
> died the night of June 20th, 1941, I think after midnight, yes, surely
> it must have been just before dawn.   (H.D. 1993: 10)

As H.D. "recovers," her palimpsestic vision intensifies: past and future are fused in a "poignant and ethereal present" that is not stasis but rather the luminous realm of the sacred, giving way to what I came to regard as her later understanding that we are not living sequentially or "after" events in time but rather in their aftermath, in the diachronous realm of the prophetic, in which the past is never behind but rather within us.

Trilogy is the birthplace of H.D.'s "imaginal self" (Hollenberg 1991: 125), restored to its creative bond with the mother, breaking patriarchal bondage, at once a fusion of psychic awareness and evidence of H.D.'s assimilation of ancient spiritual knowledge, informing her interrogation and transformation of Judeo-Christian thought. She "melt[s] down the broken, scattered fragments of her psyche in the 'fire and breath' of her poem crucible to re-create new jewels of spiritual health" (Hollenberg 1991: 129). H.D. writes,

> we are the keepers of the secret,
> the carriers, the spinners
>
> of the rare intangible thread
> that binds all humanity
>
> to ancient wisdom,
> to antiquity;   (1973: 24)

She recognizes that

> The Christos-image
> is most difficult to disentangle
>
> from its art-craft junk-shop
> paint-and-plaster medieval jumble
>
> of pain-worship and death symbol,   (H.D. 1973: 27)

In "The Walls Do Not Fall," Christos becomes Amen, pure presence, and Holy Ghost, the dream. H.D. recalls Christ's counsel that we "be wise . . . as serpents," and then, in a startling moment three years before Hiroshima, she writes,

> In no wise is the pillar-of-fire
> that went before

different from the pillar-of-fire
that comes after

chasm, schism in consciousness
must be bridged over;   (1973: 49)

She acknowledges that

> *we know no rule*
> *of procedure,*
>
> *we are voyagers, discoverers*
> *of the not-known,*
>
> *the unrecorded;*
> *we have no map;*
>
> *possibly we will reach haven,*
> *heaven.*   (H.D. 1973: 59)

The world trembles open, releasing the immanent power of presence to the regard of a transcendent but absent God.

"Tribute to Angels" opens with Hermes providing "H.D.'s speaker with a syncretic, heretical religious philosophy that enables her to re-integrate pagan myth with Christian . . . in the context of the Book of Revelation" (Hollenberg 1991: 129), whose prophecy of apocalyptic destruction she challenges, replacing John's seven angels of death with her own angels of rebirth. In "The Flowering of the Rod" H.D. reads across scriptural accounts of the birth and death of Christ, through the Mage Kaspar and the repentant prostitute Mary Magdalen, invoking us to leave the smoldering cities below and also "leave / The place-of-the-skull / to those who have fashioned it" (1973: 115). H.D. is aware of an inexorable desire for rebirth: the rising of geese to the heavens, the stars guiding the Magi to Christ: "Kaspar knew the scene was unavoidable // and already written in a star / or a configuration of stars" (1973: 144). Kaspar, the gift-bearer, could recognize the Christos without relinquishing the gods of antiquity, and he may have "apprehended more / than anyone before or after him" (H.D. 1973: 165). He looked down the deep well "of the so-far unknown / depth of pre-history" and may have understood that *this has happened before somewhere else, / or this will happen again—where? when?* (H.D. 1973: 165, 167).

In my own life, this "*when*" and "*where*" occurred in the winter of 1984. I lived in Ras Beirut in the Hotel Commodore near the old Jewish quarter, not far from the center city, a demolished and abandoned zone, trip-wired and crumbling where I walked at night with a correspondent later to be abducted and held hostage until his providential escape. He thought a poet should see this, and so we wandered under starlight through the silent ruins: windblown shops and a vacant cinema, the armless statuary of a monument to the martyrs. Days later I would take shelter in the basement of the Commodore, a derelict nightclub with an overturned piano and its walls frescoed with images from the *Arabian Nights*, while shellfire rained from East Beirut into our district, like faint thunder at first, and then as if the world above was caving in. The shelter was filled with refugees huddled under hotel blankets, sleeping off the anesthesia of drink or else nervously awake to the barrage. In the morning I accompanied a woman into the street, still and broken, the shop windows shattered open to the wind, clothing swaying in the racks, the streets a shattered puzzle of glass. Overnight this part of the city had succumbed to the war and was now otherwise. The former world of the markets, mounds of dates and tangerines, braziers of smoking lamb kabobs, and pairs of men playing backgammon, had vanished. Now the streets belonged to the warring militias. Fire had gutted the parked cars and blackened the city's trees; doves flocked above us in the smoke but refused to land. The night had been but a glimmer of the London Blitz, my single night but one of H.D.'s many, yet the world had broken, and what once seemed a city was now a scattered mosaic, awaiting restoration, in whose smoke rose all smoke, in whose cinders, all cindered possibility. One walks in such places cautiously, as if each step might further damage what has been destroyed.

"The Walls Do Not Fall" is an assertion of a poet's will. Of course the walls fell, trembling and temporal, stone by stone as once they had been erected. It was language that went on, the language that, according to Pound, "civilized Greece and Rome" (1960: 33), the language, according to poet Paul Celan, that was not lost in spite of all that happened. "But it had to go through its own lack of answers, through terrifying silence, through the thousand darknesses of murderous speech" (Celan 1986: 34).

The intricacies of poetic influence and linkage can be amorphous,

tenuous, and indirect, unreadable and indiscernible but for the assertions of the practitioner, who recognizes the effects of a forerunner
upon her art. I prefer this to the "strong" influence of misprision postulated by Harold Bloom, while acknowledging this formulation among
possible others. My first H.D. schooled my early poetic thought, but it
was decades before I would discover the confluence of circumstance,
affinity, and shared knowledge that would characterize my apprehension of her later work. My second book, *The Country between Us*, marked
a departure from the first in retaining a poetic subjectivity confident
of the legitimacy of subjective reportage but as yet unaware of the re-
configurative power of the experience of extremity. It seemed sufficient
that the "I" interrogate and question itself within the accepted lyric-
narrative form, calling into question its assertions and pronouncements.
That such work could be dismissed as the product of a certain political
intentionality was disturbing, but I had not yet begun to apprehend the
meaning of self, time, and language in the aftermath of mass death.

Five years after the publication of my second book I wrote the first
draft of *The Angel of History*. Several months later I encountered my
second H.D., the poet of *Trilogy*, while gathering work for *Against Forgetting: Twentieth-Century Poetry of Witness*, a compilation of the works
of 145 poets, writing in over 30 languages, who had themselves endured
conditions of extremity during the twentieth century. The project was
one of opening a space for the reading of such works, as the evidential
art of endurance in the context of unimaginable horror.

The whole of Western thought seemed heretofore conditioned on a
concept of the self as a rational monad: Hegel had demonstrated the
rational in concrete history, and Heidegger had shown that the root of
history lies in the historicity of the human being, grounding a deeper
understanding of the meaning of human existence in the particulars of
concrete experience. Poetry of my time had, it seemed, built a *cordon
sanitaire* around particular historical circumstance, isolating it from
philosophic and artistic query (see Wyschogrod 1985). It seemed that
the subjective "I," however challenged and interrogated, could not survive the collapse of representation, and so I endeavored to create a text
that would subsume subjectivity, relegating it to the role of passive re-
corder: the angel Metatron who listened but could not intervene, like
the *deus abscondi* of the Holocaust. Absent this God, perhaps divine in-

terlocutors could be supposed. Perhaps it was possible to move beyond the paradigm of authenticity and the primacy of the interpersonal sphere. The dissolution of this "I" opened the possibility of an I-Thou consciousness (after Martin Buber), spiritually dialectical and awake, vibrant and reciprocal, that would somehow enable the consideration of responsibility, of our ability to respond.

If personal death had been hitherto the touchstone of moral stature, marking the worth of an individual's life, what would mass-death become but the shifting tectonic plate of our sense of collective being? We mark the passing of extinct life forms while we ourselves are in the process of vanishing forever. The assurance of future time recedes from certainty. Life and death become copresent. Our consciousness of time is no longer sequential and synchronous but spatial and diachronic, H.D.'s living present. We are in the realm of the "death event," wherein "event designates the nexus of dynamic but ephemeral occurrences, the 'pieces of flotsam combed from the historical ocean,' that, taken together, form the segments of a single meaning constellation. This pattern becomes generative for the self-understanding of its time (even if this understanding is only partially glimpsed by contemporaries)" (Braudel 1972: 1243).

What I recognized in *Trilogy* was the affirmation of a precursor struggling with the insurmountable difficulty of writing her way toward restoration while conceiving a poetic form that would somehow display the ruin. However, unlike H.D., I wanted to retain hope while jettisoning the possibility of redemption (a possibility denied by spiritual refusal in the steps of Simone Weil). *The Angel of History* would be a noneschatological, nonredemptive work, denying itself the salvific comforts of a preruptural voice, speaking as though the historical cataclysm had not occurred. Yet I see in it traces of H.D., for if a consciousness suffuses H.D.'s *Trilogy*, in its transforming, recuperative rewriting of Judeo-Christian thought, it is the consciousness, however oblique and unrealized, of the extermination of the Jews and its prescience of the dawning of the nuclear age.

So in recognizing this second H.D., I recognize an influence ipso facto, an affinity with the work of a precursor who struggled toward the cataclysm that was to constitute a black hole in the cosmos of Western thought. We cannot live, as Edmund Husserl has written, if "to live is always to live-in-certainty of the world, being constantly and directly 'conscious' of the world and of oneself as living in the world" (1970: 142–43). But it is possible to live provisionally beyond the rupture and to write our way out of the ruin, aware of the fragility of civilization and the impossibility—indeed undesirability—of achieving "closure," if this means cordoning off the past as if we could escape it. It is her courage before this difficulty that most astounds me.

Poetry and Survival: H.D. and Carolyn Forché

EILEEN GREGORY

> *peril, strangely encountered, strangely endured,*
> *marks us . . .* H.D., *Trilogy*

> *Surely all art is the result of one's having been in danger, of having*
> *gone through an experience all the way to the end.*
> Carolyn Forché, *The Angel of History*

In *Within the Walls*, a series of sketches written in 1941 during the bombardment of London, H.D. describes how she finally consented to use earplugs against the noise of the bombs and artillery fire. Even though the percussion had caused her ear to bleed, she had resisted the "official" government-sponsored medical advice to do so. She "could not bear to shut out sound"—clearly because of the fear of being taken off guard. In this aberrant context, the simple choice for silence, for unfractured quiet, becomes a calculated risk. But the quiet poses another risk as well: it allows a space for self-awareness and thus for calling things into question: "then I say to myself, after all, if I am blitzed, the house will go with me and the stack of papers will go, too. This, that I now write will go with it, and why does one type pages that only have the slightest chance of survival? I asked myself that, last night, with that acute sense of silence" (H.D. 1993: 8). Why write, facing not only probable death but the obliteration of the record? H.D.'s answers to herself are lucid: because the chances of survival don't finally matter to the act of writing itself; because an imagined work is incomplete, her recurring "dreams of a book" that had, above all, "to be alive" and not dead; and because her present words, however imperfect, are part of a spell, "the words that in a sense . . . *keep me alive*" (H.D. 1993: 6–8).

The outer violence clarifies the necessities of life ("being alive," "keeping alive"), and here writing is such a necessity.

This shock also dislodges long-buried memories that merge with the present in an uncanny way. In her autobiographical narrative *The Gift*, also written during the bombardment, H.D. describes waiting with her companion Bryher through interminable waves of bombing: she feels repeatedly that she is "going down," that the floor is collapsing. This is and is not a metaphor: the floor *may* collapse, and she may be consumed in flames or trapped in rubble. But at the same time she *is* going down, Persephone-like, into distant memory, the forgotten terrors of childhood. Her memories revolve around wounds: the "passion" of her wounded father and an episode with her Moravian grandmother, who passed down to her a centuries-old secret memory: a meeting between Moravian missionaries and Indians on "Wunden Eiland," associated with a heretical cult of the wounds of Christ. For the narrator, that generational memory exists in the same time and space as the current bombardment: England itself is the "isle of wounds." She herself carries the "gift" from the dead, a "vision of power and of peace," with the responsibility to transmit it to the present (H.D. 1982: 135).

Apart from this private reckoning is H.D.'s public testimony in her war trilogy, written between 1942 and 1944. At the beginning of "The Walls Do Not Fall," among the ruins of London in the aftermath of the bombings, other questions arise:

> the bone-frame was made for
> no such shock knit within terror,
> yet the skeleton stood up to it:
>
> the flesh? it was melted away,
> the heart burnt out, dead ember,
> tendons, muscles shattered, outer husk dismembered,
>
> yet the frame held:
> we passed the flame: we wonder
> what saved us? what for?   (H.D. 1983: 510–11)

The first question—what saved us?—raises the issue, for H.D., of divine presence but also seeks to name the resources of spirit that make endurance possible. The second question—what for?—presses the issue of necessity, because survival puts one under compulsion and responsibility. Under these conditions, in the words of Terrence Des Pres, "survival and bearing witness become reciprocal acts" (1980: 31). In H.D.'s poem this question, implying a collective urgency—why, to what end, "we" have survived—leads to her imaginative recovery in the poem of the public authority of the poet. In these circumstances, poetry is not simply a private avocation but a human necessity within the social sphere, a testimony to history and memory and a vital form of resistance to violence.

That poetry is a matter of life and death—not only to the poet under compulsion but to a human world at risk of destruction—is the insistence of writers throughout this century and throughout the world, as Carolyn Forché's recent anthology, *Against Forgetting: Twentieth-Century Poetry of Witness*, forcefully demonstrates. This compilation, Forché relates, took shape gradually in response to her bewilderment at the reception of her second volume of poems, *The Country between Us* (1981), which drew from her experience as an activist in El Salvador. In the United States the book raised debate over the nature and status of "political poetry," in part because critics commonly insisted on a dichotomy between the personal and the political spheres.[1] Such a separation may be an anomaly of the American academic establishment, where, as Dana Gioia (1991) has argued, the writing of poetry has been commodified, relegated to the status of a luxury. But the idea that poetry does not "matter" in political terms, that it is powerless, as Adrienne Rich, Forché, and others point out, is a strange one in many if not most societies, especially those existing under political repression, where the writing and reading of poetry are important means of resistance, or where "art [is] assumed to be as integral to daily life as roads, laws, literacy, clean air, and water" (Rich 1993: xiv–xv).

Forché's anthology—presenting the work of 145 poets, translated from 30 languages, and spanning the whole of the century—gives body to this claim for the social necessity of poetry. As a poet's tribute to poets, a "poetic memorial to those who suffered and resisted through poetry itself" (Forché 1993: 31), the anthology is generous and inclusive. Cutting across lines of class and privilege, race, religion, political ideology, it allows one to suspend the sometimes arcane and bitter theoretical disputes of the academy in order to acknowledge a common "partisanship" among poets within situations of extremity:

Because the poetry of witness marks a resistance to false attempts at unification, it will take many forms. It will be impassioned or ironic. It will speak in the language of the common man or in an esoteric language of paradox and literary privilege. It will curse or it will bless; it will blaspheme against or ignore the holy. Its protest might rest on an odd grammatical inversion, on a heady peroration to an audience, or on a bizarre flight of fancy. It can be partisan in a limited sense but it is more often partisan in the best of senses, that is, it speaks for what might, with less than crippling irony be called "the party of humanity."   (Forché 1993: 46)

This "partisanship" has here not primarily an idealistic but a pragmatic sense, "a rejection of unwarranted pain inflicted on some humans by others, of illegitimate domination" (Forché 1993: 46).

Forché's inclusion of H.D. in this company of poets is a generative one in that it places *Trilogy*—most often considered in the limited terms of Anglo-American modernism—into a fresh and exciting context, a global record of cultural and linguistic displacement (Forché 1993: 43). In these terms, insisting on the historic and pragmatic rootedness of the poetry of witness, the very idiosyncrasy of *Trilogy* can be seen as an aspect of its resistance—as feminist critics have long proposed—and its aim, however apparently esoteric, as finally one of advocacy. Forché's gesture also defines the clearest link between herself and H.D. *Trilogy* is a remarkable and ambitious poem of testimony; H.D. is one of only five women writing in English included in *Against Forgetting*,[2] the only one among them to attempt a "long poem," as Forché also does in *The Angel of History* (1994).

It is, of course, easy to discriminate between *Trilogy* and *The Angel of History* in the way each records "the impress of extremity upon the poetic imagination" (Forché 1993: 30). The two poems reflect a century's shift in philosophical and political awareness, in particular, the shift from the late romantic assumptions of literary modernism to the skeptical positions of deconstruction and cultural studies. Where H.D. in *Trilogy* comes into her own as a modernist poet, taking on a prophetic authority and summoning ancient gods, angels, and mages in the alchemical opus of poetic transformation, Forché in *The Angel of History* reflects an austerity and restraint coming from postmodern awareness. As a poet she has moved from conventionalized modernist assumptions about the authority of voice and about the possibility of closure and resolution (Taft-Kaufman 1990: 64–68). However, in the generous spirit of Forché's anthology, I would like to emphasize not primarily the differences but the shared "partisanship" of H.D. and Forché. To reflect upon them in conjunction is not to argue for linear influence but to imagine an intertextual relationship in large part defined by their attempt to give figuration to extremity and to reflect upon its significance.

Considering these two poets together in this light makes clear one commonality: the work of each has been shaped by the experience of war. Seen in the context of global catastrophe, the careers of H.D. and Forché together span the century; at one end and the other, each has witnessed—like Walter Benjamin's angel—the debris of history piling up. H.D. began publishing in the first decade of the century; she was fully engaged as a poet in London at the beginning of Anglo-American modernism (1911–12), which was followed very quickly by the outbreak of World War I. Much of her early writing comprises an effort to work through both the personal and collective trauma of the Great War. Even in her early Hellenism, especially in her engagement with Euripides, she works history obliquely, exploring a classical palimpsest of war and imagining Greek poetry in terms of its vestigial survival within diaspora, displacement, and exile.³ With signs of the rise of another European war, she sought out Sigmund Freud, in large part to resolve her war phobia, but she instead confronted the Typhon head on, finding Vienna in 1934 coming under Fascist control and Freud's house itself marked with a swastika. During the whole of World War II she stayed in London, where she attempted her most direct poetic engagement with the violence of war in the poems of *Trilogy*. The terror of the bombardment brought back traumatized memories, as she relates in *The Gift*, and she suffered a nervous collapse in 1946. In her last years in Switzerland, where she began to be aware of the Cold War and the threat of nuclear warfare, she attempted again in her writing—particularly in *Helen in Egypt* and in *End to Torment*, her memoir of Ezra Pound—to confront the violence of history in terms of her own devastated past.⁴

Born at midcentury, Carolyn Forché comes from a Czech-American family in which the memory of fascist and Communist repression has been very much alive. She herself belongs to the American generation most decimated by the Vietnam War. Her writing and political advocacy led her as an activist into El Salvador in 1978, at the beginning of American involvement in the conflict there. Later, working as a radio correspondent and human rights liaison, she accompanied her husband, Harry Mattison, a war photographer, into some of the major war zones of the last two decades—South Africa, Lebanon, the West Bank, and Northern Ireland. Her last book, *The Angel of History*, is deliberately a fin de siècle poem, tracing a vestigial map of the ruins from "the worst of centuries" (Forché 1994: 65).

This historical actuality determines the specific radicality of each poem. "Extremity," Forché remarks, "demands new forms or alters older modes of thought. It also breaks forms and creates forms from those breaks" (Forché 1993: 42). Articulating this rupture in her own career, Forché writes in a postscript to *The Angel of History*: "The first-person, free-verse, lyric-narrative poem of my earlier years has given way to a work which has desired its own bodying forth: polyphonic, broken, haunted, and in ruins, with no possibility of restoration" (Forché 1994: 81). This fragmentary style suggests something very different from the disassociation of a modernist poem like *The Waste Land*, to which *The Angel of History* is sometimes compared. Forché attempts, according to Anita Helle, "a more radical case of fragmenting," which does not imply a lost totality (1996: 56). The frequent use of long lines that "go all the way to the margin" (Forché, quoted in Taft-Kaufman 1990: 64) is another aspect of experimentation. It implies not unboundedness and freedom (as in Walt Whitman, for instance) but rather a determination or necessity for utterance to play out. The long line pushing the margin suggests the act of recording and an awareness of the page as record: "The hand moves across the page of its own accord" (Forché 1994: 25). *Trilogy*, in terms of H.D.'s writing, represents a similar kind of breakthrough: the abandonment of a lyric style by which her career had been defined. H.D. as perfect Imagist is part of the "old self" shattered by the apocalyptic fire in "The Walls Do Not Fall"; the old repertories of style, the repetitive and overworn ecstasies, the poet sees in her meditation, no longer serve (H.D. 1983: 232–39). The poems of *Trilogy* represent, Alicia Ostriker has proposed, a formal and stylistic experiment in "open form": while loosely formal, the poem retains a lightness and accessibility, avoiding and even reversing the hierarchical and authoritarian stance of other modernist long poems, in part through the character of a choral, collective voice. However distinct the formal experiments, then, each poet in these instances works out stylistically a crisis in her conception of voice and authority, a crisis precipitated by the experience of extremity.

Forché's selection of poetry from "The Walls Do Not Fall" for her anthology makes clear its continuity with other poetry of witness, which "often seeks to register through indirection and intervention the ways in which the linguistic and moral universes have been disrupted by events" (Forché 1993: 45). These selections point to that rupture and its consequences: the violation of ordinary human life, of human habitation, by violence and political manipulation, raising questions for the survivor within the ruins of the city; the aberrant alignment of the social order, in which both "evil" and "good" serve material progress, leaving the seeker "hungry" for God; the virtue of "persistence" within conditions of minimal survival; the endurance of the written word at a time when books are burned or demanded as pulp in the making of armaments; the deathlessness of the word, in the utilitarian context of war (Forché 1993: 1, 2, 6, 9, 10).

More particularly, however, Forché emphasizes a figural aspect of the poetry of witness that one finds in *Trilogy*. "Metaphor . . . changes in extremity," Forché says. In these conditions, the poem becomes the "trace," the "historical marker," of an event; but, in making an evidentiary claim, insisting on an actuality, it resists the figurative, arresting an imaginative move away from it. It marks and is marked by the event, and, in Forché's understanding, it thus in turn marks the reader, making him or her responsible for the evidence (Taft-Kaufman 1990: 69). Referring to the work of Walter Benjamin, Forché goes further: the poem is not only evidence of an event, "the poem is *itself* an event, a trauma that changes both a common language and an individual psyche," a trauma, unlike the original event, that is entered into voluntarily (Forché 1993: 33). In particular, this trauma exposes a wounded memory: "In situations of extremity, rather than our becoming numb to pain, the pain worsens and lessens our ability to endure. . . . To write out of such extremity is to incise, with language, that same wound, to open it again, and, with utterance, to inscribe the consciousness" (Montenegro 1991: 71).

The image or metaphor as historical marker indeed characterizes the poetry in *Against Forgetting*, grounded in circumstances of imprisonment, exile, and warfare. *The Angel of History* is largely comprised of such markers—isolated, fragmentary images and snatches of speech that convey a haunted sense of the historical and real. Forché in an interview points especially to a "constellation of images having to do with rail lines, ashes, chimneys, crematoria" that signal "that you are not other than in the holocaust" (Taft-Kaufman 1990: 69). This configuration especially recurs throughout Forché's poem, serving as a kind of figural ground for still other markers. "There were trains, and beneath them, laddered fields": fields intersected by lines leading to the death camps; burnt fields, part of the effort of erasure; "truck-rutted fields" imperfectly hiding the dead; "the persistence of tracked field," suggesting the search for the lost that impels the poem itself (Forché 1994: 4, 46, 44). The nature of the marker is defined by the voices themselves as a point of ordinary human reference altered by history: "And the fields? Aren't the fields changed by what happened? / . . . / How can the fields continue as simple fields"; "A rain through raised windows, as in: you must not forget anything: the hours, hope, sleeplessness, / and the trains, you must not forgive them" (Forché 1994: 12, 10).

The historical marker in *Trilogy* is infrequent, but at pivotal moments its presence makes a clear impact. The strangeness of the title "The Walls Do Not Fall" and many other references to the city in ruins comes from the irony of "openness," in the sense that Forché refers to Hiroshima as "the last of the world's open cities" (1994: 59). The impact of the metaphor comes from the fixity of the real (though surreal) image, which is and is not metaphorical: "enter, / there as here, there are no doors"; "like a ghost, / we entered a house through a wall" (H.D. 1983: 509, 559). The lack of boundary and containment suggests a kind of liberation, a breaking open; at the same time the fact of destruction marks a bondage to the real. The customary doubleness of metaphor is made strange by the literal devastation:

> *we walk continually*
>
> *on thin air*
> *that thickens to a blind fog,*
>
> *then step swiftly aside,*
> *for even the air*

is independable,
thick where it should be fine

and tenuous
where wings separate and open,

and the ether
is heavier than the floor.   (H.D. 1983: 543)

Metaphors for danger and confusion—to "walk on thin air," to "walk in a blind fog"—are made new in this literal blundering through the smoke and dust of a bombed house. The metaphor, like the air one breathes, is warped in *"a not known, // unregistered dimension"* of power-lessness and disorientation.

At one point in "Tribute to the Angels," the speaker attempts to convey a visionary moment prompted by an actual event. Here she is called up short by an image that resists the figural: among the ruins, "a charred tree . . . burnt and stricken to the heart" but blossoming:

This is no rune nor riddle,
it is happening everywhere;

what I mean is—it is so simple
yet no trick of the pen or brush

could capture that impression;
music could do nothing with it,

nothing whatever; what I mean is—
but you have seen for yourself

that burnt-out wood crumbling   .   .   .
you have seen for yourself.   (H.D. 1983: 559)

The insistence, "This is no rune nor riddle," calls attention to another kind of sign, a part of the given. The literal image will not go beyond itself: its significance is not representable, and it is only "readable" by others who share in this condition of extremity. The reader is indeed suddenly confronted with the burden of witnessing: "you have seen for yourself." In the next section the poet tries to articulate this untranslatable quality:

. . . music? O, what I meant
by music when I said music, was—

music sets up ladders,
it makes us invisible,

it sets us apart,
it lets us escape;

but from the visible
there is no escape;

there is no escape from the spear
that pierces the heart.   (H.D. 1983: 559–60)

In this confrontation the poet in a sense defines the dislocation involved in reading a historical marker: one instinct is to draw away from the image through representation (as "music sets up ladders . . . lets us escape"), but the image rooted in a historical circumstance remains intractable ("from the visible / there is no escape"). Moreover, that image—both for the poet who confronts it here and for the reader— opens a wound ("the spear / that pierces the heart"), clearly one carrying the memory of repeated violence and devastation. H.D.'s poem marks this moment and marks the reader.

Besides the presence of this figure, *Trilogy* and *The Angel of History* share other emphases in common with poetry of witness. The opening section of "The Walls Do Not Fall" suggests some of these in its extended parallel of the ruined houses of London with the ruins of Karnak and Pompeii and with the ruined house of body and soul. The predominant image of the ruined city in both poems is a metonym for the devastation of history. H.D. traces out distant historical parallels for the besieged and destroyed city, the "smouldering cities" of Pompeii, Jerusalem, Thebes, Rome. Forché's record of lost cities is more immediate:

If a city, ruin, if an animal, hunger.
If a grave, anonymous.
If a century, this.   (1994: 6)

But these are the ruins, too, of one's own history: "The past is not where you left it, Svetko. / It is a ruined city, spackled with grief" (Forché 1994: 39). The poet in "The Walls Do Not Fall" catalogs that personal devastation, the careening path of "an erratic burnt-out comet" (H.D. 1983: 535), and *The Angel of History* begins with the image of "a woman broken into many women" (Forché 1994: 3). Within this ruin, the poem, Forché claims, becomes an "excavation site," like those of Karnak and Pompeii.[5]

A third implication of ruin suggested in H.D.'s poem is a crucial part of the record in *The Angel of History*. The bombs slice open buildings, exposing the intimate space of human habitation: "the fallen roof / leaves the sealed room / open to the air," and, going through the streets,

> . . . we pass on
>
> to another cellar, to another sliced wall
> where poor utensils show
> like rare objects in a museum;   (H.D. 1983: 509–10)

Conditions of extremity shatter ordinary human habitation, objectify what is exposed, making what was part of a living fabric of life into a specimen. This exposure of fragile life points to a general emphasis in H.D.'s poem upon the ordinary and vulnerable as focal sites of significance; indeed, the comparison of the unsealed London houses with the roofless temple insists upon the ordinary as a sacred sphere. Forché's poem persistently renders this dimension of loss. The familiar is almost obliterated:

> This is what we have taken the ordinary world to mean:
> bootprints in clay,
> the persistence of tracked field.
>
> What was there before imperfectly erased
>   and memory a reliquary in a wall of silence.
>   (Forché 1994: 44)

The past remains in isolated images, painful in marking not only an unspoken catastrophe but the loss of a shared human world: "A wedding dress hanging in a toolshed outside Warsaw" (Forché 1994: 19). In the context of this erased life, the longing that comes in memory is "the defenselessness for which there is no cure" (Forché 1994: 43, 65).

One of the most remarkable likenesses between *Trilogy* and *The Angel of History* is also a point of apparent contrast: both poems are metaphysical or spiritual in their response to conditions of extremity. Forché speaks at length in *Against Forgetting* about this dimension of the record of testimony. The language of religion, she says, has been extremely important "in this supposedly secular century," and she notes the way it serves poets in differing contexts (Forché 1993: 37–40). But in general terms, atrocity and terror test the limits of belief in the certainty and order associated with a traditional God; at the same time they impel a longing to comprehend occurrences, like the Holocaust, that appear to negate human significance altogether.

In the poems of *Trilogy* H.D. retrieves Hermeticism as an alternate to institutional religion and speaks from beginning to end in the language of presence and visionary transformation. The Christian God, Christ, and Mary are partially reclaimed through syncretism, and each of the three poems suggests a spiritual process akin to that of traditional mysticism. *The Angel of History*, however, figures a world where precisely such totality and totalizing gestures are impossible to imagine. "God" is a recurrent sign in Forché's poem, but it signifies something inexplicable and dark (*"Where an angry God, spilled blood itself, lives"*), mad (*"Le Dieu est feu"*), silent (*"the silence of God is God"*) (Forché 1994: 64, 7, 5). Here the spiritual is manifest as tragic questioning within bitterness and absence: "Put into question others, put into question God. / Whatever can be taken away is taken / to allow suffering to remain" (Forché 1994: 46).

This opposition between the two poems certainly suggests a fundamental distinction between modern and postmodern assumptions. But such obvious differences may conceal a likeness. As poets, both H.D. and Forché are finally attempting to figure not a cosmology or faith— or the lack of one—but the necessities of desire within extreme human suffering. The "divine" or "God" is a constant term within such longing, even when traditional theologies are denied and transcendence seems impossible to conceive. "To what and to whom does one say *yes*?" a voice asks in "Elegy." Another (or the same) voice immediately responds: "If God were the uncertain, would you cling to him?" (Forché 1994: 69). "God"—however problematic or displaced—signifies a need to imagine human life, both individual and collective, in terms of assent: purposefulness, justice, intelligibility, and love.

In this regard one must take seriously an obvious conjunction between the poems of H.D. and Forché: the figure of the angel. The second poem of H.D.'s *Trilogy*, "Tribute to the Angels," is conceived as an act of tribute to the "seven spirits before the throne of God" in the book of Revelation. In the midst of unremitting destruction, the poet questions the purpose of the God of the Apocalypse:

but *I make all things new*,
said He of the seven stars,

he of the seventy-times-seven
passionate, bitter wrongs,

He of the seventy-times-seven
bitter, unending wars.   (H.D. 1983: 549)

Within this anger and spiritual exhaustion, a voice reminds the poet
of her love of the angels, who are then invoked deliberately and recognized in epiphanies within the shattered, mundane landscape of the ruins. *The Angel of History* is framed by tropes of angels. It begins in an
epigraph with the famous image of the "angel of history" from Walter
Benjamin's "Theses on the Philosophy of History": "Where we perceive a chain of events, he sees one single catastrophe which keeps piling
wreckage and hurls it in front of his feet." Though the angel would like
to minister to the human world, a storm "blowing in from Paradise . . .
has got caught in his wings," so that he is propelled backward into the
future (Benjamin 1968: 257–58). The postscript of the volume is a parable by Paul Valéry: "The angel handed me a book, saying, 'It contains
everything that you could possibly wish to know.' And he disappeared."
The book, "written in an unknown character," cannot be deciphered,
and scholars debate its meaning without arriving at definite conclusions.
"Toward the close of this vision it seemed to me that the book melted,
until it could no longer be distinguished from this world that is about
us" (Forché 1994: 78).

Despite great differences in conception, the trope of the angel functions in a similar way in each of these poems: as a displaced sign of an
absent or dark God, as a figuration of the human desire to comprehend
the incomprehensible and to minister to the human world. In their
questioning of the divine, both "Tribute to the Angels" and *The Angel
of History* refer to traditions of Jewish mysticism, in which God is manifest through catastrophe and absence. This tradition of understanding
catastrophe paradoxically as the manifestation of the divine—divine
light breaking vessels too brittle to contain it—is an implicit assumption of *Trilogy*, especially the first two poems, where "presence" is
manifest only in the context of shattering. Forché notes a similar religious paradox, describing the idea of the "recession" of God in refer-

ence to the poetry of Edmond Jabès: "He draws a curtain of darkness down before Himself in order to allow light to appear, darkness serving as necessary foil for illumination" (Forché 1993: 39). One of the reiterated voices in *The Angel of History* expresses this paradox: *"le silence de Dieu est Dieu."* This is one of very many voices in the poem that struggle with "God," and though the poet clearly privileges no one of these voices, taken together they recall dimensions of human desire and intellectual search that cannot simply be rejected. The angel in this context represents a displaced, intermediary presence: a messenger within inexplicable absence.

The angels in these poems, however, are finally images of "watchers," figures for human vision, endurance, and guardianship. H.D.'s angels are not merely part of an occult symbolic machinery, they figure the poet's urgency to find a way to bear the unbearable, avoid despair, and maintain openness to and love toward the blasted visible world.[6] Similarly, the governing trope of Forché's poem, Benjamin's angel, is powerful because it figures a human desire for a "messianic" or "redemptive" sense of history and for an angelic intervention and care for the human, "to awaken the dead, and make whole what was smashed."[7] But Valéry's parable suggests that the angelic book of the knowable is "indistinguishable from the world that is about us." Likewise, angelic "redemption" and ministry belong to this world among those who remember the dead and who "watch over life" in conditions of extremity. Clearly for Forché the poet carries a special responsibility as a watcher in this "work of incessant reminding" (Montenegro 1991: 67).

Forché's articulation of the poetry of witness recovers convincingly the important social function of the poet. It also allows a way of reflecting in a new light upon the history of poetry in this century, of seeing likenesses and continuities among otherwise radically different poets. Forché's fidelities remain with the work of writing poetry and not with theoretical positions. That work, she affirms in her anthology and in *The Angel of History*, is not the "representation of experience" so much as it is an awakening of desire and remembrance through the imagination of the reader. Adrienne Rich writes about this effect of poetic language, describing a moment of listening to Wallace Stevens read a poem: "You are drawn in not because this is a description of your world, but because you begin to be reminded of your own desire and need, because the poem is not about integration and fulfillment, but about the desire . . . for those conditions. You listen, if you do, not simply to the poem, but to a part of you reawakened by the poem, momentarily made aware" (1993: 12). If one listens to H.D.'s *Trilogy*, one is recalled to one's own interiority, through its metamorphosing images and swift changes, which resolve (in the alchemical sense) into images of spiritual transformation. But *The Angel of History*, in particular, speaks not of integration and fulfillment but of their opposite: the poem is a traumatic event, voluntarily entered by the reader. Nevertheless, its power, too, lies in reminding one of one's own desire and need, of bringing the imagination into momentary awareness. Forché insists upon our remaining suspended within the ruins of the century, in a ghostly underworld of the dead and the lost, and thus she awakens a suppressed desire to grieve. Elegy is a strangely maligned form at present among critics, but, fortunately, writers are not bound by such censures.[8] Forché has succeeded in framing *The Angel of History* as a collective event of mourning within a poetics shaped by the centrality of memory.

The poetry of extremity is not as much about factual remembrance or clarification of conscience as about imaginative recollection of "[memories] through which one hasn't lived" (Forché 1994: 21). The poetic event marks the reader as a witness, as human life itself has been marked by history. That witnessing implies collective responsibility, a transmission of effects within what Forché calls a "web of indeterminacy" (Taft-Kaufman 1990: 69). In this work of testimony and reminding, H.D. and Forché find themselves in a common party, the "straggling company" of poets "who did not forgo our heritage // at the grave's edge" (H.D. 1983: 568).

NOTES

1. Forché has repeatedly discussed this incident in her career. See Forché (1993: 30–31; 1986).

2. Others are Gertrude Stein, Denise Levertov, Irena Klepfisz, and Muriel Rukeyser.

3. I argue this concept of H.D.'s Hellenic engagement in Gregory (1997: esp. chaps. 1 and 2).

4. Among the many studies that treat H.D.'s late poetry, Susan Friedman's *Psyche Reborn* (1981) most clearly focuses upon H.D.'s consciousness of war and its figuration in her writing.

5. The remark about the "excavation site" comes from a comment on *The Angel*

of History on Forché's website. The sense of ruin at the basis of the poem is described by Forché in a recent interview: "Moving around so abruptly between war zones, I began to inhabit a ruin—a ruin of my own life, but also a much more public and historical ruin which I began to see the twentieth century as. So, as a poet . . . I felt myself to be somewhat of an archaeologist, wandering around in wreckage, picking up pieces of it and fitting them together" (Price 1995).

6. This way of understanding the angels in "Tribute to the Angels" was suggested by Marina Camboni in conversations in Rome in 1997.

7. Forché frequently refers in interviews to the "redemptive" motive of poetry in the sense suggested by Benjamin and Adorno. She speaks of "[Adorno's] messianic dream of a redemptive literature, a culture read against the grain so as to spark a light against the darkness."

8. Three commentaries on *The Angel of History* associate its elegiac form and its emphasis upon memory with "nostalgia," perhaps because the elegy is one of the chief objects of attack in deconstruction—the mourning of a lost totality. The elegy is also associated with nineteenth-century sentimental poetry by women, and critics propose that Forché's poem, in giving repeated priority to female voices, continues this—to them—illegitimate poetic tradition in which women are seen to do the cultural work of mourning. See Mitchell and Skoler (1995: 74–77), Helle (1996: 52–59), and Rushforth (1996).

Works Cited

Abraham, Nicolas, and Maria Torok. 1994. *The Shell and the Kernel: Renewals of Psychoanalysis*. Vol. 1. Ed. and trans. Nicholas T. Rand. Chicago: University of Chicago Press.

Ahl, Frederick. 1985. *Metaformations: Soundplay and Wordplay in Ovid and Other Classical Poets*. Ithaca, N.Y.: Cornell University Press.

Albright, Thomas. 1985. *Art in the San Francisco Bay Area, 1945–1980*. Berkeley: University of California Press.

Andrews, Bruce, and Charles Bernstein, eds. 1984. *The L=A=N=G=U=A=G=E Book*. Carbondale: Southern Illinois University Press.

Baccolini, Rafaella. 1995. *Tradition Identity Desire: Revisionist Strategies in H.D.'s Late Poetry*. Bologna: Patrona.

Bailey, Derek. 1993. *Improvisation: Its Nature and Practice in Music*. New York: Da Capo Press.

Basho. 1968. *Backroads to Far Towns*. Trans. Cid Corman and Susumu Kanaike. New York: Ecco Press. Reprinted 1996.

Bede the Venerable, Saint. 1968. *Ecclesiastical History*. Rev. ed. Book 2, *A History of the English Church and People*. Trans. Leo Sherley-Price. Harmondsworth, England: Penguin Classics.

Benitez-Rojo, Antonio. 1992. *The Repeating Island: The Caribbean and the Postmodern Perspective*. Trans. James Maraniss. Durham and London: Duke University Press.

Benjamin, Walter. 1968. *Illuminations*. Ed. Hannah Arendt. Trans. Harry Zohn. New York: Schocken.

Bernstein, Charles. 1992. "In the Middle of Modernism in the Middle of Capitalism on the Outskirts of New York." In Charles Bernstein, *A Poetics*. Cambridge, Mass.: Harvard University Press. 90–105.

Bertholf, Robert J. 1992. *A Great Admiration: H.D./Robert Duncan, Correspondence 1950–1961*. Venice, Calif.: Lapis Press.

Blake, William. 1964. *William Blake*. Ed. J. Bronowski. London: Penguin Books.

Blokker, Roy. 1979. *The Music of Shostakovich: The Symphonies*. London: Tantivy Press.

Bloom, Harold. 1972. *The Anxiety of Influence*. Oxford: Oxford University Press.

Boughn, Michael. 1993. *H.D.: A Bibliography, 1905–1990*. Charlottesville: University Press of Virginia.

Braudel, Frenand. 1972. *The Mediterranean and the Mediterranean World in the Age of Phillip II*. Pt. 2. Trans. Sian Reynolds. New York: Harper and Row.

Buck, Claire. 1991. *H.D. and Freud: Bisexuality and a Feminine Discourse*. New York: Harvester Wheatsheaf.

Burnett, Gary. 1990. *H.D.: Between Image and Epic*. Ann Arbor, Mich.: UMI Research Press.

Butler, Judith. 1990. *Gender Trouble: Feminism and the Subversion of Identity*. New York: Routledge.

Carruth, Hayden, ed. 1970. *The Voice That Is Great within Us: American Poetry of the Twentieth Century*. New York: Bantam.

Celan, Paul. 1986. "Speech Made at Bremen, 1958." In *Collected Prose*. Trans. Rosemary Waldrop. New York: Sheep Meadow Press.

Char, Rene. 1973. *The Dog of Hearts*. Trans. Paul Mann. Santa Cruz, Calif.: Green Horse Press.

Chisholm, Dianne. 1992. *H.D.'s Freudian Poetics: Psychoanalysis in Translation*. Ithaca, N.Y.: Cornell University Press.

Cixous, Hélène. 1981. "The Laugh of the Medusa." In *New French Feminisms: An Anthology*. Trans. Keith Cohen and Paula Cohen. Ed. Elaine Marks and Isabelle de Courtivron. New York: Schocken Books. 245–64.

Collecott, Diana. 1999. *H.D. and Sapphic Modernism*. Cambridge: Cambridge University Press.

Conte, Joseph M. 1991. *Unending Design: The Forms of Postmodern Poetry*. Ithaca, N.Y.: Cornell University Press.

Cook, Pamela. 1992. "Secrets and Manifestoes: Alicia Ostriker's Poetry and Politics." *Borderlands: Texas Poetry Review* 2: 80–86.

Crown, Kathleen, ed. 1998. "The Contemporary Long Poem: Feminist Intersections and Experiments: A Roundtable Conversation." *Women's Studies: An Interdisciplinary Journal* 27: 507–36.

Culler, Jonathan. 1988. "The Call of the Phoneme: Introduction." In *On Puns: The Foundation of Letters*. Ed. Jonathan Culler. London and New York: Blackwell. 1–16.

DeKoven, Marianne. 1986. "Gertrude's Granddaughters." *Women's Review of Books* 4, no. 2: 13–14.

Dembo, L. S. 1966. *Conceptions of Reality in Modern American Poetry*. Berkeley: University of California Press.

Des Pres, Terrence. 1980. *The Survivor: An Anatomy of Life in the Death Camps*. Oxford: Oxford University Press.

Dickinson, Emily. 1994. *Selected Letters*. Ed. Thomas H. Johnson. Cambridge, Mass.: Harvard University Press.

Dinnerstein, Dorothy. 1976. *The Mermaid and the Minotaur*. New York: Harper and Row.

di Prima, Diane. 1971. *Revolutionary Letters, etc*. San Francisco: City Lights.

Doubiago, Sharon. 1982. *Hard Country*. Minneapolis: West End Press.

———. 1986. "Perdita's Father." Unpublished manuscript.

———. 1988. *The Book of Seeing with One's Own Eyes: Stories by Sharon Doubiago*. Saint Paul, Minn.: Greywolf Press.

———. 1990. "The Reddest Rose Unfolds." *American Voice* 18: 56–61.

———. 1992. *South America Mi Hija*. Pittsburgh: Pittsburgh University Press.

———. 1993. "Introduction." In *Myrrh/My Life As a Screamer*. By Judith Roche. Seattle: Blue Heron Press.

Duncan, Robert. 1967. *The H.D. Book*. Pt. 1, chap. 2. *Coyote's Journal* 8: 27–35.

———. 1968. *Bending the Bow*. New York: New Directions.

———. 1969. *Roots and Branches*. New York: New Directions.

———. 1970. *Tribunals: Passages 31–35*. Los Angeles: Black Sparrow Press.

———. 1983. "*The H.D. Book*: Outline and Chronology." *Ironwood* 22 11, no. 2: 65.

———. 1993. *Selected Poems*. Ed. Robert J. Bertholf. New York: New Directions.

Duncan, Robert, and David Meltzer. 1989. *Wallace Berman Retrospective*. Venice, Calif.: Lapis Press.

DuPlessis, Rachel Blau. 1975. "George Oppen: 'What do we believe to live with?'" *Ironwood* 5, no. 1: 62–75.

———. 1979a. "Psyche, or Wholeness." *Massachusetts Review* 20, no. 1: 76–96.

———. 1979b. "Romantic Thralldom in H.D." *Contemporary Literature* 20, no. 2: 178–203.

———. 1980. *Wells*. New York. Montemora Foundation.

———. 1981. "Objectivist Ethics and Political Vision: A Study of Oppen and Pound." In *George Oppen: Man and Poet*. Ed. Burton Hatlen. Orono, Maine: National Poetry Foundation. 123–48.

———. 1982. "A Note: (Reflections on Louise Bogan)." In *Feminist Poetics: A Consideration of the Female Construction of Language*. Ed. Kathleen Fraser. San Francisco: San Francisco State University Press. 108–13.

———. 1985. *Writing beyond the Ending: Narrative Strategies of Twentieth-Century Women Writers*. Bloomington: Indiana University Press.

————. 1986. *H.D.: The Career of That Struggle*. Bloomington: Indiana University Press.

————. 1987a. "'The Familiar / Becomes Extreme': George Oppen and Silence." *North Dakota Quarterly* 55, no. 4: 18–36.

————. 1987b. *Tabula Rosa*. Elmwood, Conn.: Potes and Poets Press.

————. 1988. "No Moore of the Same: The Feminist Poetics of Marianne Moore." *William Carlos Williams Review* 14, no. 1: 6–32.

————. 1990a. *The Pink Guitar: Writing as Feminist Practice*. New York: Routledge.

————, ed. 1990b. *The Selected Letters of George Oppen*. Durham: Duke University Press.

————. 1991. *Drafts*. Elmwood, Conn.: Potes and Poets Press.

————. 1992a. "Lorine Niedecker, the Anonymous: Gender, Class, Genre and Resistances." *Kenyon Review* 14, no. 2: 96–116.

————. 1992b. "'Seismic Orgasm': Sexual Intercourse, Gender Narratives, and Lyric Ideology in Mina Loy." *Studies in Historical Change*. Ed. Ralph Cohen. Charlottesville: University Press of Virginia. 264–91.

————. 1993. "Reader, I Married Me: A Polygamous Memoir." In *Changing Subjects: The Making of Feminist Literary Criticism*. Ed. Gayle Greene and Coppelia Kahn. New York: Routledge. 97–111.

————. 1994. "'Corpses of Poesy': Some Modern Poets and Some Gender Ideologies of Lyric." *Feminist Measures: Soundings in Poetry and Theory*. Ed. Lynn Keller and Cristanne Miller. Ann Arbor: University of Michigan Press.

————. 1996a. "f-Words: An Essay on the Essay." *American Literature* 68, no. 1: 15–45.

————. 1996b. "Manifests." *Diacritics* 26, nos. 3–4: 31–53.

————. 1996c. "On Drafts: A Memorandum of Understanding." In *Onward: Contemporary Poetry and Poetics*. Ed. Peter Baker. New York: Peter Lang. 143–55.

————. 1997. *Drafts 15–XXX: The Fold*. Elmwood, Conn.: Potes and Poets Press.

Edmunds, Susan. 1994. *Out of Line: History, Psychoanalysis, and Montage in H.D.'s Long Poems*. Palo Alto, Calif.: Stanford University Press.

Eliot, T. S. 1962. *The Complete Poetry and Plays*. New York: Harcourt, Brace and World.

Ellison, Ralph. 1952. *Invisible Man*. New York: New American Library.

Faas, Ekbert. 1983. *Young Robert Duncan*. Santa Barbara, Calif.: Black Sparrow Press.

Fenellosa, Ernest. 1936. *The Chinese Written Character as a Medium for Poetry*. Ed. Ezra Pound. San Francisco: City Lights.

Forché, Carolyn. 1981. *The Country between Us*. New York: Harper and Row.

———. 1986. "A Lesson in Commitment." In *The Writer in Our World: A TriQuarterly Symposium*. Ed. Reginald Gibbons. Boston: Atlantic Monthly Press. 30–38.

———. 1993. *Against Forgetting: Twentieth-Century Poetry of Witness*. New York: Norton.

———. 1994. *The Angel of History*. New York: Harper Perennial.

———. N.d. "Culture, Canon, and Curriculum." Published on the Carolyn Forché website, http://osf1.gmu.edu/~cforchem/index.html.

Foster, Ed. 1992. "An Interview with Leslie Scalapino." *Talisman: A Journal of Contemporary Poetry and Poetics* 8: 32–41.

Fraser, Kathleen. 1988. "Line. On the Line. Lining up. Lined with. Between the Lines. Bottom Line." In *The Line in Postmodern Poetry*. Ed. Robert Frank and Henry Sayre. Urbana: University of Illinois Press.

———. 1989. "The Tradition of Marginality." *Frontiers* 10, no. 3: 22–27.

———. 1993. *When New Time Folds Up*. Minneapolis: Chax Press.

———. 1997. *Il Cuore: The Heart (Selected Poems 1970–1995)*. Introduction by Peter Quartermain. Hanover: Wesleyan University Press.

Friedman, Susan Stanford. 1975. "Who Buried H.D.? A Poet, Her Critics, and Her Place in 'The Literary Tradition.'" *College English* 36: 801–14.

———. 1981. *Psyche Reborn: The Emergence of H.D.* Bloomington: Indiana University Press.

———. 1990. *Penelope's Web: Gender, Modernity, H.D.'s Fiction*. Cambridge: Cambridge University Press.

Friedman, Susan Stanford, and Rachel Blau DuPlessis, eds. 1990. *Signets: Reading H.D.* Madison: University of Wisconsin Press.

Frost, Elisabeth A. 1995. "Signifyin(g) on Stein: The Revisionist Poetics of Harryette Mullen and Leslie Scalapino." *Postmodern Culture: An Electronic Journal of Interdisciplinary Criticism* 5, no. 3: n.p. Available at http://jefferson.village.virginia.edu/pmc/contents.all.html.

———. 1996. "An Interview with Leslie Scalapino." *Contemporary Literature* 37, no. 1: 1–23.

Gelpi, Albert. 1987. *A Coherent Splendor: The American Poetic Renaissance, 1910–1950*. New York: Cambridge University Press.

Gilbert, Sandra, and Susan Gubar. 1988. *No Man's Land: The Place of the Woman Writer in the Twentieth Century*. New Haven, Conn.: Yale University Press.

Gioia, Dana. 1991. "Can Poetry Matter?" *Atlantic Monthly* 267, no. 5 (May): 94–106.

Glissant, Edouard. 1989. *Caribbean Discourse: Selected Essays*. Trans. and with an introduction by J. Michael Dash. Charlottesville: University of Virginia Press.

Goodman, Jenny. 1997. "An Interview with Sharon Doubiago." *Contemporary Literature* 38, no. 1: 1–43.

———. 1998. "Bearing an Unbearable History: The Adoption of the 'Feminine I' in Sharon Doubiago's *Hard Country*." Special issue on American Women Poets and the Long Poem, ed. Kathleen Crown, *Women's Studies* 27: 447–64.

Gregory, Eileen. 1997. *H.D. and Hellenism: Classic Lines*. Cambridge: Cambridge University Press.

Griaule, Marcel. 1970. *Conversations with Ogotommêli: An Introduction to Dogon Religious Ideas*. London: Oxford University Press.

Gubar, Susan. 1978. "The Echoing Spell of H.D.'s *Trilogy*." *Contemporary Literature* 19: 196–218.

———. 1982. "The Blank Page and Female Creativity." In *Writing and Sexual Difference*. Ed. Elizabeth Abel. Chicago: University of Chicago Press.

Guest, Barbara. 1984. *Herself Defined: The Poet H.D. and Her World*. New York: Doubleday.

Hall, Nor. 1980. *The Moon and the Virgin: Reflections on the Archetypal Feminine*. New York: Harper and Row.

Hart, George. 1995. "'A Memory Forgotten': The Circle of Memory and Forgetting in H.D.'s *Helen in Egypt*." *Sagetrieb* 14, nos. 1–2: 161–77.

Hartman, Geoffrey, and Sanford Budick. 1986. *Midrash and Literature*. New Haven, Conn.: Yale University Press.

H.D. 1934. *Kora and Ka with Mira Mare*. Dijon, France: Imprimerie Darantière. Reprint 1996, ed. Robert Spoo. New York: New Directions.

———. 1961. *Helen in Egypt*. New York: New Directions.

———. 1968. *Palimpsest*. Carbondale: Southern Illinois University Press.

———. 1972. *Hermetic Definition*. New York: New Directions.

———. 1973. *Trilogy*. Reprint 1998, ed. Aliki Barnstone. New York: New Directions.

———. 1974. *Tribute to Freud*. Introduction by Kenneth Fields. Boston: David R. Godine.

———. 1979. *End to Torment: A Memoir of Ezra Pound*. Ed. Norman Holmes Pearson and Michael King. New York: New Directions.

———. 1981. *HERmione*. New York: New Directions.

———. 1982a. *The Gift*. New York: New Directions. Reprint 1998, ed. Jane Augustine. Gainesville: University Press of Florida.

———. 1982b. *Notes on Thought and Vision and The Wise Sappho*. Introduction by Albert Gelpi. San Francisco: City Lights Books.

———. 1983. *Collected Poems 1912–1944*. Ed. Louis L. Martz. New York: New Directions.

———. 1986. "Notes on Recent Writing." *Iowa Review* 16, no. 3: 174–221.

————. 1988. *Selected Poems*. Ed. Louis L. Martz. New York: New Directions.

————. 1992a. *Asphodel*. Ed. Robert Spoo. Durham: Duke University Press.

————. 1992b. *Paint It Today*. Ed. Cassandra Laity. New York: New York University Press.

————. 1992c. *Vale Ave*. Introduction by John Walsh. Redding Ridge: Black Swan Books.

————. 1993. *Within the Walls*. Designed by Kim Merker and Don Howell. Iowa City: Windhover Press.

Helle, Anita. 1996. "Elegy as History: Three Women Poets 'by the Century's Deathbed.'" *South Atlantic Review* 61, no. 2: 51–68.

Hillman, Brenda. 1992. *Death Tractates*. Middletown, Conn.: Wesleyan University Press.

————. 1993. *Bright Existence*. Middletown, Conn.: Wesleyan University Press.

Hirschman, Jack. 1971. *Aur Sea*. Berkeley, Calif.: Tree Press.

Hogue, Cynthia. 1995. *Scheming Women: Poetry, Privilege, and the Politics of Subjectivity*. Albany: SUNY Press.

————. 1998. "Interview with Kathleen Fraser." *Contemporary Literature* 39, no. 1: 1–26.

————. 1999. "Infectious Ecstasy: On the Poetics of Performative Transformation." In *Women Poets of the Americas: Symposium of Critical Essays*. Ed. Jacqueline Vaught Brogan and Cordelia Candelaria. Notre Dame, Ind.: University of Notre Dame Press.

Hollenberg, Donna Krolik. 1991. *H.D.: The Poetics of Childbirth and Creativity*. Boston: Northeastern University Press.

————. 1997. *Between History and Poetry: The Letters of H.D. and Norman Holmes Pearson*. Iowa City: University of Iowa Press.

Howe, Susan. 1993. *The Birthmark: Upsetting the Wilderness in American Literary History*. Middletown, Conn.: Wesleyan University Press.

Husserl, Edmund. 1970. *The Crisis of European Sciences and Transcendental Phenomenology*. Trans. David Carr. Evanston, Ill.: Northwestern University Press.

Irigaray, Luce. 1985. *This Sex Which Is Not One*. Trans. Catherine Porter with Carolyn Burke. Ithaca, N.Y.: Cornell University Press.

Jaffer, Frances. 1977. *Any Time Now*. Berkeley, Calif.: Effie's Press.

————. 1981. *She Talks to Herself in the Language of an Educated Woman*. Berkeley, Calif.: Kelsey St. Press.

————. 1985. *ALTERNATE Endings*. San Francisco: HOW(ever) Book Series. No. 1.

Johnson, Jeannine. 1998. "This Green Sprout Why: Defending Poetry in the Twentieth Century." Ph.D. dissertation, Yale University.

Kamboureli, Smaro. 1991. *On the Edge of Genre: The Contemporary Canadian Long Poem.* Toronto: University of Toronto Press.

Keats, John. 1968. "Letter to George and Thomas Keats." In *Norton Anthology of English Literature.* New York: W. W. Norton.

Keller, Lynn. 1997. *Forms of Expansion: Recent Long Poems by Women.* Chicago: University of Chicago Press.

Kelly, Robert. 1978. *The Convections.* Santa Rosa, Calif.: Black Sparrow Press.

———. 1995. *Red Actions: Selected Poems 1960–1993.* Santa Rosa, Calif.: Black Sparrow Press.

King, Michael, ed. 1986. *H.D.: Woman and Poet.* Orono, Maine: National Poetry Foundation.

Kinnahan, Linda A. 1994. *Poetics of the Feminine: Authority and Literary Tradition in William Carlos Williams, Mina Loy, Denise Levertov, and Kathleen Fraser.* Cambridge: Cambridge University Press.

Kizer, Carolyn. 1965. *Knock upon Silence.* New York: Doubleday.

Korg, Jacob. 1995. *Ritual and Experiment in Modern Poetry.* New York: St. Martin's Press.

Kristeva, Julia. 1980. *Desire in Language: A Semiotic Approach to Literature and Art.* Ed. Leon S. Roudiez. Trans. Thomas Gora, Alice Jardine, and Leon S. Roudiez. New York: Columbia University Press.

Laity, Cassandra. 1996. *H.D. and the Victorian Fin de Siècle: Gender, Modernism, Decadence.* Cambridge: Cambridge University Press.

Lawrence, D. H. 1973. *The Escaped Cock.* Ed. Gerald M. Lacy. Santa Rosa, Calif.: Black Sparrow Press.

Mackey, Nathaniel. 1974. "Call Me Tantra: Open Field Poetics as Muse." Ph.D. dissertation, Department of English, Stanford University.

———. 1985. *Eroding Witness.* Urbana and Chicago: University of Illinois Press.

———. 1993a. *Discrepant Engagement: Dissonance, Cross-Culturality, and Experimental Writing.* Cambridge: Cambridge University Press.

———. 1993b. *Djbot Baghostus's Run.* Los Angeles: Sun & Moon Press.

———. 1993c. *School of Udhra.* San Francisco: City Lights.

———. 1994. "Interview with Ed Foster." In *Postmodern Poetry: The Talisman Interviews.* Ed. Ed Foster. Hoboken, N.J.: Talisman House. 69–83.

———. 1997. *Bedouin Hornbook.* Los Angeles: Sun & Moon Press. Originally published Lexington, Ky.: Callaloo Fiction Series, 1986.

McClure, Michael. 1993. *Lighting the Corners on Nature, Art, and the Visionary: Essays and Interviews.* Albuquerque: University of New Mexico Press.

McHale, Brian. 1987. *Postmodernist Fiction.* New York: Methuen.

Mitchell, Nora, and Emily Skoler. 1995. "History, Death, Politics, Despair." *New England Review* 17, no. 2: 67–71.

Montenegro, David. 1991. "Carolyn Forché: An Interview with David Montenegro." In *Points of Departure: International Writers on Writing and Politics.* Ed. David Montenegro. Ann Arbor: University of Michigan Press.

Morris, Adalaide, ed. 1997. *Sound States: Innovative Poetics and Acoustical Technologies.* Durham: University of North Carolina Press.

Neumann, Erich. 1956. *Amor and Psyche: The Psychic Development of the Feminine.* Trans. Ralph Manheim. New York: Pantheon.

———. 1963. *The Great Mother: An Analysis of the Archetype.* Trans. Ralph Manheim. Bollingen Series XLVII. 2d ed. Princeton, N.J.: Princeton University Press.

Nielsen, Aldon Lynn. 1997. *Black Chant: Languages of African-American Postmodernism.* Cambridge: Cambridge University Press.

O'Leary, Peter. 1997. "An Interview with Nathaniel Mackey." *Chicago Review* 43, no. 1: 30–46.

Olson, Charles. 1983. *The Maximus Poems.* Berkeley: University of California Press.

Oppen, George. 1975. *Collected Poems.* New York: New Directions.

Ostriker, Alicia. 1974. *Once More out of Darkness and Other Poems.* Berkeley, Calif.: Berkeley Poets Cooperative.

———. 1982. *A Woman under the Surface.* Princeton, N.J.: Princeton University Press.

———. 1983. *Writing Like a Woman.* Ann Arbor: University of Michigan Press.

———. 1986a. *The Imaginary Lover.* Pittsburgh: Pittsburgh University Press.

———. 1986b. *Stealing the Language: The Emergence of Women's Poetry in America.* Boston: Beacon Press.

———. 1989. *Green Age.* Pittsburgh: Pittsburgh University Press.

———. 1990. "No Rule of Procedure: The Open Poetics of H.D." In *Signets: Reading H.D.* Ed. Susan Stanford Friedman and Rachel Blau DuPlessis. Madison: University of Wisconsin Press. 336–51.

———. 1993. *Feminist Revision and the Bible.* Cambridge: Blackwell.

———. 1994. *The Nakedness of the Fathers: Biblical Visions and Revisions.* New Brunswick, N.J.: Rutgers University Press.

———. 1996. *The Crack in Everything.* Pittsburgh: Pittsburgh University Press.

Pound, Ezra. 1960. *ABC of Reading.* New York: New Directions.

———. 1968. *Literary Essays.* New York: New Directions.

———. 1972. *The Cantos of Ezra Pound.* New York: New Directions.

———. 1987. *Selected Letters of Ezra Pound and Louis Zukofsky.* Ed. Barry Ahearn. New York: New Directions.

Price, Leslie. 1995. "A Symphony of Utterance: A Discussion with Carolyn Forché." *Ivy.*

Prins, Yopie, and Maeera Shreiber, eds. 1997. *Dwelling in Possibility: Women Poets and Critics on Poetry*. Ithaca, N.Y.: Cornell University Press.

Quartermain, Peter. 1997. "Introduction." In *Il Cuore: The Heart (Selected Poems 1970–1995)*. By Kathleen Fraser. Middletown, Conn.: Wesleyan University Press.

Rainey, Lawrence. 1998. *Institutions of Modernism: Literary Elites and Public Culture*. New Haven, Conn.: Yale University Press.

Rich, Adrienne. 1993. *What Is Found There: Notebooks on Poetry and Politics*. New York: Norton.

Riddel, Joseph. 1979. "H.D.'s Scene of Writing—Poetry As (and) Analysis." *Studies in the Literary Imagination* 12: 41–59.

Rilke, Rainer Maria. 1972. *Duino Elegies*. Trans. Stephen Garney and Jay Wilson. New York: Harper and Row.

Robinson, Janice. 1982. *H.D.: The Life and Work of an American Poet*. Boston: Houghton Mifflin.

Roche, Judith. 1988. "Myrrh: A Study of Persona in H.D.'s *Trilogy*." *line* 12: 63–110.

Rukeyser, Muriel. 1994. *A Muriel Rukeyser Reader*. Ed. Jan Heller Levi. New York: Norton.

Rushforth, Leonie. 1996. "Memory as Religion." Review of *The Angel of History*. *Long Poem Newsletter* 2.

Scalapino, Leslie. 1988. *way*. San Francisco: North Point Press.

———. 1989. *How Phenomena Appear to Unfold*. Elmwood, Conn.: Potes and Poets Press.

———. 1994. *Objects in the Terrifying Tense/Longing from Taking Place*. New York: Roof Books.

———. 1996. *The Front Matter, Dead Souls*. Middletown, Conn.: Wesleyan University Press.

Schweik, Susan. 1991. *A Gulf So Deeply Cut: American Women Poets and the Second World War*. Madison: University of Wisconsin Press.

Scott, Bonnie Kime, ed. 1990. *The Gender of Modernism*. Bloomington: Indiana University Press.

Seltzer, Robert. 1980. *Jewish People, Jewish Thought: The Jewish Experience in History*. New York: Macmillan.

Shostakovich, Dmitri. 1979. *Testimony: The Memoirs of Dmitri Shostakovich*. Ed. Solomon Volkov. New York: Harper and Row.

Silliman, Ron, ed. 1986. *In the American Tree*. Orono, Maine: National Poetry Foundation.

Spicer, Jack. 1989. *The Collected Books of Jack Spicer*. Ed. with a commentary by Robin Blaser. Santa Rosa, Calif.: Black Sparrow Press.

Spivak, Gayatri. 1980. "Finding Feminist Reading: Dante to Yeats." *Social Text* 1, no. 3: 73–87.

Spoo, Robert. 1997. "H.D. Prosed." In *The Future of Modernism*. Ed. Hugh Witemeyer. Ann Arbor: University of Michigan Press.

Stein, Gertrude. 1990. *Tender Buttons*. Reprint ed. Los Angeles: Sun & Moon Press.

Stewart, Garrett. 1990. *Reading Voices: Literature and the Phonotext*. Berkeley: University of California Press.

———. 1997. "Modernism's Sonic Waiver: Literary Writing and the Filmic Difference." In *Sound States: Innovative Poetics and Acoustical Technology*. Ed. Adalaide Morris. Durham: North Carolina University Press. 237–73.

Stewart, Susan. 1995. "Lyric Possession." *Critical Inquiry* 22: 34–63.

Stimpson, Catherine R. 1993. "Demeter in South America." *Parnassus: Poetry in Review* 17, no. 2, 18, no. 1: 258–71.

Stricker, Meredith. 1989. "New Species." *HOW(ever)* 5, no. 4: 1, 19–20.

Taft-Kaufman, Jill. 1990. "Jill Taft-Kaufman Talks with Carolyn Forché." *Text and Performance Quarterly* 10: 61–70.

Twitchell-Waas, Jeffrey. 1996. " 'Set in Eternity but Lived In': H.D.'s *Vale Ave*." *Sagetrieb* 15, nos. 1–2: 203–27.

Ulmer, Gregory. 1988. "The Puncept in Grammatology." In *On Puns: The Foundation of Letters*. Ed. Jonathan Culler. London and New York: Blackwell. 164–89.

Watten, Barrett. 1984. *Total Syntax*. Carbondale: University of Southern Illinois Press.

Williams, William Carlos. 1957. *Selected Letters*. Ed. with an introduction by John Thirlwall. New York: Doubleday.

———. 1963. *Paterson*. New York: New Directions.

Wilson, Rob. 1991. *American Sublime: Genealogy of a Poetic Genre*. Madison: University of Wisconsin Press.

Wyschogrod, Edith. 1985. *Spirit in Ashes: Hegel, Heidegger, and Man-Made Death*. New Haven, Conn.: Yale University Press.

Zilboorg, Caroline. 1992. *Richard Aldington and H.D.: The Early Years in Letters*. Bloomington: Indiana University Press.

———. 1995. *Richard Aldington and H.D.: The Later Years in Letters*. Manchester: Manchester University Press.

Zumthor, Paul. 1990. *Oral Poetry: An Introduction*. Minneapolis: University of Minnesota Press.

Contributors

ALICIA OSTRIKER, a poet and critic, is professor of English at Rutgers University and author of *Stealing the Language: The Emergence of Women's Poetry in America* as well as other books and essays. Her two most recent books of poems, *The Crack in Everything* (1996) and *The Little Space: Selected and New Poems, 1968–1998* (1998), were National Book Award finalists.

DONNA KROLIK HOLLENBERG is associate professor of English at the University of Connecticut. Her books are *H.D.: The Poetics of Childbirth and Creativity* (1991) and *Between History and Poetry: The Letters of H.D. and Norman Holmes Pearson* (1997), and she has also published essays on Adrienne Rich, Kay Boyle, Timothy Findley, and Alice Walker.

ROBERT KELLY has long been associated with the writing program at Bard College, where he continues the practice of his own writing. He has published more than fifty books of poetry and fiction, the latest of which are *Mont Blanc* and *Queen of Terrors*, respectively. *Red Actions: Selected Poems 1960–1993* is his most recent publication. In 1994 he was honored with the degree of doctor of letters awarded by the State University of New York.

JANE AUGUSTINE is a poet, fiction writer, mixed-media artist, and scholar of women in modernism. Her poems appear in three chapbooks, *Lit by the Earth's Dark Blood*, *Journeys*, and *French Windows*, in the anthology *Beneath a Single Moon: Buddhism in Contemporary American Poetry* and in many literary magazines. Her awards include the H.D. Fellowship in American Literature at Beinecke Library, Yale University, and two fellowships in poetry from the New York State Council on the Arts. She is the editor of *The Gift by H.D.: The Complete Text* (University Press of Florida, 1998).

SHARON DOUBIAGO, poet and fiction writer, is the author of several collections of poetry, including two book-length poems, *Hard Country* (1982, reprinted in 1999) and *South America Mi Hija* (1992), and two collections of short stories, *The Book of Seeing with One's Own Eyes* (1988) and *El Niño* (1989). Her honors include the Oregon Book Award and two Pushcart Awards. She has taught in many writing programs around the country and is currently visiting writer at the University of Wyoming.

KATHLEEN CROWN, a critic and poet, is assistant professor of English at Kalamazoo College. In addition to her dissertation, "This Ecstatic Nation: History, Trauma, and Vision in American Poetry since World War Two," she has published essays on H.D., Virginia Woolf, and several contemporary poets. Her poetry has appeared in *Calyx* and *Southern Poetry Review*.

FRANCES JAFFER, poet, is the author of three books of poetry: *Any Time Now* (1977), *She Talks to Herself in the Language of an Educated Woman* (1981), and *ALTERNATE Endings* (1985). She was a founding editor of *HOW(ever)*, a journal of experimental writing by women. During the 1970s she organized a workshop that convened regularly to read and discuss the work of H.D. Her work is available from Small Press Distribution, Berkeley, California.

KIM VAETH, poet, is the author of one book of poetry, *Her Yes* (1994), and the song cycle "Elegy" (1997). She is completing a second book of poetry.

RACHEL BLAU DUPLESSIS, critic, poet, and editor, is professor of English at Temple University. Her critical work on twentieth-century writers includes *Writing beyond the Ending: Narrative Strategies of Twentieth-Century Women Writers* (1985), *H.D.: The Career of That Struggle* (1986), and her edition of *The Selected Letters of George Oppen* (1990). DuPlessis is known for her practice of innovative essays in *The Pink Guitar: Writing as Feminist Practice* (1990). In 1986 she began her long poem project, now in its third volume: *Tabula Rosa* (1987), *Drafts 3–14* (1991), and *Drafts 15–XXX: The Fold* (1997). *Live, from Feminism: Memoirs of Women's Liberation*, edited by DuPlessis and Ann Snitow, appeared in 1998.

BURTON HATLEN is professor of English at the University of Maine, where he also serves as director of the National Poetry Foundation. He is the editor of *Sagetrieb*, a journal devoted to scholarly and critical work on poetry in the Imagist and Objectivist traditions. He has published a book of his own poetry, *I Wanted to Tell You*, as well as many articles on Shakespeare, Renaissance poetry, modernist and postmodern poetry, and literary theory.

KATHLEEN FRASER, poet, is the author of fourteen books of poetry, most recently *Il Cuore: The Heart (Selected Poems 1970–1995)* (Wesleyan University Press, 1997). For twenty years she was professor of creative writing at San Fran-

cisco State University, as well as director of the Poetry Center there, and foun-
der of the American Poetry Archives. She was also a founding editor of the
feminist/experimental poetry journal *HOW(ever)*, which she is now editing as
a website and archive with support from the Rutgers CETH program. Her
collection of essays, *Translating the Unspeakable*, was published by the University of Alabama Press in 1999.

CYNTHIA HOGUE, a poet and critic, is associate professor of English at Buck-
nell University and director of the Stadler Center of Poetry. She has published
two collections of poetry and a critical book on American women's poetry
titled *Scheming Women: Poetry, Privilege, and the Politics of Subjectivity*. She has
just completed her third collection of poems, titled *The Never-Wife*, and is at
work on a second collection of essays.

BRENDA HILLMAN, poet, is the author of five books of poetry published
by Wesleyan University Press: *White Dress, Fortress, Death Tractates, Bright Ex-
istence*, and, most recently, *Loose Sugar* (1997). Her work has won the Delmore
Schwartz Memorial Award for Poetry and the Poetry Society of America
Norma Farber First Book Prize. She teaches at St. Mary's College in Moraga,
California.

ALIKI BARNSTONE, poet, editor, and critic, is associate professor of English
at the University of Nevada, Las Vegas. She co-edited *A Book of Women Poets
from Antiquity to Now* (1992) and *The Calvinist Roots of the Modern Era* (1997),
and she wrote the readers notes for H.D.'s *Trilogy* (1998). Her book of poems
Madly in Love (1997) was nominated for the Pulitzer Prize.

LESLIE SCALAPINO, poet, is the author of *The Return of Painting, The Pearl,
Orion/A Trilogy*, just reprinted, and *Green and Black: Selected Writings*, as well as
of *Defoe* (1995) and *The Front Matter, Dead Souls* (1996). A new book, *New Time*,
is forthcoming from Wesleyan University Press.

ELISABETH A. FROST, critic and poet, is assistant professor of English at
Fordham University. She has published several essays on modern and contem-
porary poets, including Mina Loy, Gertrude Stein, Wallace Stevens, Harryette
Mullen, and Leslie Scalapino. Her poetry has been published in *Poetry*, the *New
England Review*, and *Shenandoah*, as well as other journals. She is currently com-
pleting a book titled *The Feminist Avant-Garde in American Poetry*.

NATHANIEL MACKEY, poet and critic, is the author of four chapbooks of
poetry and two books of poetry, *Eroding Witness* (1985) and *School of Udhra*
(1993). *Strick: Song of the Andoumboulou: 16–25*, a CD recording of poems with
Royal Hartigan and Hafez Modirzadeh, was released in 1995 by Spoken Engine

Company. Two volumes of his ongoing prose composition, *From a Broken Bottle Traces of Perfume Still Emanate*, have been published: *Bedouin Hornbook* (1986) and *Djbot Baghostus's Run* (1993). He is editor of the literary magazine *Hambone*, co-editor (with Art Lange) of the anthology *Moment's Notice: Jazz in Poetry and Prose* (1993), and author of a book of critical essays, *Discrepant Engagement: Dissonance, Cross-Culturality, and Experimental Writing* (1993). He teaches at the University of California, Santa Cruz.

ADALAIDE MORRIS teaches and writes on modern and contemporary poetry and poetics at the University of Iowa, where she is a professor and chair of the English Department. She has published a book on Wallace Stevens and several essays on H.D., as well as essays on Emily Dickinson, Adrienne Rich, and the state of the profession. Most recently, she edited *Sound States: Innovative Poetics and Acoustical Technologies* (University of North Carolina Press, 1997).

CAROLYN FORCHÉ, poet and translator, is the author of three award-winning books of poetry: *Gathering the Tribes, The Country between Us*, and, most recently, *The Angel of History* (1994). She is also the editor of *Against Forgetting: Twentieth-Century Poetry of Witness*. She teaches at George Mason University.

EILEEN GREGORY is professor of English at the University of Dallas. She has published numerous essays on H.D. and was the editor of the *H.D. Newsletter*. The recipient of an NEH research grant, she recently published *H.D. and Hellenism: Classic Lines* (Cambridge University Press, 1997).

Index